The Seer of Bayside

The Seer of Bayside

Veronica Lueken and the Struggle to Define Catholicism

JOSEPH P. LAYCOCK

OXFORD
UNIVERSITY PRESS

OXFORD
UNIVERSITY PRESS

Oxford University Press is a department of the University of Oxford.
It furthers the University's objective of excellence in research, scholarship,
and education by publishing worldwide.

Oxford   New York

Auckland   Cape Town   Dar es Salaam   Hong Kong   Karachi
Kuala Lumpur   Madrid   Melbourne   Mexico City   Nairobi
New Delhi   Shanghai   Taipei   Toronto

With offices in

Argentina   Austria   Brazil   Chile   Czech Republic   France   Greece
Guatemala   Hungary   Italy   Japan   Poland   Portugal   Singapore
South Korea   Switzerland   Thailand   Turkey   Ukraine   Vietnam

Oxford is a registered trademark of Oxford University Press
in the UK and certain other countries.

Published in the United States of America by
Oxford University Press
198 Madison Avenue, New York, NY 10016

Library of Congress Cataloging-in-Publication Data
Laycock, Joseph, 1980
The seer of Bayside : Veronica Lueken and the struggle to define
Catholicism / Joseph P. Laycock.
pages cm
Includes bibliographical references and index.
ISBN 978–0–19–937966–8 (hardcover : alk. paper)—ISBN 978–0–19–937967–5
(ebook)—ISBN 978–0–19–937968–2 (ebook)
1. Mary, Blessed Virgin, Saint—Apparitions and miracles—New York (State)—
New York.   2. Lueken, Veronica.   3. Catholic Church—
United States—History—20th century.   4. Prophecies.   I. Title.
BT660.B35L39 2014
282'.747243—dc23
2014011235

1 3 5 7 9 8 6 4 2
Printed in the United States of America
on acid-free paper

For my parents

Contents

Preface

IN 1893 CHICAGO hosted the World's Columbian Exhibition to celebrate and honor the world's cultures. The center of the exhibition was dominated by "The White City" where visitors could find displays of Western technology. On the periphery was the Midway Plaisance, which featured living exhibits of the "primitive cultures" of the world. The Midway performances generally reflected Western fantasies of exotic cultures. Visitors could see an exhibit in which Chinese actors recreated an opium den or watch exotic dancing at the Persian "Palace of Eros."[1] The architecture of the White City and the Midway defined who was an insider and who was an outsider, who was civilized and who was primitive. Like any effective hegemony, the assumptions inherent in the Columbian Exhibition were difficult to challenge because they operated beneath the level of discourse. It was a model of the world that could only be navigated and explored using the categorical assumptions of its designers. And yet, one wonders what would have happened if one of the living exhibits from the Midway Plaisance had set up camp in The White City and declared that their culture's discoveries were just as significant, just as central to the project of civilization, as Western technocracy.

As a historian and ethnographer of American religious cultures I am drawn to groups that are understudied, misunderstood, and maligned. I learned early in my career that the academic study of religion was built with similar architectural features to ensure that outsiders remain on the outside. I cannot count how many times I spoke with peers and mentors about research projects that excited me only to be told, "Ah! You study new religious movements!" I was always frustrated by this response because the subjects of my ethnography never think of themselves as practicing new religious movements (NRMs). While the study of NRMs is important work, the category can be employed to maintain a two-tier model of religion. As J. Z. Smith wrote, "Difference is seldom a comparison between entities judged to be equivalent. Difference most frequently entails a

hierarchy of prestige and the concomitant political ranking of superordi-
nate and subordinate."[2] Like the Columbian Exhibition's White City, some
religious traditions enjoy a privileged status in the center of the field of
study. Surrounding these are the "sideshows" of religious studies—the
NRMs, the folk pieties, the "little traditions"—that are deemed worthy of
inclusion in the field but tacitly regarded as a distraction from the "real
work" occurring in the center.

I became interested in the Baysiders—who have claimed the site of the
1964–65 World's Fair as their own—because they openly challenge these
definitional boundaries. The Baysiders insist that they are *not* an NRM or
a vernacular variation of Catholicism but loyal and *normal* Catholics. From
their perspective, center and periphery are reversed and it is everyone
else who has accepted strange variations on normative Catholic belief and
practice. Unwilling to accept a place on the margins, the Baysiders regularly visit Rome and write letters to the Vatican hoping that their views
and practices will be embraced by the magisterium. They also lobby local
Church authorities and the media to take them seriously. In the Archives
of the Diocese of Brooklyn, I found a card from a Baysider addressed to
Bishop Francis J. Mugavero. It was unsigned and posed only one question,
"Why is Bayside a cult?" Could there be a more naked or honest challenge
to the two-tier model of religion?

The forty-year struggle of the Baysiders to be accepted as normal Catholics
reminds us that definitional boundaries like "religion" and "cult" are not
self-evident but exercises of power. They are the product of previous contests and they remain contestable. Just as Western imperialism provided the
categories employed in the Columbian Exhibition, vested interests, notably
Protestant theology, have shaped the way we think about religious categories.
Ultimately there is no "center" to the field of religious studies. This means
that the categories religion scholars use to organize their data are at best heur-
istic. At worst, they constitute what Robert Orsi has called a "hidden moral
framework" that works to define "true religion" by quietly keeping certain
forms of religiosity separate from and elevated above the exotic other.[3]

The history of the Baysiders is a case study in how these battles for
religious legitimacy are fought. As in war, there are not only winners and
losers but clever gambits and desperate charges, mutinies and betray-
als, heroes and casualties. The conflict is important to study not only
because it determines the victor but because it changes the combatants.
The Baysiders have formed their understanding of themselves through
their tensions with Church authorities and with society-at-large. Thus, the

two-tier model of religion not only presents a distorted view of the religious landscape, but actively molds the development of its subjects.

Research for this book consisted of archival research, oral history, and ethnography with the two Baysider groups that have access to Flushing Meadows Park. The Archives of the Diocese of Brooklyn hold several boxes of material sent to them regarding Veronica Lueken, and the archivist graciously allowed me to access this material. These boxes contained angry letters from Baysiders as well as angry letters from lay Catholics who had spoken to Baysiders. There were numerous Polaroid pictures that had been sent in by Baysiders which feature strange anomalies in the film. Accompanying letters beseeched Church authorities to recognize the streaks and shapes in the film as evidence of the supernatural. There were medical charts showing the inexplicable recovery of individuals who suffered from deadly diseases before attending Baysider vigils. Catholic leaders from every inhabited continent had written the diocese demanding why some in their flock had suddenly begun to believe that Paul VI was an imposter. People from across the country had mailed in five-dollar bills to contribute to the construction of a great basilica at St. Robert Bellarmine's. (The Church had dutifully returned all of these donations.) There were also numerous letters from Lueken herself including descriptions of her visions, strongly worded retorts to statements made by the diocese, and a Christmas card sent to the chancellor of the diocese. The files were also filled with sacramentals: Many Baysiders had mailed in letters with rosaries, saint medals, and blessed rose petals attached to them with scotch tape. Sacred objects continually tumbled out of the files as I went through them.

In June 2012, I travelled to Queens, New York, to attend the forty-second anniversary of the original apparition of Bayside. While there, I was also able to make contact with both Saint Michael's World Apostolate (SMWA) and Our Lady of the Roses Shrine (OLR). I conducted participant observation at three Sunday holy hours and three vigils, each lasting several hours, at Flushing Meadows. I took a personal tour of SMWA's workshop in College Point where I saw their offices and printing equipment and had lunch. I also attended an annual banquet organized by SMWA. In addition to speaking with Baysiders from around the world, I was also able to interview former leaders of the Bayside Hills Civic Association, Kevin Farrelly and Adrian Cornell, who witnessed the controversy in Bayside and were willing to share their memories with me. I was also able to interview Lueken's grandson, Jeremy, who speaks fondly of his grandmother but does not consider himself a Baysider.

This has not been an easy history to write. History, as they say, is written by the winners but so far this conflict has many factions and no decisive victor. I have spoken with clergy and archivists from the Diocese of Brooklyn, former presidents of the Bayside Hills Civic Association whose lives were disrupted by Baysider vigils, Baysiders from around the world, and leaders from two rival Baysider organizations that resulted from a bitter schism in 1997. Each of these factions has their own version of events and I have developed sympathies for all of them. I have tried to take all of their claims and perspectives seriously while also remaining critical and applying the rigor expected by my peers. The result is that when I sat down to write, I felt as though an entire room full of people was staring over my shoulder, clamoring that this was not how it happened, that I was being unfair, that I was being too critical of one side and too credulous of another. It is possible that the version of events told here will be upsetting to everyone involved and that I will be written off equally as an intellectual with anti-Catholic bias, a cult apologist, and an agent of Satan sent to discredit the Bayside Prophecies. If all parties involved find my version of history objectionable, I will take this as a sign that I have achieved some degree of objectivity or at least spread my prejudices equally.

I have many people to thank for the completion of this project. I should begin with the wonderful faculty at Boston University, especially Stephen Prothero, David Frankfurter, Jon Roberts, Christopher Lehrich, and Thomas Michael. I am also deeply grateful for the input of Robert Orsi, Julie Byrne, and Ronald Brown. I am indebted to Joseph Coen, the archivist of the Diocese of Brooklyn, for allowing me to access primary documents and for always maintaining historical neutrality, and to Katherine Newburg who spent two days in a basement helping me sort through said documents. I am grateful to the workers of Saint Michael's World Apostolate for speaking with me and showing me hospitality even though they had every reason not to trust a nosey academic. Jeremy Lueken was very generous in providing an oral history of his family. Kevin Farrelly and Adrian K. Cornell were extremely helpful in providing oral history as well as historical documents. Alison McKay of the Bayside Historical Society helped to locate archival materials. Gerald P. Fogarty, S.J., and Landislas Orsy, S.J., provided important help in interpreting Vatican documents and canon law. I am grateful to Natasha Mikles who spent a very cold winter afternoon with me in Mount Saint Mary Cemetery. Finally, I must thank the wonderful editorial staff, Cynthia Read and Charlotte Steinhardt, without whose help this book could not have been written.

The Seer of Bayside

I

Who Speaks for Mary?

FROM 1964 TO 1965, Flushing Meadows Corona Park in Queens, New York, was the site of the World's Fair. Half a century later, the remains of the fair still define the park. The New York State Pavilion, once an exhibition hall, is now derelict. Its abandoned observation towers hover over the landscape like rusty flying saucers. Dominating the park is a twelve-story-high stainless-steel model of the Earth known as "The Unisphere." From the base of this monument, paved walkways radiate outward, leading visitors past skate-boarders, soccer fields, and ice-cream vendors. Visitors who stroll through Flushing Meadows on a Sunday morning can see another unusual sight: Near the southeast corner of the park is a small monument with a fiberglass statue of the Virgin Mary sitting atop it. Gathered around the statue is a collection of people of many ethnicities saying the rosary and reading Catholic litanies. The leaders of this group are easy to spot by their berets. The women wear pale blue berets, and the men's are white with the words "Saint Michael" embroidered across the front in green. A stone's throw away from this group is another, nearly identical statue of Mary, surrounded by a different group of people in blue and white berets also saying the rosary. The two groups do not speak to each other. In fact, they hardly acknowledge each other's presence at all. The scene resembles some sort of optical illusion. It seems more plausible that this is some trick of the light than that two similarly garbed groups would hold identical vigils so close together.

On a beautiful Sunday morning in June, I spoke with a man from Poland who had bicycled nearly ten miles that morning just to ride through the park. He was Catholic and, seeing the two Virgin Mary statues, decided to investigate. He rode up to the group closest to the road where a friendly man in a white beret handed him some literature. On learning he was from Poland, the man in the beret brought over an older woman, her hair covered by a shawl, who was also from Poland. I watched the two speak briefly in Polish before the woman excused herself to return to her rosary. The man in the white beret went to take his turn leading the liturgy and I was left alone with the cyclist.

"Why are there two Marys?" he asked me.
I knew the answer to his question, but felt it was not my place to explain. "They disagree on some things," I answered.
Looking puzzled, the cyclist asked, "Well, which one is Roman Catholic?" "They both are," I said.

Like many other encounters I had as an outsider studying Marian devotion in the park, my brief exchange with the cyclist presented an ethical dilemma. I did not tell the cyclist, who was already sufficiently confused, that some Catholic authorities contest whether either group is actually Roman Catholic or are both quasi-schismatic movements condemned by the Mother Church. In fact, this scene in the park calls into question what it means to be Catholic. Catholic according to *whom*? The cyclist's question also reminded me that I was an active player in these contested definitional boundaries. As an ethnographer, I was supposed to somehow be present to witness this struggle for sacred space and legitimacy without taking sides. But even my refusal to take a side was problematic. Far from being something akin to Emerson's transparent eyeball, I was keenly aware of being an embodied being, trying not to interfere while observing a site where meaning was being created through embodied ritual practices.

The chain of events that led to there being two Marys in Flushing Meadows every Sunday actually began just after midnight on June 5, 1968, when Palestinian immigrant Sirhan Sirhan shot Senator Robert Kennedy. The next day, as Kennedy lay in the hospital, a Roman Catholic housewife named Veronica Lueken (1923–95) from Bayside, New York, was praying for his recovery when she became enveloped by an overwhelming fragrance of roses. Although the senator died late that night, Lueken's mystical experiences had only begun. The inexplicable smell of roses continued to haunt her. She would wake up to find she had written poetry that she could not remember writing. She had prayed to St. Therese of Lisieux to save Senator Kennedy and suspected that Therese was somehow the true author of these poems. She discussed these experiences with the priests at her parish church, St. Robert Bellarmine's, but she felt they did not take her seriously. Her husband Artie also discouraged any discussion of miracles.

As time went on, her visions became darker. In the sky over Bayside, she saw a vision of a black eagle screaming "Woe, woe, woe to the inhabitants of the earth!" She became convinced that these experiences signaled an impending disaster. She wrote Cardinal Richard Cushing in Boston and warned him that something terrible was going to happen. She also felt that her looming sense of dread was somehow connected to the Second Vatican Council, which had concluded in 1965. The Council had done away with the Tridentine mass, replacing Latin with English. Lueken felt that priests had begun to dismiss the Catholic traditions she had practiced since she was a girl. In 1969, she wrote a letter to Pope Paul VI and asked him to reverse these reforms.

In April 1970, the Virgin Mary appeared to Lueken in her apartment. She announced that she would appear at St. Robert Bellarmine's church in Bayside "when the roses are in bloom." On the night of June 18th, 1970, Lueken knelt alone in the rain praying the rosary before a statue of the Immaculate Conception outside her church. Here, Mary appeared to Lueken and instructed her that she was a bride of Christ, that she wept for the sins of the world, and that everyone must return to saying the rosary. Lueken announced that a national shrine should be built on the church grounds and that Mary would henceforth appear there on every Catholic feast day. Over the next two years, a small body of followers joined Lueken in her vigils in front of the statue. At each appearance, Lueken would deliver a "message from heaven," spoken through her by Mary as well as a growing cast of saints and angels. These messages typically included jeremiads about the weight of America's sins and warnings of a coming chastisement.

In 1973, Lueken's visions drew the attention of The Pilgrims of Saint Michael, a conservative Catholic movement from Quebec. The Pilgrims were also known as "the White Berets" for the hats they wore. Like Lueken, they were greatly alarmed over the reforms of Vatican II. In particular, they wanted to restore the tradition of saying the Prayer of St. Michael after mass, a tradition that had been suppressed in 1965. The White Berets declared Lueken to be "the seer of the age" and printed her messages from heaven in their newsletter. They also began organizing buses that transported hundreds of pilgrims to attend vigils in front of Lueken's parish church. Lueken's messages began to hint at global conspiracies, a coming nuclear war, and a celestial body called "The Fiery Ball of Redemption" that would soon strike the Earth, causing planet-wide destruction.

Church authorities had tolerated Lueken's activities for three years, but now her growing movement was creating a crisis. Meanwhile, the Bayside Hills Civic Association (BHCA) was horrified by the crowds of pilgrims who had descended on their quiet neighborhood. St. Robert Bellarmine's church was surrounded by private homes on all sides. The residents objected to the crowds of pilgrims who often stayed until midnight. Pilgrims, they claimed, were trampling their manicured lawns and driving down the property values of their homes. The BHCA put immense pressure on the parish and the Diocese of Brooklyn to bring Lueken and her followers to heel.

When a hurried investigation by the diocese concluded that her experiences were not supernatural, Lueken was asked to cease holding her vigils at St. Robert Bellarmine's. When she refused, diocesan officials began interrupting her vigils with a bullhorn, reading a letter from the bishop and ordering all loyal Catholics not to participate. Lueken and her followers responded that such tactics only proved how far a Satanic conspiracy had spread through the Church since Vatican II. The BHCA began holding counter-vigils and heckling pilgrims. The situation became dangerous and growing numbers of police were dispatched to keep the peace. Several residents were arrested for disorderly conduct and assaulting police officers. A few were even hospitalized after violent confrontations with police or pilgrims. These events came to be called "The Battle of Bayside." The situation was finally resolved in 1975 when the Supreme Court of New York issued an injunction barring Lueken from holding her vigils near St. Robert Bellarmine's. The night before agreeing to the injunction, Lueken received a message from Mary and Jesus to relocate the vigils to Flushing Meadows Corona Park.

The new vigil site was a monument marking the spot where the Vatican Pavilion had stood during the World's Fair. Followers purchased a fiberglass statue of the Virgin Mary, which was brought to the park for vigils. The crowds only continued to grow. The Pilgrims of Saint Michael eventually withdrew their support and returned to Canada. But Lueken's followers created an organized mission to bring the messages from heaven to the entire world. They drew in Catholics who, like Lueken, regarded the reforms of Vatican II as a betrayal of Catholic tradition. The movement created the corporation "Our Lady of the Roses Shrine," which managed an international mailing list of thousands. Missionary efforts were led by a group called the Order of St. Michael, who lived as a community and devoted all of their time to the mission. On June 18th, 1983, fifteen thousand pilgrims from around the world gathered in Flushing Meadows Park for the thirteenth anniversary of the apparition at Bayside.

Catholics who believed in Lueken's messages came to call themselves "Baysiders" after the original location of the apparition. Ironically, the residents of Bayside, New York, also referred to themselves as "Baysiders." They regarded the pilgrims as an invading and foreign force and were confused that they would claim this title for themselves. During the 1980s, independent Baysider chapters were established across the United States and in Canada. Lueken's messages were translated into many languages and disseminated to Catholic communities on every continent.

The Baysiders professed to be traditional Catholics loyal to canon law and the Holy See. However, their defiance of the Brooklyn diocese caused many Catholics to regard them as an insubordinate and schismatic movement. Shortly after arriving in Flushing Meadows, Lueken delivered a revelation that resolved this paradox—at least for her followers. Pope Paul VI, who had endorsed the reforms of Vatican II, was an imposter. The true pope was kept heavily sedated by the conspirators and the man now claiming to be Paul VI was actually a communist doppelganger created by plastic surgery. The Baysiders were not in rebellion against their Church; they were only questioning the orders of conspirators and imposters who had infiltrated the Church hierarchy.

In 1986, Francis J. Mugavero, bishop of Brooklyn, made an announcement reiterating that Lueken's visions were false and contradicted Catholic doctrine. Mugavero's findings were sent to three hundred bishops throughout the United States and one hundred conferences of bishops throughout the world. Despite this censure from Church authorities, Lueken's followers still identify as Catholics in good standing and they defend their views citing canon law. They contend that Lueken's visions never received a proper investigation led by a bishop, and that the diocese's dismissal of Lueken is therefore not legitimate. If anyone has violated Church law, they argue, it is the modernists whom Lueken condemned for receiving communion in the hand and other ritual transgressions that go against long-established Catholic tradition.

Lueken continued to give regular messages from heaven until her death in 1995. In total, Mary, Jesus, and a variety of other heavenly beings spoke to her over three hundred times. These messages were consolidated into a canon known as the Bayside Prophecies. Although the crowds are nowhere near the size they were before Lueken's death, Baysiders still travel to Flushing Meadows from as far away as India and Malaysia. On the Internet, Lueken's messages have become part of a larger milieu of conspiracy theories and millennial speculation. Baysiders still await "The Chastisement" described in Lueken's messages. Many Baysiders believe that when God punishes mankind for its sins, the chastisement will take two forms—World War III, which will include a large-scale nuclear exchange, and a fiery comet that will collide with Earth and devastate the planet.

After Lueken's death, Our Lady of the Roses Shrine continued to hold vigils, promote the Bayside Prophecies, and coordinate pilgrimages to Flushing Meadows with followers from around the world. But in 1997, a schism occurred between the shrine's director, Michael Mangan, and Lueken's widower, Arthur Lueken. A judge ruled in favor of Arthur Lueken, declaring him president of Our Lady of the Roses Shrine (OLR) and award- ing him all of the organization's assets and facilities. Undaunted, Mangan formed his own group, Saint Michael's World Apostolate (SMWA). Both groups continued to arrive at the movement's sacred site in Flushing Meadows where they held their rival vigils. Once again, police were sent out to keep the peace. Today, this conflict has thawed into a sort of detente. The two groups have scheduled their access to the park much as divorcees might arrange custody of their children. Their celebrations of Catholic feast days are sometimes timed such that only one group will be present in the park on a given day. For events where both groups must be present, such as Sunday morning holy hour, they alternate which group will have access to the monument. One group may set its statue of the Virgin Mary on the Vatican monument; the other must use a nearby traffic island. There is little love lost between the two groups, but they have decided it is in everyone's interest to appear professional while in the park.

The vigils continue to attract newcomers who seem drawn to the sin- cerity of the attendees and the aura of sanctity surrounding their outdoor rituals. Many of those who have only recently begun saying rosaries in the park seem unaware of the history of Lueken's conflict with Church authorities or the details of the schism that led to there being two Marys in the park. Many report witnessing miracles near the vigil site or share stories of people recovering from terrible illnesses after praying there. For some, Flushing Meadows is simply a special place to say the rosary.

Like the various monuments left behind from the World's Fair, the vig- ils are evidence of amazing events that once occurred in the park. This book is a chronicle of these amazing events. The history of the Baysider movement is a series of contests over who has the authority to articulate a religious group's core tradition. In telling this story, I draw attention to the mechanisms by which lay communities impose their understanding of tradition over and against those of their ecclesiastical and lay opponents. The Baysiders assert their worldview not through legal arguments or proclamations but through daily, embodied practices and the strategic use of space and ritual. The Vatican Pavilion monument at Flushing Meadows Park is not only a sacred site, it is a site of epistemic power. The public rituals held there produce their own form of authority through which Baysiders are able to legitimate their understanding of the cosmos and—when they deem it necessary—even resist the authority of the magisterium.

Catholicism as an Imagined Community

As a movement, the Baysiders are defined by their seemingly paradoxical relationship with the Mother Church. Baysiders are simultaneously deeply critical of and profoundly deferential to Catholic authority. They hold vigils in Flushing Meadows against the wishes of the local diocese and yet they feel they are loyal Catholics—perhaps the last loyal Catholics left. Church authorities have also demonstrated contradictory attitudes toward the Baysiders. The official position of the Diocese of Brooklyn is that Lueken's visions are inauthentic and should not be supported. John Whelan, Archbishop of Hartford, Connecticut, took a stronger stance, claiming that in his opinion the Baysiders are heretical.[1] However, there have always been priests, monks, and nuns who support the Baysiders and attend vigils. I attended a vigil at Flushing Meadows where at least three priests were present. During the vigil, shrine leaders set up folding chairs behind the statue of Mary where these priests could take confessions from attendees. The relationship between Baysiders and Church authorities is neither static nor strictly oppositional. As Baysiders continue to try to make sense of the reforms of Vatican II, they engage Church authorities in a dance of deference and defiance. Church authorities have responded with their own dance of tolerance and censure. It is a dance that has lasted for more than forty years.

To make sense of this complicated relationship it is necessary to understand that the idea of the Catholic Church as a global and monolithic polity is an *imagined* community. In his work on nationalism, Benedict Anderson argued that all forms of community larger than a primeval village are imagined. This is not to say that communities are illusory or "fake" but rather that ongoing conceptual work is necessary in order for individuals to feel a sense of connection with others whom they never see face to face. Religious traditions, in particular, are continuously imagined and reimagined. Leonard Primiano claimed that " 'official' religion does not, in fact, exist."[2] Rather, normative religion exists only as an ideal type. The beliefs and practices of any given individual are always a vernacular expression of an "official" tradition that exists only in the abstract. This situation in which vernacular practices are united by an imagined normative ideal is especially true of Catholicism, which has countless varied and local expressions throughout the world. But despite these differences, Catholics are able to understand themselves as part of a global polity unified through such institutional symbols as apostolic succession, the body of canon law, and, especially, the office of pope and the authority of the magisterium.

While the imagined boundaries of Catholicism frequently seem natural and undisputed, historical circumstances can call them into question, forcing a renegotiation of what it means to be Catholic. Clifford Geertz noted the paradox that religion is concerned with ultimate and immutable truth, and yet inevitably changes over time, remarking, "Nothing, apparently, alters like the unalterable." Catholic leaders already knew this. Nearly a century before Geertz, the American Bishop John Ireland addressed the same problem when he wrote, "The church never changes and yet she changes."[3] Catholics have adopted different strategies for negotiating this paradox, leading to rival understandings of what normative Catholicism is. After Vatican II and the social changes of the 1960s, American Catholics became divided over how they remembered their own tradition. Reform-minded Catholics moved to dismiss pre-Conciliar devotional culture as a relic of the past while traditionalists celebrated and canonized it. The emergence of the Baysiders in the decade following Vatican II can be read as a historical moment in which the imagined boundaries of the Catholic polity faltered. Two Catholic cultures that had always taken for granted that they shared a common tradition became unexpectedly alienated from one another. Anthony Bevilacqua, an auxiliary bishop for the Diocese of Brooklyn, said of Lueken, "She has condemned Communion in the hand. She's condemned the Eucharistic Ministers. She said Pope Paul VI was an imposter, that somebody else took his place. I can go on with a thousand things. If that is authentic, we're in two different churches."[4] Conversely, the Baysiders felt it was Church authorities who had strayed from authentic Catholicism. As Dan, a sixty-one-year-old mechanical engineer and Baysider, explained to me, "It wasn't us lay Catholics who started changing all of the traditions."[5] In 1974, Lueken delivered an angry message from Jesus warning the clergy, "You have brought into My House all manners of whims and fancy, giving in to your carnal natures. Will you stand before Me as My representatives and say that your teaching has been pure in My sight? I shall spit you out and cast you into the fires!"[6] This exchange of condemnations was really a debate about how the imagined boundaries of the Catholic polity ought to be drawn.

It is this mutual sense of alienation and betrayal that makes the relationship between Baysiders and Church authorities so complex, so bitter, and so tragic. Baysiders lament the reforms of Vatican II and feel that the Catholic hierarchy has been compromised by modernism. But they also reject the so-called sedevacantist movements that formed after the Council. These were groups of traditionalist Catholics who declared that the Seat of Peter is empty and that the Catholic hierarchy is no longer legitimate. Even when Lueken was most at odds with her diocese, she urged her followers not to leave the Church. The Baysiders believe in a prophecy that one day the Mother Church will come around: Waters will spring forth from the ground at St. Robert Bellarmine's as they did at Lourdes, a great basilica will be erected in Bayside, and Veronica Lueken will be canonized as "Veronica of the Cross." A leader from Our Lady of the Roses Shrine explained that when this happens, the shrine will be under the direct control of the Church and lay leadership will no longer be necessary. For Baysiders, this prophecy presents the hope that they, their clergy, and their tradition will one day be restored to a harmonious whole.

Historicizing the Definitional Boundaries of Catholicism

In the contest to define Catholic tradition, Church authorities wield an enormous advantage over the Baysiders. A stark example of this occurred in 1978 when Lueken and her followers attempted to form the legal entity "Our Lady of the Roses Shrine." The Supreme Court of New York initially denied Lueken's application for incorporation because the proposed organization did not meet the state's standards for a Catholic organization.

Article 5 of the New York Religious Corporations Law specifies that a certificate of incorporation for an unincorporated Catholic Church "shall be executed and acknowledged by the Roman Catholic archbishop or bishop, and the vicar-general of the diocese in which its place of worship is, and by the rector of the church, and by two laymen, members of such church who shall be selected by such officials, or by a majority of such officials."[7] Needless to say, Lueken's group had no hope of meeting these requirements. In fact, the Diocese of Brooklyn actively attempted to block the application.[8] Of course, Lueken and her followers did not seek to establish themselves as a Catholic "church" per se. Their application described the group's purpose as "to print, mail, disseminate Roman Catholic information, to conduct prayer vigils, and with divine guidance keep the knowledge of God and His plan for peace and security in the hearts of all mankind." However, Judge Arthur W. Lonschein deemed this purpose sufficient to invoke Article 5 and added in his opinion that the very *name* "Our Lady of the Roses" was suggestive of Catholicism and therefore would require the approval of Church authorities. Lonschein added:

> I make no determination as to the propriety or social desirability of the incorporator's purposes. Nor is it for me to presume to pass judgment on the religious quality or spiritual probity of the purposes of the proposed corporation.... It is not my determination that Ms. Lueken may not seek to incorporate as a religious corporation or may not seek to incorporate as a not-for-profit corporation where their purposes may not involve worship.[9]

In other words, whatever Lueken was doing was fine, so long as she conceded it was *not* Catholicism. This decision from a secular court demonstrates the incredible leverage that Church authorities have over the laity in defining the boundaries of Catholicism.

If the Baysiders were not "really" Catholics, then what were they? In the 1970s, the American media was preoccupied with the threat of subversive "cults" and several journalists applied this pejorative label to Lueken and her followers. An article in *New York Magazine* drew a parallel between Lueken and Jim Jones. *The National Enquirer* blasted the Baysiders as a cult and accused Lueken of "brainwashing" her followers.[10] The few religion scholars who have written on the Baysiders have framed this group as a "new religious movement," a form of "re-enchantment," or "folk piety."[11] While these categories have their uses, they can also obscure the inherent messiness of the Baysiders' Catholicism. These scholarly designations all assume that Baysider Catholicism is not normative. This assumption is decidedly not shared by the Baysiders themselves, who feel that they have preserved Catholic tradition while everyone else has deviated from it. Meredith McGuire notes that the definitional boundaries that permeate the field of religion are contested and represent the exertion of power. Categories such as "mainstream Catholic" and "cult" are not objective realities but the result of a series of battles for legitimacy. In order to have a historically accurate understanding of religion, McGuire argues, scholars must historicize these definitional boundaries and pay attention to their contested nature.[12]

The Baysiders' dance of deference and defiance has countless historical precedents. While a religious tradition cannot be neatly bifurcated along the axis of "popular" and "elite," there has always been a fault-line between the vernacular practices of lay Catholics and the doctrinal positions of the Church hierarchy.[13] While these two faces of Catholicism share much in common, they often see the world in different ways. Where vernacular Catholicism blurs the lines between sacred and profane, finding the miraculous in the local and the everyday, the hierarchy generally works to consolidate access to the sacred within prescribed times, spaces, and rituals. They employ different mechanisms and traditions for evaluating truth claims, especially claims of the supernatural and the miraculous. Perhaps most importantly, they are concerned with different audiences. Church authorities are concerned with how Catholic practices will be regarded by governments, theological and political opponents, and the culture at large. By contrast, lay Catholics rarely worry about what outsiders might think of their devotions.

Despite these differences, the two faces of Catholicism share an imagined community. Much of Catholic devotional culture represents the work of priests, nuns, and laity constructing a shared culture together. However, certain historical circumstances motivate Church authorities to police the definitional boundaries of Catholicism in ways that alienate lay Catholics. As was the case at Bayside, outside criticism often motivates the hierarchy to rein in devotional practices, either condemning them as superstition or assimilating them into an authorized canon of Catholic tradition. The Counter-Reformation was in essence a prolonged attempt by the hierarchy to assimilate and control local expressions of Catholic devotion in response to Protestant critiques. As was always the case, some of these reforms were embraced by lay Catholics while others inspired conflict and resistance. Church authorities made similar efforts to redefine Catholic tradition in response to rationalist critics following the Enlightenment and to American Protestants who accused Catholics of "Romanism" during the nineteenth century. Different circumstances, however, have inspired Church authorities to embrace devotional culture in order to channel popular support against an outside threat. Historically, popes have endorsed popular Marian apparitions when they are associated with opposition to secular opponents such as Italian nationalists in the nineteenth century and communism in the twentieth century. In the United States, the *Roe v. Wade* decision of 1973 brought about a similar moment of alignment between Church authorities and lay Catholic culture. Cardinal Joseph John O'Connor of New York organized protests of abortion clinics and, in the mid-1980s, Baysiders came out in droves to support demonstrations organized by O'Connor. In the summer of 2012, the Obama administration's "HHS mandate," which would require employers to provide health coverage for contraception, inspired another moment of alignment. Baysider leaders spoke out against the mandate and felt they were fighting alongside their bishops for their rights as Catholics.

It is through this model of Catholicism as a process of conflict and collaboration between lay Catholics and Church authorities that the Baysiders are best understood. The Baysiders do not represent a deviant sect or a localized variation of Catholicism, but rather an ongoing and asymmetrical debate about what Catholicism is. Just as Baysiders have expressed reluctance to defy Church authorities, the Diocese of Brooklyn appeared torn between their desire to let lay Catholics enjoy their devotional culture and a need to protect the public image of the Church. Were it not for the disruptions created by holding massive vigils in a densely populated neighborhood and the complaints of the BHCA, Lueken might have been able to continue her vigils without censure for much longer.[14] Instead, pressure continued to mount, causing the two faces of Catholic culture to become increasingly exasperated and alienated from each other. When she argued with Church authorities, Lueken discovered aspects of her own Church that were unfamiliar to her. Her parish church was not simply God's house, it was also a legally constituted institution controlled by a parish council. The Church hierarchy was not simply an abstract symbol of the connection between her parish priests and the pope, it was revealed as a bureaucracy in which clergy obey a strict chain of command and ideals are often mitigated by political expediency. Likewise, diocesan officials felt bewildered by the response of Lueken and her followers.

Internal documents express disbelief that so many lay Catholics would take Lueken's visions seriously. When authorities attempted to stop the vigils at Bayside, they were demoralized by how little power they had to control the pilgrims. But despite this process of estrangement, there were some lines that were never crossed. Lueken always insisted that Catholics were not to leave the Church. Likewise, Church authorities never threatened Lueken or her followers with excommunication. The conflict between Baysiders and their Church does not resemble a heresiological battle between rival religions so much as a painful separation between partners whose feelings for each other have changed. In thinking about this conflict, it is relevant that the Catholic Catechism defines divorce as immoral, arguing that it "introduces disorder into the family and into society." "This disorder," it is argued, "brings grave harm to the deserted spouse, to children traumatized by the separation of their parents and often torn between them, and because of its contagious effect, which makes it truly a plague on society."[15] The Catholic understanding of divorce as a social evil also applies to the relationship between the Baysiders and Church authorities, who have continued their partnership long after it has ceased to be convenient or pleasurable. This image of alienated practitioners who remain committed to their Church in bad times as well as good is often a tragic one, but it is also noble in its stoic commitment to an ideal.

Technologies of Power

Marian apparitions demonstrate the kinds of power that lay Catholics can bring to bear in defining the boundaries of Catholic culture. Scholars have disagreed as to whether the symbolic power of Mary in Catholic tradition is an inherently destabilizing influence that perpetually challenges the status quo or a form of social control exerted over lay Catholics. Victor and Edith Turner, in their analysis of Marian pilgrimages, see Mary as firmly aligned with the nonhierarchical face of Catholicism. They argue that Marian apparitions "point to the hidden, nonhierarchical domain of the Church and stress the power of the weak; the community; the rare and unprecedented, as against the regular, ordained, and normative."[16] Conversely, feminist critics of Catholicism frequently argue that Mary has served as a tool for imposing patriarchal gender roles.[17] In reality, Mary is neither inherently subversive nor inherently stabilizing. Like all potent religious symbols, Mary has the power to either maintain cultural institutions or challenge them. Robert Orsi describes the figures of Catholic devotional life as "cultural double agents, constituting and destabilizing both culture and self."[18] When conflicts arise between ecclesiastical and popular Catholicism, the Virgin Mary often acts as a sort of fulcrum that determines the balance of symbolic power. This is particularly the case with Marian apparitions. While apparitional movements cannot convene councils or issue papal bulls, they have a powerful ability to shape Catholic culture through the strategic use of sacred space and embodied rituals. This power is well known to Catholic authorities as well as secular governments around the world. At various times, Church authorities have sought either to harness this power of apparitional movements or else to stamp them out.[19] The fact that the Baysider movement has survived the death of its seer and continues to resist an unsupportive diocese is a testament to their power to assert their interpretation of Catholicism. While Baysiders have become conversant in canon law and presented legal arguments for the legitimacy of their movement, their ability to resist Church authority really comes from the fact that they have continuously occupied public space that they have rendered sacred through ritual. Roger Friedland and Richard Hecht describe the religious center as a "technology of power."[20] Baysiders discovered that their ability to impose their own meaning onto sacred space and to assert their presence through sound gave them a kind of authority. Ironically, as the Baysiders developed into a global movement, these same technologies of power were used in internecine conflicts between rival factions of Baysiders. Jonathan Z. Smith once defined religion as "the quest, within the bounds of the human, historical condition, for the power to manipulate and negotiate one's 'situation' so as to have 'space' in which to meaningfully dwell."[21] The history of the Baysiders is the story of such a quest. As a case study, it reveals much about how vernacular forms of religion employ technologies of power to alter their situation, even in the face of contested definitional boundaries.

The most important technology of power for any apparitional movement is the control of sacred space. Marian apparitions have been reported from Mexico to Cairo and from Rwanda to Japan. In almost every case, the apparition is closely linked to the location where it first appeared. Apparitional movements generally assume a powerful connection between supernatural presence and physical space. Baysiders feel that prayers are more efficacious if they are performed at the vigil site in Flushing Meadows. By saying the rosary at Flushing Meadows, they believe they are mitigating the weight of the world's many sins and staving off the coming Chastisement that will punish humanity. I spoke with one Baysider who had recently lost his wife. A shrine leader assured him that not only was the community praying for his wife, they were doing so at the vigil site where their prayers would have maximum potency. Significantly, the supernatural power of place applies to demonic forces as well as heavenly ones. The former Jesuit Malachi Martin (whose books on conspiracies within the Vatican are popular with Baysiders) describes the significance of physical space in *Hostage to the Devil*, his book about exorcism. Martin writes that cases of possession are often linked to physical locations and that there is a "puzzle of spirit and place" that cannot be explained but must be accepted as a fact of exorcism.[22]

Scholars theorizing this puzzle of spirit and place have shifted from poetical interpretations of sacred space to political ones. Eliade understood sacred space as a site where the sacred "erupts" into the chaotic world of the profane and imposes order.[23] This model is more or less how Baysiders themselves understand the significance of the vigil grounds: as a place where heavenly beings descend to bestow blessings and knowledge to the Earth and its inhabitants. Smith modified Eliade's theory in two ways. First, he noted that sacred space is disjunctive rather than conjunctive. That is, sacred sites do not function to connect the sacred to the profane but to separate them by mapping out exactly where one ends and the other begins. Sacred and profane are shifting, mobile categories and the creation of sacred space is one way through which religious communities effect these shifts. Second, the sacredness of a sacred site does not simply erupt from heaven but is created by human efforts. There is symbolic labor that goes into establishing and consecrating sacred space in the form of repeated and embodied practices. Smith explained, "Repetition is the human mode of articulating absolute Reality."[24]

Foucault noted that "space is fundamental in any exercise of power."[25] Smith's insights reveal that the ability to create sacred space as the Baysiders did at St. Robert Bellarmine's church and Flushing Meadows is inherently an exercise in epistemic power. By continually holding vigils at these sites, Baysiders gained an ability to legitimize their worldview as normative and impose their own meaning onto the world. During my ethnography with the Baysiders, I found that many of the controversial ideas expressed in the Bayside Prophecies, such as conspiracy theories, were not especially important to many Baysiders. The only point that was non-negotiable was the belief that Jesus and Mary really are appearing in Flushing Meadows Park. Sacred space, then, is the foundation for the entire Baysider worldview. This use of consecrated space is a technology of power that makes it possible to resist if not overcome the rival power of the magisterium. When a nominally Catholic group has been holding vigils continuously for forty years, it becomes increasingly implausible to claim that their beliefs and practices are not part of Catholic tradition.

The connection between space and power is not lost on the opponents of apparitional movements. This is one reason why the residents of Bayside Hills were so upset that Lueken's movement appropriated the name "Baysiders" for themselves. David Chidester and Edward Linenthal note that "sacred space is inevitably contested space."[26] Authorities seeking to suppress apparitional movements invariably attempt to separate them from their sacred site. Before the apparitions at Lourdes received Church approval, the local government forbade pilgrims from visiting the grotto and even erected barricades, which pilgrims repeatedly tore down. At Medjugorje in Bosnia-Herzegovina, police blocked access to the apparition site for more than two years. Pilgrims met at local churches or in private homes until they could return. Baysiders went through a similar round of banishment and reclamation. They are now somewhat unique among apparitional movements in that they effectively have two sacred sites. St. Robert Bellarmine's church in Bayside, where Lueken had hoped to establish a basilica, is still considered the true home of the Baysider movement. After the injunction effectively exiled them from this site, the Baysiders established a secondary sacred site, which has now become a technology of power in its own right. The ongoing struggle between rival Baysider factions to control the site at Flushing Meadows is evidence of its power.

Along with space, sound is a crucial technology of power in the Baysider story. The Baysiders used the sounds of their vigils to claim space as their own and to consecrate it as sacred. Controversy over religious sounds is particularly common in urban settings where multiple religious polities coexist in a finite space. In his recent work on religion and sound, Isaac Weiner points out that sound frequently spills over the normative boundaries meant to keep religion contained. Sound is well suited to claiming space because it imposes on others in ways that sights do not. Weiner quotes John Dewey, "Vision is a spectator. Hearing is a participator."[27]

The attempt to impose meaning using sound soon led to "acoustic warfare," as others sought to disrupt the work of the Baysiders. J. Z. Smith framed sacred space in terms of communication, writing: "A sacred space is a place of clarification (a focusing lens) where men and gods are held to

be transparent to one another. It is a place where, as in all forms of communication, static and noise (i.e., the accidental) are decreased so that the
exchange of information can be increased."[28] During the Battle of Bayside,
the Baysiders' opponents sought to impose static onto the consecrating
sounds of the vigils. Residents organized concerts during vigils, led angry
chants, or ran their lawnmowers to counter the sound of prayers. As tensions with Church authorities worsened, diocesan officials tried reading a
letter from the bishop aloud through a bullhorn. The Baysiders responded
to all of these tactics with more sound, by saying the rosary louder. In
Flushing Meadows, both groups lead the rosary using portable micro-
phones. Standing between the two vigils, one experiences the dissonance
of two discordant sets of rosaries. The words are the same but the prayers
are out of sync with each other. This effect creates an invisible barrier between the two groups in the form of a sonic "no man's land." At stake in
these sonic battles is an attempt to claim sacred space and, in turn, to seize
the power to impose one vision of tradition over and against another. It is
through such technologies of power that contested and vernacular expressions of religion like the Baysiders defend themselves and create space in
which to meaningfully dwell.

A Word about Fieldwork

Doing ethnographic work with the Baysiders presented several difficulties.
Robert Orsi comments that fieldwork often comes with the sense of "in-
trusion, interruption, and prying." I certainly had this sense throughout
this project. The Baysiders are an embattled group and are particularly
wary of the media, who they feel have consistently attempted to distort
their movement and portray Lueken as either mentally ill or a fraud. I repeatedly had to explain that I was not a journalist, whom Orsi describes
as "the dreaded doubles" of field researchers.[29] Even academic researchers
who have met with the Baysiders have sometimes been dismissive of their
worldview. Because of this, Baysiders were understandably suspicious
of yet another outsider seeking to interview them. Compounding this
problem, several of the leaders I spoke with associated academia with a
modernist and politically liberal agenda that was at odds with their values.
On the other hand, when Baysiders asked about my prior research, they
were impressed that I had been to the diocese's archives. Many Baysiders
regarded the diocese as secretive and unhelpful. They were curious to

learn what I found through my archival research and this became an en-trée to conversation about the shrine.

An additional problem was that the two rival groups almost always gathered in the same place at the same time. This made it extremely diffi-cult to negotiate entry with both groups. When two vigils were being held, no one went back and forth between the two groups. Generally, members of one group regarded the members of the other as invisible. When I ini-tially arrived at the park, I went to meet the contacts I had made through e-mail with SMWA. Only after approaching one group did I realize the social barriers that kept me from approaching the other. I simply found it too awkward to approach both groups during a single event.

I was far more successful at negotiating entry with the larger group, SMWA. SMWA's vigils typically drew forty to fifty people. During the course of my research I was able to have several lengthy conversations with members of this group from around the country and around the world. I was able to form a closer working relationship with SMWA leaders the more I returned to the vigil site. One leader explained to me, "All we ask is that you be fair."[30]

OLR is a considerably smaller group and rarely had more than a dozen people present for an event. The group's leadership did not respond to my e-mails or phone calls. I decided to show up unannounced at one of their vigils on an evening when they were alone in the park. Upon arriving, I explained that I was a researcher. The group's leader responded that OLR has an official policy of not granting interviews. When I asked if I could observe their vigil, I was told that vigils are open to the public and that anyone may participate. This allowed me to do participant observation for over three hours. When the vigil was over, I was able to speak infor-mally with some of the other attendees, who were cordial. Before I left, the group's leader made it clear that e-mails and phone calls would not be answered. She did express interest in my archival research and suggested I mail it to a PO Box maintained by the shrine. "But your other stuff," she added, "It's not Catholic. And it's not good."[31] From this comment I inferred that leaders from the shrine had received my initial e-mails, researched my background on the Internet, discovered my previous pub-lications on topics such as religion and popular culture and new religious movements, and concluded that I was an unwholesome or untrustworthy person. Following this encounter, I focused my ethnography exclusively on SMWA. Had I made initial contact with OLR instead of SMWA and suc-cessfully negotiated entry, my subsequent experience with the Baysiders would likely have been very different.

It is sometimes said that the task of a religion scholar is to render the strange familiar and the familiar strange.[32] From an initial textual encounter, the messages of Veronica Lueken are certainly strange. In addition to describing a conspiracy within the Vatican and a comet that will devastate the planet, the Bayside Prophecies also mention such details as invading Soviets armed with death rays, UFOs, and vampires—demonically possessed beings who require human blood. Without any sort of cultural context through which to interpret these messages, the Baysiders can appear totally other. But by spending time at the vigil site talking to Baysiders, I came closer to understanding how Baysiders see the world. Baysiders firmly believe in the supernatural and that miracles regularly occur during vigils. Most of them also believe that society is in moral decline and that their freedoms as Catholics and Americans are threatened by powerful and insidious forces. However, the Baysiders I met were neither irrational nor hysterical. As with all cultural traditions surrounding a sacred text, some parts of the Bayside Prophecies are emphasized, others less so. Of the hundreds of Baysiders present, no one spoke of death rays, UFOs, or vampires. Many believed in the coming of a comet and that Paul VI was an imposter. However, these beliefs did not prevent them from participating in mainstream society. As one Baysider explained it, "Our Lady doesn't want us to go crazy. We believe and we pray the rosary. I'm not going to dig myself a hole in the backyard and hide in it."[33] Another remarked, "If I die of old age before the Chastisement comes, that's fine with me."[34]

Furthermore, from their perspective, it is the rest of the world that has turned away from common sense. Baysiders expressed deep concern over violence and sexuality in the media, gay marriage, and, especially, the issue of abortion. They also felt that their Church had neglected its duty to speak out on these issues and had capitulated to changing social mores. Compared to what the modern Church had become, Lueken's messages seemed far more sensible to them.

The Plot of the Book

This book chronicles the history of the Baysiders from Veronica Lueken's early visions to the present, framing the movement's development as the result of an evolving relationship with Church authorities. Chapter 2 describes Lueken's early biography through her first visions and the formation of her new identity as a Marian seer. A number of theorists have considered the problem of how and why ordinary people became seers, prophets, and shamans.[35] Without making claims about what the ultimate source of Lueken's revelations was, I argue that her *social role* as a seer was effectively created for her by the contests over Catholic tradition underway in the early 1970s. When Lueken talked about her experiences, she received both a "push" effect from Church authorities, who regarded her mysticism as embarrassing, and a "pull" effect from traditionalist lay Catholics, who sought some sort of agency in resisting liturgical reforms. These social factors worked to transform frightening and anomalous experiences into prophecies and Lueken into a channel for popular dissent over the reforms of Vatican II.

Chapter 3 documents the Battle of Bayside in which the BCHA and the Diocese of Brooklyn sought to remove Lueken and her followers from St. Robert Bellarmine's. This was a period of intense struggle between the two faces of Catholicism, in which Church authorities were motivated by pressure from Bayside residents and national media. The response of both Baysiders and Church authorities escalated as the two groups became increasingly exasperated with each other. The Battle of Bayside reveals much about how emerging religious movements are shaped by conflict.

Chapter 4 explores the blossoming of Baysider culture after their arrival in Flushing Meadows following the Battle of Bayside. Without being hindered by their Catholic and secular opponents, the Baysiders were able to continue their project of creating a space in which to meaningfully dwell. In addition to formalizing an institutional hierarchy and a liturgical structure for vigils, this period saw the creation of a prophetic worldview through which the numerous social changes of the 1970s were rendered sensible.

Chapter 5 examines the spread of the Baysider movement throughout the world. This rapid dissemination of Lueken's messages across continents was particularly alarming for Church authorities. As the Baysider movement grew, it too became an imagined community consisting of numerous vernacular expressions. Baysider leaders were now faced with their own set of definitional boundaries to police. Just as Church authorities had been unable to control pilgrims in Bayside, Baysider leaders found that they had little authority over individuals whose zeal threatened to slow their movement's progress toward legitimacy.

Chapter 6 describes the history of the movement from Lueken's death in 1995 to the present. With the death of their seer, the Baysiders suffered a heavy loss of members and resources. In 1997 the group split into OLR and SMWA, as well as a number of independent groups and ministries. This opened yet another battle over who could speak for a tradition, and the same technologies of power were deployed that had been used during the Battle of Bayside. Unlike the Battle of Bayside, the schism has become a bitter war of attrition that has lasted nearly two decades. Like the Unisphere and New York Pavilion, the Baysider vigils in Flushing Meadows are a reminder of past glories. The vigils no longer attract the crowds of thousands that they did when Lueken was alive. However, the Baysiders have persevered and still continue to draw newcomers. A new generation of Catholics who never knew Lueken or experienced the changes of Vatican II has begun to attend vigils. In the final analysis, the ability of the Baysiders to endure for almost half a century in the face of censure from Church authorities demonstrates that they are not helpless in defining Catholic tradition and that their vigils are rituals of power. The Baysiders serve as a reminder that while the center defines the periphery, the periphery also has the power to define the center.

2

Making Sense of the Anomalous

ON A NOVEMBER night a worried mother lay awake in bed. She had been in poor health and feared that she would not be well enough to care for her husband and her seven children. Like many Catholic women in this situation, she prayed to Mary and Jesus for help. She heard a voice in the hallway and at first thought it was one of her children. She rose from bed and stepped into the hall where she saw a veiled stranger staring back at her. Terrified, she retreated into the bedroom praying the Hail Mary. The figure followed her. Too frightened to look, she lay in bed with her back to the figure until it disappeared. It was a month before she related this experience to her husband, who suggested that the supernatural visitor might have been the Virgin Mary. Mary had most likely come because of "the wickedness of the world." For months, the woman prayed to be forgiven for spurning the apparition. On Good Friday, the crucifix on her bedroom wall began glowing in the dark. She heard a voice, which she now identified as Mary's, tell her, "I will be back but not in this room, but where and when the flowers bloom, trees and grass are green."[1]

This is not the story of Veronica Lueken, but of Mary Ann Van Hoof of Necedah, Wisconsin. In 1950, Van Hoof was the seer for a series of apparitions that attracted crowds of thousands and drew heavy censure from Church authorities. Like Lueken's, many of Van Hoof's messages were apocalyptic and conspiracy driven. Both women underwent similar transformations, changing in a relatively short period of time from mild Catholic housewives and mothers into charismatic leaders of controversial Marian movements. Lueken's career as a seer began just as Van Hoof's was going into decline. Some scholars have suggested that some of the content of Lueken's messages seems derivative of Van Hoof's.[2] Lueken's detractors have claimed that the two seers knew each other or that Lueken was callously attempting to mimic Van Hoof's career.[3] Baysider leaders deny any such connection. The only evidence that the two ever spoke comes from Lueken's confidante, Ann Ferguson. In an interview for *These Last Days Radio Program*, an independent Baysider radio show, Ferguson said that Lueken telephoned Van Hoof in 1969, when her own mystical experiences were just beginning. According to Ferguson, the alleged conversation was very short. Van Hoof's only advice was, "You had better forget about giving out Heaven's messages as you will be persecuted."[4]

Even if there was no direct contact between the two seers, the culture of Marian apparitions functions as a " chain of memory" by which believers are united through a shared knowledge of Marian lore.[5] It is expected that tropes and signs from one apparition will reappear at another. Critics sometimes point to the similarities between Marian apparitions to argue that a particular vision is derivative and therefore false. Sociologists, however, understand that a mystical experience can only be interpreted and described within a particular cultural context. David Yamane points out that sociologists and historians cannot study religious experiences themselves but only the meaning that is extracted from them. He explains, "By the time the individual comes to understand the experience, it has past. What remains is the memory, the interpretation, the linguistification, the recounting, the emplotment, the narrativization. This is the 'data' which sociologists must study."[6] This data is more useful to historians of religion than the "truth" of a mystical experience. As Courtney Bender suggests, scholars should pay attention to how accounts of religious experiences are not only descriptive but also prescriptive and inscriptive. By attending to the mechanisms through which these experiences are interpreted, mystical experiences can be examined as sites of religious history.[7]

Many people have reported having a mystical experience at some point in their lives. Typically these experiences are discussed with only a few and the effect on the experiencer's worldview is minimal.[8] It is when the experiencer seeks confirmation from others and multiple people become invested in negotiating and contesting what happened that mystical experiences become historically significant. For both Lueken and Van Hoof, their experiences were initially frightening and confusing until they could be interpreted through a tradition of Marian apparitions. The process of interpretation was not a solitary undertaking but a collective one that involved friends, family members, lay Catholics, and clergy—both sympathetic and critical. The various interests of all of these parties came to influence the meaning that these anomalous experiences ultimately acquired. People paid attention to the visions of Van Hoof and Lueken because they seemed relevant to larger social and religious issues. As the seers themselves tried to understand what these experiences meant, those around them sought to bring their visions to bear on such problems as the Cold War, changing social mores, and the reforms of Vatican II. The individual task of interpreting an anomalous experience became entangled in a collective effort to impose meaningful order onto the world.

Certain social and historical conditions must be in place for an "ordinary" mystical experience to be received as a vision or a prophecy. For Van Hoof and Lueken, an ongoing struggle to define "normal" Catholic tradition created the conditions under which the public became invested in interpreting their experiences. Both women experienced rejection from Church authorities that caused them to feel isolated and defensive. This rejection drove them to seek support from lay Catholics who were drawn to the symbolic capital of a Marian seer. In both cases, it was the "push" of Church authorities and the "pull" from interested lay Catholics, together, that steered a woman with anomalous experiences into her new public role as a seer and a voice of popular dissent.

The Case of Mary Ann Van Hoof

Van Hoof's career followed a trajectory similar to Lueken's. The forces that aligned around their visions were similar, and the response of Church authorities to Van Hoof set a precedent that was frequently invoked in debates surrounding Lueken. Van Hoof was born Mary Ann Bieber. Though baptized Catholic at birth, she received no religious training. Her mother, an immigrant from Hungary, had been active in a Spiritualist lodge where Mary Ann may have attended séances. Her connection to Catholicism became stronger after her marriage to Godfred Van Hoof in 1935. Life was hard for the Van Hoofs, who struggled to maintain their 142-acre farm. When her experiences first began on November 12, 1949, Mary Ann was suffering from heart pain and a kidney ailment, and was profoundly worried about the future of her farm and her family. Her initial interpretation of the apparition vacillated between the cultural views of her Catholic husband and her Spiritualist mother. She thought it might have been a visitation by a saint or by a spirit of the dead. It was her husband who suggested that the apparition had actually been the Virgin Mary and that Mary does not appear simply to comfort troubled mothers but to deliver messages of global importance. On April 7, Good Friday, 1950, Van Hoof received a message from Mary to go to her parish priest and ask that a rosary be offered every evening at eight o'clock. She related this message to her parish priest, Father S. R. Lengowski, who was initially supportive.

On May 28, 1950, Pentecost Sunday, Van Hoof witnessed a full apparition. Mary appeared hovering in her yard amid a small grove of ash trees. She gave Van Hoof a commission, explaining that she was to be a "victim soul," suffering in order to redeem others. Mary promised that she would return on four future dates: June 4, June 16, August 15, and October 7. This sort of "schedule" is part of the lore of Marian apparitions. At Fatima, Portugal, the most important apparition of the twentieth century, three child seers reported that Mary appeared to them on May 13, 1917, and promised to return five more times, always on the 13th of the month.

Fatima was an important lens through which Van Hoof and the public came to interpret her experiences. Lucia Dos Santos, the only one the three child seers to survive to adulthood, published three books of memoirs between 1935 and 1941. She claimed that on July 13, 1917, the Virgin had imparted three secrets to the children. The first had been a vision of hell. The second was a desire that Russia be consecrated to Mary's immaculate heart. If this was not done, Russia would spread its errors throughout the world, bringing war and persecutions of the Church. The third secret was sealed in the Vatican and not released until the year 2000. For North American Catholics, Dos Santos's memoirs linked patriotic and religious opposition to communism with Marian piety. Many who came to see Van Hoof expected an "American Fatima." Some even reported seeing the sun spin as it had in Portugal in 1917.

Since the Council of Trent, it has been the duty of bishops to assess claims of private revelation, including Marian apparitions. While local priests supported Van Hoof's visions, John R. Treacy, Bishop of La Crosse, Wisconsin, did not. On June 15, 1950, he sent a team of priests, one of whom was the editor of the diocesan newspaper, to investigate Van Hoof. After interviewing the seer, the investigators shut themselves in a dark room with Van Hoof's crucifix to see if it would glow. It did not. Following this interrogation, Van Hoof's visions began to take a defensive and even paranoid turn.

The next day, more than a thousand people arrived at the Van Hoof home for the expected apparition. One woman burst in uninvited, weeping and announcing that she had been cured of asthma. After that, Father

Lengowski had a guard placed in the home to keep out strangers. As the crowds around the house grew, six pilgrims gathered on the cellar door, causing it to collapse. Van Hoof's message from Mary stated, "My child, Satan will approach you in the form of a man dressed in lamb's clothing and question you and try to confuse you."[9] This was an apparent indictment of Bishop Treacy and his investigation. Van Hoof conveyed Mary's wish that a shrine be built on that spot. She also described a vivid scene of a ruined city in which people were dying of what appeared to be radiation poisoning. This was followed by a call to return to righteousness and to pray for the conversion of Russia.[10]

For the next apparition, on August 16, reporters from *Newsweek*, *Time*, *Life*, and *The New York Times* arrived in Necedah. At the Van Hoofs' parish, the bishop had to authorize mass every half hour to accommodate pilgrims. Police were needed to escort the family in and out of the church. When she delivered her message, pilgrims stood as far as half a mile away. State police estimated that 100,000 people from around the United States and beyond had gathered. Van Hoof warned of a Satanic, communist conspiracy threatening to engulf America. She described plans for an invasion (presumably by Russia) that would start in Alaska and spread down through the West Coast. She also asked for prayers for American politicians, especially Wisconsin senator Joseph McCarthy. Within Van Hoof's body of messages, McCarthy—a Catholic whose name has become synonymous with fanatical opposition to communism—is presented as a sort of saint and later a martyr. The final apparition on October 7 drew approximately 30,000 people. This marked the end of Van Hoof's large-scale messages but not her mystical experiences. A number of followers moved to Necedah where they formed a community and continued to promote her messages until her death in 1985. Van Hoof's conflict with Church authorities continued to escalate. Indeed, an article in *The Bayside Times* suggested that in developing its strategy for dealing with Lueken, the Diocese of Brooklyn had examined the case of Van Hoof.[11]

Van Hoof's messages were initially very personal. On May 30, 1950, Mary explained to her, "You received no love, which you longed for in your home." Diocesan investigators interpreted this statement as referring to Van Hoof's father, who had beaten her repeatedly as a child.[12] This statement, along with Mary's message that Van Hoof was "a victim soul" served to articulate and interpret the seer's personal pain and suffering. However, as Van Hoof's experiences went on, the messages shifted from having a personal significance to one of global and historical import. Her visions often reflected popular Cold War anxieties about nuclear war and subversive threats from communist infiltrators. In some of Van Hoof's messages, Mary sounds like a general relaying the locations of Russian submarines and the strategic significance of various nations. Her followers had a great deal of leeway in arranging these inchoate warnings and visions into a coherent narrative of past and future events. Eventually, Van Hoof and her followers outlined a "super-conspiracy" in which many forces were arrayed against America in a system she called "Satan's Chain of Command." Among these forces were "The Learned Elders of Zion."[13] This suggests that at some point Van Hoof was tutored in the global conspiracy outlined in the anti-Semitic forgery *The Protocols of the Elders of Zion*. Somehow the messages shifted from a focus on personal pain and suffering to expression of much broader cultural concerns about the Cold War, the perceived secularization of American culture, and fears of subversive conspiracies.

This change from a sickly housewife struggling to interpret an inexplicable experience to an apocalyptic seer rallying America against its spiritual and physical enemies occurred through both a "push" from Church authorities who rejected her and a "pull" from interested lay Catholics who endorsed her role as seer and influenced the interpretation of her experiences. While her parish priest, Father Lengowski, was supportive, his superiors eventually forbade him from visiting the Van Hoof farm and finally transferred him to another parish seventy-five miles away. Similarly, those priests and nuns who were supportive of Van Hoof were compelled to visit the farm in plain clothes and maintain a low profile. Meanwhile, continued investigations organized by the diocese seem to have made Van Hoof feel defensive and alienated from Church authorities. During Holy Week in 1952, Bishop Treacy ordered Van Hoof to report to Marquette Medical School for a ten-day medical examination. Van Hoof cooperated, possibly viewing the medical study as a chance to validate her experiences to the Church. A panel of three psychiatrists concluded that she suffered from "hysteria and repressed sexual anxiety."[14] Three years later Van Hoof's visions were officially condemned. In 1975, Treacy's successor, Bishop Frederick W. Freking, ordered Van Hoof's movement to disband. When they refused, Freking issued a formal interdict against Van Hoof and six of her followers. This barred them from receiving the sacraments, and Van Hoof and her followers were denied communion at their parish church.

As Van Hoof's relationship with her church continued to deteriorate, she turned increasingly to support from lay Catholics who were convinced she had an important message for the world. She surrounded herself with a coterie of friends she called her "Chosen Ones," who screened all of her visitors. One of the most important of these, Henry Swan, became a manager and publisher of sorts for Van Hoof. He is credited with helping her organize her messages into a coherent "theology of history" that outlines the forces of Satan's Chain of Command, the current end-times scenario, and what followers must do to prepare.[15] As the Church pushed Van Hoof away, Swan pulled her closer. The conspiratorial worldview espoused by Swan helped her to make sense of the escalating attacks from Church authorities: They were trying to discredit her because they were under the influence of the conspiracy. Had Church authorities not alienated Van Hoof or made her defensive about her experiences, she might never have come to rely so heavily on figures like Swan. Instead, the diocesan officials effectively ceded their influence over Van Hoof and her visions, giving her lay Catholic followers a greater role in shaping how the messages were interpreted and the narrative that ultimately emerged from them.

Veronica Lueken's First Visions

The woman who would become the seer of Bayside was born Veronica Kearn on July 12, 1923, in Jamaica, Queens. Her mother remarried when Veronica was young and Veronica was adopted by her stepfather, whose surname was McDonald.[16] The McDonalds were a poor working-class family. Veronica dropped out of high school and worked a variety of jobs. Photographs from the 1930s show that she was a beautiful young woman. She aspired to an acting career and as a teenager she worked as a substitute dancer at the Roxy Theatre in Manhattan.[17] Her interest in show business continued throughout her life. Her favorite celebrities were Jeannette MacDonald and Nelson Eddy, the singing duo known as "America's Sweethearts."[18]

During World War II, Veronica enrolled as a nurse with the Red Cross. After the war she met her husband, Arthur, at the skating rink in Flushing Meadows Park where she would hold vigils thirty years later. Arthur later told his family that the day he met Veronica he had been feeling depressed and told himself, "The next woman who comes around the rink, I'll marry."[19] Arthur was originally from Indiana. After serving in the Navy, he sought work as a construction engineer. The couple generally referred to each other as "Artie" and "Ronnie." They had five children together: Linda, Arthur Jr. (Butch), Thomas, Larry, and Raymond. Arthur often struggled to find steady work and the Luekens changed addresses frequently. In 1965, the family moved into a five-room apartment in Heather Gardens, in Bayside. Lueken began to attend services at St. Robert Bellarmine's church, which was only about a mile from her apartment.[20] The church was located in the middle of Bayside Hills, a prosperous neighborhood with an active homeowner's association. While Lueken was part of the same parish as the residents of Bayside Hills, she was regarded as an outsider.

A series of unfortunate events occurred after the move to Heather Gardens. Veronica's brother, who suffered from multiple sclerosis, moved into the apartment in 1966. Not long after that came Veronica's stepfather, who was out of work and homeless. Now the apartment was home to nine. To make more room, Veronica and Artie moved their bed into the dining room.[21] At this time Artie fell ill and lost his job as a construction engineer. Next, the Lueken's eldest child, Butch, left home to spend a year as a yoga devotee in Berkeley, California, and Linda dropped out of high school.[22] By 1968, the family's situation had improved somewhat in that Artie had recovered and returned to work.

Like Mary Ann Van Hoof, Lueken and her family were under a great deal of stress when her visions began. Ronald Brown, a historian who has observed the Baysiders in New York for over twenty years, has suggested that Lueken may have also felt disappointed with her husband's lack of financial success and left behind by the prosperity that many Americans experienced in the postwar years. While many returning veterans took advantage of the G.I. Bill, Arthur Lueken continually struggled to find work. This situation may have made it painful to attend St. Robert Bellarmine's alongside more affluent homeowners. Lueken's eventual persona as a seer gave meaning to this disappointment. A life of suffering and simplicity is consistent with popular Catholic expectations for mystics and seers, although after Lueken became a seer her family finally did achieve a middle-class lifestyle.

Lueken's visions began on the morning of June 5th, 1968. She had dropped off her husband Artie at a Flushing construction site. On her car radio, she listened to news coverage of the attack on Robert Kennedy and the prayer sessions being organized for his recovery. It suddenly occurred to her that she should pray to St. Therese of Lisieux, known as The Little

Flower of Jesus, to intercede.²³ Lueken had only a dim memory of this saint from her childhood, but she somehow felt that if she prayed to St. Therese, Kennedy would recover. As she began praying, she was suddenly overcome with the smell of roses. She recalled, "It wasn't as though I was smelling one flower—it was like walking through a flower shop!"²⁴ After a few moments, the anomalous fragrance departed as suddenly as it had come.

Later that afternoon, Lueken drove her stepfather to the hospital for a check-up. As she waited outside the doctor's office, she took out her rosary and again began to pray for Kennedy's recovery. The fragrance of roses returned. When she got home, Lueken went to St. Robert Bellarmine's for confession. She described the strange smell to her confessor, Father Sullivan, who reassured her that she should be neither disturbed nor excited by her experiences, that Heaven works in mysterious ways, and to continue praying for guidance. That night Lueken continued to say the rosary as Kennedy's condition deteriorated. After midnight, her husband urged her to retire, at which point she blurted out, without knowing why, that the senator would die at 2:00 a.m. Then she went to bed. At 1:44 a.m., Robert Kennedy was pronounced dead.

Robert Kennedy's body was brought to St. Patrick's Cathedral in New York where a viewing was held for two days. Lueken consulted Father Sullivan again who once again advised her not to be upset and to continue to pray for guidance. She went home and watched Kennedy's funeral service. She stepped out onto the porch and, looking toward heaven, began to say the rosary again for the senator's soul. The smell of roses returned for the third time. Lueken recalled, "This time I was frightened. I said, 'Oh, please not again!' and instantly it was gone."²⁵ That night, Lueken was awakened at 3:00 a.m. by an "inner voice," which told her, "Veronica, I want you to write. Get out of bed. You must write what I tell you." In a trance, Lueken wrote a short message and returned to bed. The next morning, she and Artie found she had produced the following poem:

A Minor Miracle Bobby and Therese

A delicate petal scented by Heaven
Fell from her bower of roses
As her hand led the way
Up the path on that day
That Bobby kissed Mary and Moses.²⁶

It is not entirely clear why Lueken was so affected by Robert Kennedy's death, but the assassinations of John and Robert Kennedy were a blow to all Americans, especially Catholics.[27] In the headquarters of SMWA, there is a large framed painting of Robert Kennedy. One shrine worker explained to me that Robert had been a devout Catholic, more righteous than his brother John, and that the forces of evil had been determined to assassinate him before he could become president.

At this point Lueken had experienced a revelation but she was not yet a seer. She sought confirmation for her experiences and, like prophets from Mohammad to Joseph Smith, turned first to her family. But Lueken's husband did not believe her for at least the first two years of her experiences. He would cry when Lueken reported new mystical experiences, fearing his wife was losing her mind. Lueken recalled, "Every time I told him something new that happened, he would write it down on a piece of paper, and call this doctor who is our friend and say, 'She's getting WORSE. She saw this ... NOW she said St. Theresa said THAT ...' "[28] Because her husband would not believe her and her parish priests were decidedly neutral, Lueken began looking for affirmation elsewhere. She wrote several letters to Cardinal Richard Cushing in Boston. While Cushing never endorsed Lueken's revelations, he did answer her letters. One response included a mass card for a service dedicated to Bobby Kennedy and his family, which she framed and hung on her living room wall.

On August 4, 1968, at 5:30 a.m., Lueken was preparing for early morning mass when she saw the framed letter from Cushing "float" off the wall and crash at her feet. She hurried to St. Robert Bellarmine's where she burst in on a group of four priests to tell them about this new development. She recalled, "They ushered me out of the place, 'Be a good girl, please go home,' they said. This was about the fifth visit I had made there." Lueken left in tears. As she neared home, she heard the voice of Therese comfort her. It instructed her to open the Bible to a random page. She did this and turned to Job 27. A bright light shined forth from the page and obscured all of the text except for the words, "I am the Almighty. I will teach by the hand of God what the Almighty has in store."[29] This en-counter demonstrates the "push" effect of Church authorities. By sending Lueken home, the priests forfeited an important opportunity to shape the meaning of her experience. The rejection did not cause Lueken to ignore her experiences or attribute less significance to them. Instead, she attrib-uted even greater meaning to what was happening, seeing it as part of God's divine plan.

The next day, Lueken sent Arthur to a Catholic shop to buy a small statue of St. Therese. She made this the center of a small shrine on top of her dresser. At 10:00 a.m. on August 6, the statue fell off the dresser and Lueken feared it was broken. Picking it up, Lueken said, "Oh, Theresa, I'm so happy you didn't break your neck!" As she set the statue back, she saw a pinpoint of white light coming out of the wall behind the dresser. The pinpoint grew until an enormous circle of light appeared to be coming through the wall. Lueken would later struggle to articulate this experience:

> I felt—the only way I can explain it is I felt like my head was stick-ing out in some kind of vast space. It was so quiet. There seemed to be like a mist going across my face. I still remember the deep grayness of it.... Suddenly as the light came sort of—oh, around me, I saw a face; but it was like miles away—just a tiny little face, but getting larger as it came towards me.... She had a face but there was no body, although I didn't feel that that made any difference.
>
> So as I was looking at her, I said: "Who's that?" But just as I said that, there was like a blast, a force, or an explosion, but it didn't hurt. It hit me on the right side of the face and pushed my head up and to the left.
>
> The same face was still there but the light that was coming out from under her skin made her look so beautiful! It made her skin look so very white. In fact, the light was so bright that I can't re-member her nose and her mouth. But I remember her eyes, be-cause they were flashing with such happiness.
>
> And then as I looked, I didn't hear a word, let's say earwise, but I knew she was saying, "This is what Heaven is like!" And oh! I was so thrilled that I screamed out, "Saint Theresa!"[30]

This exclamation attracted the attention of her youngest son, Raymond, who was then ten years old. Two years later, after much coaxing from his mother, Raymond made a tape recording of his testimony that he too had seen St. Therese in his mother's bedroom. Raymond was mocked by his playmates for claiming he saw a being from heaven. Of all of Lueken's children, Raymond was the only one who consistently supported his mother's visions.

While the vision subsided, Lueken remained in an altered state of consciousness. She felt that St. Therese had "entered into her in spirit." She stayed awake for three days and nights transcribing "poem-messages" for the saint. These early messages were eventually collected into a document called "Occulations from Heaven." Like "A Minor Miracle Bobby and Therese," they have a warm and sentimental quality that distinguishes them from the prophetic and apocalyptic tone of Lueken's later messages. All of these writings were to be signed "Veronica," but with a cross surrounded by the letters JMJT (Jesus, Mary, Joseph, Therese).[31] Lueken would continue to use this form of signature in her letters to Church authorities. When Lueken finally slept, she was awoken by a pulling sensation that she interpreted as St. Therese leaving her body. She described this as a painful experience, as if she was losing a piece of herself.

In August, Lueken began seeing a number of visions in the sky over Bayside: a cross, the face of Jesus, and the sun spinning as it had at Fatima. While shopping on August 20, she saw a vision of a black eagle that filled the entire sky. The eagle screamed at her, "Woe, woe, woe to the inhabitants of the earth."[32] Badly frightened, Lueken ran into a store and used the phone to call her husband at work. Arthur advised her to go home and relax. Instead of relaxing, Lueken wired Cardinal Cushing to describe her vision. "You've got to DO something!" she urged the Cardinal. Next she called the priests at St. Robert Bellarmine's, who were similarly unreceptive. The following day the Soviet Union invaded Czechoslovakia.[33] This connection seems to have confirmed Lueken's suspicion that her experiences were of global significance. It also solidified a theme of opposition to communism that ran throughout her visions.

Lueken continued to receive more messages from Therese discussing both the nature of divine love and the threat of Satan, whom she occasionally referred to as "Luciel." On September 1, 1969, Lueken received a message from Therese for Pope Paul VI asking him to reverse the changes of the Second Vatican Council and restore the Tridentine Mass.[34] A similar message on September 7 chided priests for not properly upholding their calling. Since the apparition of La Salette in 1846, Marian seers have frequently given voice to jeremiads about the ritual transgressions of their fellow Catholics. In time, the body of Lueken's messages would increasingly express concerns about the Cold War and the threat of nuclear weapons, shifting cultural mores, the activities of Satanic cults, and the rise of a fascist one-world government. However, the liturgical reforms of Vatican II remained a kind of anchor to which all cultural and political problems were ultimately connected. To this day, Baysiders strongly oppose liturgical reforms such as the vernacular mass and receiving communion in the hand. For many traditionalist Catholics, ritual transgression lies close to the heart of all the world's troubles.

At some point Lueken began to attribute some of her messages to the Virgin Mary as well as Therese. As the messages shifted to matters of pressing and global significance, Mary gradually became more prominent than Therese. That September, Lueken kneeled at the altar rail at St. Robert Bellarmine's following confession. She looked up at the statue of Mary and saw that its face had changed: Instead of its usual serene countenance, it had become a mask of pain. Mary's face was aged with worry and heartache. Lueken felt that Mary was so distressed because women were attending mass without head coverings and sporting modern, immodest clothing. After this experience, Lueken began regularly visiting a statue of Mary outside the church.

St. Robert Bellarmine's was built in 1939—only four years after the neighborhood of Bayside Hills was constructed on the site of a former golf course. The original church was simply a converted house. Its first mass drew 225 worshippers. The police deemed a crowd of this size to be hazardous in a residential area—a complaint that foreshadowed future conflicts surrounding religious gatherings in Bayside Hills. By 1941, the parish had acquired an entire block between 56th and 58th avenues and 212th and 213th streets. Here, the parish built a church, a rectory, and a recreation hall. A school was added in the 1950s. By the 1960s, the parish had grown to 8800 Catholics and further expansion was needed. A larger church was completed in 1969 and the old building was converted into a gymnasium for the school.[35] Between the new church and the gymnasium was a small courtyard with a statue of the Immaculate Conception. Lueken would leave rosaries in its hands and place crowns of flowers on its head. On October 8, this statue "spoke" to her, saying, "I will come when the roses are in bloom." Lueken took this to mean June. She described her response to this announcement, "I told everyone. So I wired Billy Graham, Cardinal Cushing, everyone that I knew, Our Lady's coming when the roses are in bloom, in June."[36]

Lueken was seeking affirmation wherever she could find it. And by setting a date for a future Marian apparition—as had Van Hoof and the children of Fatima—she was attracting the attention of people and organizations interested in Marian lore. On May 19, Lueken had coffee with her friend and neighbor Grace "Gracy" Pera, a twenty-seven-year-old whom Lueken described as "a working girl." Both women claimed they looked out the window and saw a vision of Mary standing atop a "big ball with a cross on it." This description sounds like a *globus cruciger*—an object commonly depicted in medieval Christian art. Pera's confirmation of her early visions was important to Lueken, as were those of her son Raymond and another neighbor, a single mother of three whom Lueken calls "Carol M." She later said of Pera, "Jesus decided to send me what Theresa called a 'companionable spirit,' to sort of console me, I guess, and someone I could talk to."[37] Pera made a taped testimony of her vision with Lueken and sent a transcript of it to *Vers Demain*, the newspaper of the Canadian Pilgrims of Saint Michael.[38]

Lueken also wrote to networks related to other Marian apparitions. Her telephone call to Mary Ann Van Hoof was likely made at this time. While Van Hoof was unsupportive, Lueken did find another "companionable spirit" in Joey Lomangino, who led a group that organized pilgrimages from the United States to an apparition site in Garabandal, Spain. In the 1960s, a group of girls claimed to receive numerous messages from the Virgin Mary in Garabandal. Like many apparitions, those at Garabandal are not approved by Church authorities, but have also not been censured. Lomangino had been blinded in an accident in 1947 when he was sixteen. In 1963 and 1964, he made two trips from the United States to Garabandal in search of a cure. On his second visit, one of the seers prophesied that he would receive "new eyes." With this prophecy, some of the seers' charisma was transferred to Lomangino. He expressed his belief in Lueken, who later recalled, "Well, I told Joseph this by telephone and I was so happy, because I knew that he—at that time, he did believe me, and it was kind of being worldly still, I haven't lost enough of my own feelings that I could stand alone, and it was wonderful to know that there was someone who believed me."[39] By affirming Lueken's experiences, Lomangino was also able to shape their interpretation. Lueken told him that Mary had set a definite date for her arrival—June 18. Lomangino responded that this date was also the anniversary of the apparitions at Garabandal. Many Baysiders still maintain that there is a link between these two apparitions.

Lueken continued to prepare for Mary's arrival at St. Robert Bellarmine's. Every morning, rain or shine, she would send her children off to school and then visit the statue of Mary to say the rosary. Children from the parish school would pass her during these morning rosary sessions and ridicule her. Lueken complained about this to her pastor, who brought the children to heel. In late May, Mary began giving Lueken more explicit instructions for her arrival. A shrine was to be erected at St. Robert Bellarmine's and called "Our Lady of the Roses Shrine." Lueken made a sketch of this shrine, which consisted of a simple concrete oval that could house the statue of Mary, with an inscription that read "Mary Help of Mothers." She also explained that Mary had asked her to have a special gown constructed of blue or white, to be worn with a head covering. This gown was essentially a "Mary costume" similar to what might be seen in a nativity scene. A friend created such a dress for her and Lueken would later wear it during vigils.[40]

While some of Lueken's neighbors were excited about Mary's arrival, her church was less than amenable to Lueken's requests for assistance. Mary specified that Lueken was to send a letter and a phone call to each of the priests at St. Robert Bellarmine's about the apparition coming on June 18. There would need to be folding chairs for the elderly and facilities available for all the pilgrims. The priests were to announce the date during every Sunday mass. Lueken also wrote to nuns at a local convent asking them to come. She sent her drawing of the shrine to Monsignor Emmet McDonald so that he could begin making arrangements for its construction. The parish priests seemed uncertain how to respond to these requests. Lueken described a phone conversation with a Father Dunne. She explained Mary's request that he "bring all peoples" to St. Robert Bellarmine's. Lueken acknowledged that "peoples" was an odd phrasing but insisted that was how Mary spoke. Father Dunne explained he was not willing to do this. When Lueken asked him why not, he replied, "I'll be deposed." Father Dunne did, at least, offer to bring some flowers. Lueken asked her parish Rosary Society if they would say a continuous rosary on June 18, but they would not. On June 16, Lueken passed the statue of Mary outside the church and saw it was crying. She wrote, "I passed by Our Lady's statue setting on the lawn, and I got a terrible fright, because the face had changed and there, the statue, I saw her eyes swelled up, swelled shut as though She had been crying a long time. And her lip was curled under, and everything."[41] This vision of the weeping Madonna likely mirrored Lueken's own feelings of rejection.

When June 18 finally arrived, only a handful of supporters came to Lueken's vigil. She later described how she began kneeling before the statue of Mary at St. Robert Bellarmine's at 9 a.m. and remained there until 1 a.m. the following morning. It was so hot that day that one of Lueken's companions—a woman from Indiana who had come to record any messages from Mary—fainted. The heat was followed by pouring rain. However, Mary did eventually appear to Lueken, telling her: "My tears fall on you. Pray, My children. So many souls will be lost. It is because I love you that I have come. You will have to suffer, My child. Cry with me, My child, for I have never stopped crying."[42] Lueken did cry. Mary went on to explain that a great darkness was coming, that not enough prayers were being offered to heaven, and that people must say the rosary. She also explained to Lueken that she was a bride of Christ. After the apparition departed, Lueken's sixteen-hour ordeal had left her bedridden and unable to walk for three days. She wrote Monsignor McDonald and the other priests and explained that Mary would henceforth appear by the statue at St. Robert Bellarmine's on all Catholic feast days. At this point, Monsignor McDonald was uncertain what to do and notified Francis J. Mugavero, Bishop of Brooklyn.

Victim Soul and Voice Box

By the end of the summer of 1970 Lueken was holding regular vigils attended by a small group of followers. Attendees would gather at 9 p.m. the night before Catholic feast days and say the rosary until midnight.[43] Near the middle of these vigils, Lueken would enter a state of ecstasy in which Mary would appear to her. She would then deliver a divine message that her followers would record. These messages are referred to as "locutions," a term from Catholic tradition that refers to the audible equivalent of visions.[44] In the summer of 1973, Lueken acquired an old mimeograph machine and began sending copies of her locutions to a growing circle of followers.

Now that Lueken was surrounded with a sufficient community of companionable spirits, her abilities as a seer began to flourish. Over the course of her life she delivered over three hundred locutions as well as many private messages from Jesus and Mary. Whether they believed in her or not, everyone who witnessed her giving these messages agreed that Lueken had an amazing ability to draw the audience into her visions. I spoke with a shrine worker from SMWA who recalled being with Lueken during a vision in which Mary showed her an image of hell. Lueken described her horror at seeing the glow of the flames and smelling burning bodies. She begged Mary to stop the vision, but Mary explained that it was necessary for her to witness it. The shrine worker was so engrossed with listening to Lueken that he felt he too was witnessing hell itself. He said that no actor could possibly have given such a performance.

Many of Lueken's visions were frightening and included graphic descriptions of future disasters including floods, earthquakes, plagues, stock market crashes, terrorism, and "roaming bands of homosexuals."[45] However, Lueken also described images of heavenly beings that are as lovely as the images of death and destruction are frightening. Unlike many Marian seers, Lueken's visions were not limited to Mary but featured an enormous cast of saints and angels. An incomplete list of these beings includes Jesus, Moses, the Archangels Michael, Gabriel, and Rafael, Saint Therese of Lisieux, Saint Joseph, the Apostle Paul, John the Evangelist, Joan of Arc, Teresa of Avila, Francis of Assisi, Saint Anne (the mother of Mary), Joachim of Fiore, Bernadette of Lourdes, John Neumann of Philadelphia, Gemma Galgani, Aloysius Gonzaga, Thomas Aquinas, Robert Bellarmine, Catherine Laboure, Jacinta Marto, and Padre Pio. She also encountered numerous departed popes and Marian seers, some of whom had not yet been canonized. She even learned the names of new angels such as the guardian angels Tusazeri, Sactorius, Tomdarius, Nadinia, and Razene, as well as Exterminatus, the angel of death. Because of this large cast, Baysiders often speak of "heaven" rather than a single entity such as God, Mary, or Jesus. For instance, the Bayside Prophecies are described as "messages from heaven."

Anyone who takes the time to read through the Bayside Prophecies will notice the lavish attention Lueken gives to sartorial details. In each vision, every article of clothing is described in exquisite detail, from the Virgin Mary's gown to the Archangel Michael's armor. The Virgin Mary typically wears a different gown, crown, and jewelry in each vision. However, there would occasionally be repeats, which Lueken would note in her descriptions. The following message is typical of these descriptions:

> Now through the light, Our Lady is coming forward. She is dressed beautifully in Her whole Fatima habit. I've always called it Her Fatima habit when She wears the Fatima crown upon her head. Our Lady has the Fatima crown, and She also has under it Her mantle, the beautiful white mantle with golden edging. The edging is so fantastically golden that I'm sure it must be spun gold, pure spun gold. Our Lady has on her a beautiful gown that comes high up upon Her neck, and is also lined with border of I would say, about a half an inch of gold about Her neck; and Our Lady's gown is white, pure white. Now Our Lady has a belting, a gold-corded belting now which cinches in, sort of, Her gown.[46]

Lueken explained that the rich description of her visions was necessary to reach a fallen generation. She remarked, "In appearing in New York City, Our Lady has come to the capital city of a nation of television addicts. They have been conditioned to demand the details of the visual. And with Her typical graciousness, Our Lady seeks to accommodate them."[47]

These details also constitute a form of what David Morgan calls "visual piety" in which images—even as described by a seer—connect people to their cultural heritage and create a meaningful understanding of the world. The richness of Lueken's descriptions, along with other visual cues such as the statue of Mary, marked the vigil grounds as a sacred space. Most importantly, the visual elements of Baysider culture contributed to a sense of interactivity with the sacred during vigils. Baysiders regarded Lueken's vigils as a special time and space in which heavenly beings could hear their prayers and sorrows and reciprocate with blessings.[48]

This daily sense of interaction with heavenly beings also transformed how Lueken understood herself. As a seer, Lueken was able to form a coherent self-narrative that made sense of her personal sufferings, changes in her Church, and her inexplicable experiences. Like Van Hoof, she described herself as both a "victim soul," one who sufferers to atone for the sins of others, and a "voice box," one who communicates messages for heaven. Victim souls are believed to share in "co-redemption" with Christ, meaning that human suffering helps Christ to continue to save sinners. The theology of victim souls evolved alongside the Marian apparitions of the nineteenth century. Victim souls are also linked to a Marian theology of history because it is understood that particularly dark and sinful times necessitate the suffering of innocent victims for the salvation of others.[49] Many of Lueken's favorite saints, including St. Therese, Gemma Galgani, and Padre Pio were closely associated with victim soul theology. In at least one locution, Mary stated explicitly that Lueken has suffered as a victim soul for the world's sins.[50] Lueken emphasized that many victim souls would be needed to mitigate a chastisement that would soon punish humanity for its sins. Mary Ann Van Hoof also described herself as a victim soul.

Lueken truly did suffer numerous medical problems over the course of her life, as well as emotional pain and hardship. Her identity as a victim soul was a sort of personal theodicy through which she could make sense of these misfortunes. But this identification also enhanced her personal charisma. Her followers catalogued her suffering, seeing each new unfortunate development as further evidence of her saintliness. SMWA's website maintains a webpage entitled, "Gethsemani to Calvary: Sufferings of Veronica of the Cross," which chronicles in detail all of the torment she endured from 1968 until her death in 1995. It lists not only her numerous health problems, including a heart attack, spinal arthritis, and tumors in her spine and kidney, but also her emotional pains: facing a lawsuit against her own church, hate mail, and death threats.[51] For her followers, each of these misfortunes came as further confirmation of Lueken's authority as a seer and the urgency of her millennial prophecies. Victim soul theology remains important for SMWA. One shrine worker was disabled from multiple sclerosis. Another long-time community member was diagnosed with lung cancer. Others described the suffering of these individuals to me in hallowed tones. One woman remarked, "He's got lung cancer and he never even smoked! This man is a saint!"[52]

As Lueken came to terms with her own pain and suffering, her relationship with the anomalous experiences that had intruded into her life also stabilized. Nothing resembling the three-day possession by St. Therese occurred again. Instead, heaven spoke to her primarily through locutions and during the designated ritual times of the vigils. In 1971, she described herself as "a voice box" for heaven.[53] Often Marian seers must first hear messages and then repeat them back to an audience, in a manner similar to an interpreter. Lueken, however, delivered her locutions instantaneously. She explained this process, "There is no need for Jesus and our Mother to speak out. The words go back and forth, sort of mind to mind, spirit to spirit. That is the only way that I can explain it." Being a voice box for heaven was also physically taxing. Lueken reported that the day after delivering a locution she would feel extremely dehydrated and drink quarts of water.[54]

It also became easier to tell where Lueken's personality ended and the personality of the heavenly personages began. She began to manifest two sets of traits, distinguishing her ordinary personality from her role as heaven's voice box. Her followers claimed that, while in ecstasy, Lueken never blinked and that they could distinguish her voice from Mary's by pitch.[55] In one locution, Lueken's voice suddenly became rapid and high pitched. Speaking as Mary, she announced, "My child, I am giving you a different voice because I want you to sound exactly as I do."[56] Lueken also displayed two different vocabularies and would frequently explain that she did not know the meaning of some words used by Mary and other heavenly beings. In an interview taken shortly before her first public vigil she gave the following anecdote:

I asked Our Lady, "Will you cure Joey [Joseph Lomangino]?" Our Lady said, "I cannot tell you now, as you are [not] wont to keep a secret. Your love of sharing makes your heart open for all to read, so patiently watch the signs." I had to look up the word 'wont' W-O-N-T, and I read that, "You are not used to." So I really had to laugh, Our Lady knows me exactly! Because I do find it difficult to keep a secret![57]

In an interview with Roberta Grant, she explained that her "mind blanks completely" during locutions, adding, "Afterward when I listen to the tapes and read the messages, I have to use a dictionary to look up some of those big words!"[58]

Maintaining two distinctive vocabularies made her locutions more plausible in several ways: it provided some evidence that there really were multiple personalities communicating through Lueken and it helped her to conform to a popular expectation of a Marian seer as an uneducated woman of humble origins.[59] It also gave Lueken the rhetorical ability to communicate from two different positions simultaneously—that of the submissive Catholic housewife and the commanding Queen of Heaven. This sort of dual communication would later appear in a letter to Chancellor King and Bishop Mugavero, reprimanding them for actions taken against her vigils. The letter shifts between first accusing Church authorities of having lost their holiness, lying, and doing the will of Satan, and then deferentially asking that the bishop and chancellor pray for her. In one paragraph, Lueken writes, "God is our Judge and our only concern. He asks that this Mission continue—until the Chastisement—and it will." In the next, she writes, "My Human words can not compare in any measure to the Words of Our Blessed Mother or Jesus—so please forgive my lack of Higher Education evidenced in this letter. I can only offer the truth in my limited means of Communication."[60] This dual voice as both submissive Catholic housewife and voice box of heaven also reflects the fundamental paradox of the Baysider movement: the dance of deference and defiance in which Church authorities are both beloved and vilified almost simultaneously.

A Culture of Prophecy

With Lueken's transformation from housewife to seer complete, a unique culture with its own beliefs and practices began to take shape around her. One of the first traditions to form was that of "miraculous Polaroids."

Pilgrims who took pictures of vigils using quick-developing cameras began to report anomalies in their photographs.[61] Usually these were limited to inexplicable streaks of light, which skeptics attributed to mishandling the film as it developed or to using cameras in dark settings for which they were not designed. As early as 1968 a miraculous Polaroid was sent in to the Polaroid Company for analysis. The photograph was examined by Dr. Edwin Land, the inventor of the first commercial instant camera. Land conceded that he had no explanation for the image. However, he cautioned, "So many things occur in our daily lives which have no explanation and we wonder if this isn't one of them."[62] Many more anomalous Polaroids followed. Looking at the streaks and blurs, pilgrims were able to discern letters, numbers, the faces of saints, demons, and other images thought to be the keys of prophecy. Lueken seemed especially adept at interpreting these images. By 1971, dozens of pilgrims were snapping such pictures and bringing them to Veronica for interpretation.[63] Eventually a document was created explaining how to interpret the various numbers, letters, symbols, and colors that appear in the Polaroids. Green indicated the presence of the archangel Michael, blue meant the presence of Mary, a letter "W" stood for warning, a letter "A" stood for "anno" and indicated that the Polaroid was communicating an important date, and so on.[64] In 1972, Polaroid invented the SX-70, an affordable, quick-developing camera.[65] Now everyone could visit Lueken and receive their very own "Polaroids from heaven."

Miraculous photographs are common at Marian apparition sites around the world. A picture taken during one of Van Hoof's vigils in Necadah, Wisconsin, on October 7, 1950, is generally considered to be the first photograph of a Marian apparition.[66] However, the history of supernatural photography began a century earlier during the Spiritualist movement. The ability to "capture" nature in a photograph lent itself to the idea that supernature could likewise be captured.[67] Daniel Wojcik suggests that the first miraculous photograph in Christian tradition is the so-called "Hidden Christ Picture" or "The Sacred Heart in the Branches." The picture, which has significance in both Catholic and Protestant traditions, is said to have been taken in the late 1930s. Various accounts from the 1940s and 1950s claim that the picture was taken by a skeptic who either doubted the existence of God or took the Lord's name in vain, allegedly declaring, "If God is everywhere, I'll take his picture." When the film was developed and revealed a picture of Jesus, the skeptic either converted, went mad, or died of shock depending on which version of the story is told. An alternative origin claims that the photograph was taken by someone suffering a spiritual crisis and that the photograph restored their faith.[68] Jessy Pagliaroli argues that miraculous photography became more popular in Catholic culture during the 1970s partly because Polaroids were available to the public but also because Vatican II created a new demand for "external signs" of Catholic faith. A wider cultural interest in the paranormal may also have been a factor. For instance, E. Ann Matter points out that supernatural photography is part of the plot of 1976 apocalyptic horror film *The Omen*.[69]

Jean Baudrillard described the Polaroid as a magical process in which an "ecstatic membrane" is peeled away from an object. This understanding of Polaroids gives them a special kind of authority. As Edward Berryman notes, miraculous photographs are understood to *impose* belief rather than elicit it.[70] This type of evidence also has a democratizing effect.[71] At Bayside, it gave lay Catholics the agency to argue with Church experts. As one irate Baysider wrote in a parish newsletter from 1982:

> Bishop Bevilacqua suggests that apparitions "should be accompanied by unusual signs, tangible evidence that God is communicating with his children." And gives as an example the miracle of the sun at Fatima. There is, at Bayside, concrete, visible and unalterable proof of divine assistance in the form of miraculous photographs that confound the imagination and defy explanation. This proof is not secret, it is not available to a select few only, it is *available to all*. Anyone may, by attending a Vigil, get proof of this. It is not limited to Veronica and close friends.[72]

As a form of irrefutable and irreproducible religious knowledge, miraculous Polaroids descend from an ancient Christian tradition of icons known as *acheiropoietos* (not made by hand). *Acheiropoietos* are also known under Latin or Latin-Greek hybrids including *vera imago*, *vera icon*, and *veronica*. The most famous cases of such images include the Shroud of Turin and the older story of Veronica's veil. In that story, a woman named Veronica used her veil to wipe the sweating and bleeding face of Christ as he carried his cross toward Golgotha whereupon the cloth was marked with an image of the face of Jesus. Many Baysiders are familiar with the story of Veronica's veil. They believe that the name Veronica is derived from the Latin for "true icon" and that this is evidence that Veronica Lueken was destined for her role as a seer. Actually, the name Veronica is a Latin form of the name Berenice and not derived from *vera icon*. However, for both the legendary Veronica and Veronica Lueken there is a sense that *nomen est omen*.[73] Like Veronica's veil, miraculous Polaroids are understood to be sacred objects unto themselves. Within some apparitional movements, miraculous pictures have been said to exude oil or exhibit other supernatural properties.

In Bayside, one of the earliest and most important miraculous Polaroids was taken by Robert Franzenburg on September 14, 1971. Franzenburg lived a few blocks north of St. Robert Bellarmine's and was one of Lueken's early supporters. He was passing the statue of Mary where a group of about five women were gathered to say the rosary. One of these women, Clara Kreitmeyer, asked if he would take a picture of them praying the rosary. Franzenberg had an early model of Polaroid. After taking a picture, it was necessary to pull the film out, wait sixty seconds, and then peel back a cover from the film. As Lueken (who was not present) told the story, Franzenberg held the developing photo in his hand when there was "a snap! A crack! That went through his fingers holding the photo!" When he pulled back the film he was shocked by what he saw. In some versions of the story he nearly fainted. In others, he dropped the photograph and the camera and ran away.[74] The photograph showed the message "Jacinta 1972" written in luminescent script. This was not an unusual streak of light but an unmistakable message that seemed to spontaneously appear on the film. Some time after taking this picture, Franzenburg ceased his involvement with Lueken.

Baysiders assumed the name Jacinta referred to Jacinta Marto, one of the child seers who had witnessed the Marian apparition at Fatima, Portugal, in 1917. Many believed that this message contained a clue to the mysterious third secret of Fatima. The photograph became a sort of icon for Bayside, appearing on newsletters, books, and eventually the Internet. One Baysider explained to me that someone had finally interpreted the message correctly: Apparently if you turned the Polaroid on its side the date "2015" could be discerned. This, she explained, was the date of the Chastisement when God would punish the world for its sins. Lueken wrote the diocese about this photograph and tried to convince them of its significance. The Polaroid, dubbed "The Jacinta 1972 photograph," became a stark example of how two groups of Catholics could see the world in completely different ways. For the community that had formed around Lueken and her messages, the picture was undeniable proof that something supernatural was taking place in Bayside and that Lueken's visions were true. For Church authorities and skeptics, the photograph was an obvious forgery that proved someone in Lueken's movement was engaged in deliberate deception.

Bill Wuest, a professional photographic technician and columnist for *The Long Island Press*, said that the Jacinta 1972 photograph was "an intentional double exposure by someone with photographic sophistication." To prove this, he created his own "miraculous photograph" in which the words "Bill Wuest 1973" appear in the same ghostly text.[75] In the 1990s, researcher Michael Cuneo met a group of apostate Baysiders who claimed to have met "the photographer," whom they refused to name. In this story, the photographer confessed that he created the image by simply writing on the coversheet of the film as it was developing. This is a plausible explanation.[76] Lueken recalled that Franzenberg had an artistic talent and would create drawings and design rubber stamps to promote her messages. But if Franzenberg simply drew the message on the Polaroid, this does not explain his motives. Ann Cillis, another apostate Baysider, claimed that Franzenberg faked this picture to test Lueken. She explained, "When she accepted it as true and as 'miraculous' he realized that she was not all that she claimed to be. He withdrew from the group."[77]

In 1980, Lueken recorded some of her memories about her early messages, which her followers developed into a text entitled "Conversations with Jesus." Here, she offers her own explanation for why Franzenberg left. In January 1971, she received a private message from Jesus that Lucifer himself was coming to St. Robert Bellarmine's in the body of a priest. When Lueken asked why Lucifer would do this, Jesus answered, "Because to divide is to conquer." Jesus specified that Lueken, Franzenberg, and "Carol M." were not to attend a specific mass on January 23 at which this priest would be present. But when the three arrived for a different mass, the "possessed" priest was there waiting for them. Lueken believed this encounter with the possessed priest happened because she spoke her message from Jesus aloud, giving the enemy a chance to hear her and change their plans. Lueken did not say which priest had become a host for the spirit of Satan, but she refers to him as "Father McL." She adds, "I would say he looked the picture of satan, with short cropped beard, Van-Dyke-like black; black hair all combed straight."[78] A footnote to "Conversations with Jesus" explains that Lucifer was only able to enter a Catholic mass because the liturgy had ceased to include the prayer to St. Michael. Lueken told her two comrades not to look at Father McL's face and under no circumstances to take communion from him. Heaven helped them not to look at Father McL and a sort of mist appeared over his face. But when it was time for communion Franzenberg consumed the host offered by Father McL. When Lueken asked him why he disobeyed her, he answered, "I thought whatever was in him maybe left by now."[79] When Lueken next saw Franzenberg, he had changed. His eyes resembled "deep pools of nothingness." Not long after this encounter he drifted away from the group. Lueken attributed this to the corrupting influence of the mysterious Father McL.

This story is difficult to interpret. A great deal of context is missing and elements of this narrative may have been created after the fact to account for the loss of Franzenberg. The *Long Island Press* article that discusses the Jacinta 1972 photograph describes meeting an anonymous Bayside man who left the fold, which may well have been Franzenberg. The apostate Baysider remarked, "Each time I wanted to say my own thing, I couldn't. You have to say 'yes' the way she [Veronica] wants. Once you get around her crowd, they don't let you go. I don't like to talk to her anymore because when I do, she starts to cry and get emotional and I can't take that."[80] Lueken also ends her account of Franzenberg and Father McL with another possible explanation, "Being a shy fellow, he did not want to be exposed to any publicity, or anything of the trials that are necessary for the propagation of Heaven's Message."[81] It is possible that Franzenberg saw his involvement with miraculous Polaroids and prophecies as something akin to a game he was playing with Lueken and that he withdrew when the play became too serious.

Nothing quite as spectacular as the Jacinta 72 Polaroid has manifested since; however, Baysiders have produced hundreds of miraculous Polaroids over the years. Many of these images are difficult to account for and are visually striking. Those outside Lueken's movement began to suspect that the miraculous Polaroids were a deliberate hoax, designed to collect donations from the gullible. Chancellor James P. King of the Brooklyn Diocese suspected that whoever was doctoring these Polaroids sought to exploit Lueken's beliefs for financial gain. Bayside residents, who were increasingly alarmed by the growing momentum behind Lueken's movement, suspected that Ann Ferguson, one of Lueken's early supporters, might be manipulating her.[82] Ferguson apparently had a facility for taking miraculous Polaroids that Lueken did not. In a locution in 1975, Mary explained to Lueken, "Your spouse will instruct My child Ann to bring forth two photographs. Only you will know the meaning of these photographs. It is the proof you will need." After this, whenever Lueken had to make an important decision she would phone Ferguson, who would take a Polaroid. Then Lueken would interpret it to discern what she ought to do. When a priest from another country wanted to visit Lueken, she had Ferguson take his picture. In this picture, Lueken discerned the shapes of a goat, a demon, and a flying saucer. She took this as a sign not to meet with the priest.[83] Outsiders repeatedly accused the Baysiders of deceiving people to raise money, but there is little evidence to support this. It does not seem that Lueken was being manipulated by her friend. Rather, the miraculous Polaroids demonstrate a source of shared meaning and a community of prophecy that was forming around Lueken and her companionable spirits.

Lueken kept a portfolio of Polaroids in the hopes that a bishop would one day investigate it. After her death, the portfolio became an important relic as Baysider factions vied for control of Lueken's legacy. According to one Baysider website, the inside cover of the portfolio contained the following message:

> This Book is the Sole Property of the Records of the Corporation of "Our Lady of the Roses" for the Future Church Review (Archives). No One Must Either Remove a Photo or Mutilate Portfolio Under Penalty of Legal Action When Made Necessary. Veronica adds these Words of Warning from Jesus, January 24, 1981: "Should thieves or robbers take by force or cunning this Book, Woe to them, for a cruel fate shall they meet with, until the return of the Book. Amen."[84]

Baysiders still take miraculous pictures at vigils, although perhaps not with the same zeal they did in the 1970s. Most pilgrims now use modern digital cameras and the anomalies continue to manifest. Some of these anomalies can be explained by the numerous light sources present at vigils, especially candles. The vigil site at Flushing Meadows is also oriented such that the Long Island Expressway is behind the statue of Mary, although a row of bushes usually screens out light from passing cars.

At a vigil on June 16, a Baysider who had come from California approached me with a vintage Polaroid camera. He explained that since this was my first time at Flushing Meadows, he wanted me to take a picture of Our Lady. I was flattered. I took the camera from him and saw that two saint medals had been affixed to it with Scotch tape: Saint Benedict and Our Lady of the Roses, a medal designed by Lueken's followers in 1971. "I even got it blessed by a priest with holy water," he said. I asked him if the priest knew about Bayside. He responded that the priest had no idea why he wanted an old camera blessed. Apparently, the priest had thought it best not to ask. Standing at the back of the crowd, I aimed the camera at the statue of Mary and snapped a picture. It was dusk and bright lights had been brought out to illuminate the statue. The resulting Polaroid was very blurry and did have a kind of otherworldly quality to it. It is unlikely that anyone looking at the Polaroid would be able to guess what it is a picture of. The audience, the trees, and the sky all appear as an indistinguishable dark mass. Mary appears in the center of the photo as a dazzling blob of light with only a vaguely anthropomorphic shape. I was surprised both by how far away and how bright the statue appears in the picture. In the foreground above and below Mary are broad bands of dim light. I have no guess as to what caused them. It was not an especially spectacular Polaroid and I did not ask anyone to analyze it for me. But I could not help trying to imagine a possible meaning for the picture. Perhaps Mary seemed so far away because I was an outsider who had only come to the vigil to do research. Perhaps the inexplicable bands that appeared in front of Mary symbolized how my academic training "barred" me from understanding the truth of Bayside.[85]

Based on this experience, I think that a large part of the appeal of miraculous photographs is the sense of agency and participation they give to Baysiders. Only Lueken receives detailed messages from the Virgin Mary, but anyone can receive a message from heaven through a photograph. Furthermore, the meanings found in miraculous Polaroids are often far more personal than Lueken's messages, which were usually of global import. A woman from Ecuador showed me a Polaroid that she kept in her purse. It had what appeared to be the profile of a face in it. She explained that she had been praying for someone in Purgatory (probably a family member) when she took this picture. For her, the appearance of a face in the picture meant that her prayers had succeeded. These are the sorts of personal problems and concerns that, for Baysiders, can sometimes be answered through a miraculous Polaroid.

Another defining aspect of the Baysider culture of prophecy is the anticipation of a divine Chastisement. The end-time scenario for Baysiders is very complex and incorporates millennial tropes from several previous apparitions, notably Fatima and Garabandal. There are many elements to the scenario including a "great Warning" and a "great Miracle" giving humanity a final chance to repent, a third world war, and "fiery ball" resembling a comet. Later visions describe the Rapture, a seemingly

Protestant element. Generally, Lueken simply described inchoate visions of future calamities such as ruined cities and rampaging armies. It was left to others to assemble these visions into a meaningful millennial scenario. However, one locution given on June 8, 1974, provides a fairly concise chronology of the events leading up to the Chastisement. The heavenly being that delivered this message to Lueken was none other than Jacinta Marto, one of the child seers of Fatima, who died in the Spanish influenza pandemic only two years after her visions. Lueken, speaking on behalf of Jacinta, told the assembled audience, "It is true that I gave a final message, but I, too, could not give the date—only to warn the world that a great Warning would come to mankind. It would be a great cataclysm Warning, and then there would be a great Miracle, and after that, if nothing changes and man continues to offend the Father, He would have to start this terrible, terrible trial. For there will be a great War and there will be a great, terrible Chastisement."[86]

Of all of these elements, the "Ball of Redemption" became the most important. The first cryptic reference to the Ball of Redemption appeared in a message from the Virgin Mary delivered on June 17, 1971. The origin of this ball may lie with the so-called sun miracle of Fatima. During the final apparition at Fatima, Portugal, on October 13, 1917, some 20,000 people witnessed "the miracle of the dancing sun," one of the most famous events of Marian lore. The sun spun wildly, changed colors, and appeared to "dive-bomb" the pilgrims. Just when thousands of pilgrims feared they would be burned to death, the sun returned to its ordinary position in the sky. It had been raining that day, and many reported that after this encounter, their clothes were dry. Dr. Jose Maria de Almeida Garrett was a member of the Faculty of Sciences at Coimbra University and an eyewitness to the event. In an interview given two months after the sun miracle, he recalled:

> Suddenly, one heard a clamor, a cry of anguish breaking from all the people. The sun, whirling wildly, seemed all at once to loosen itself from the firmament and, blood red, advance threateningly upon the earth as if to crush us with its huge and fiery weight. The sensation during those moments was truly terrible.... All the phenomena which I have described were observed by me in a calm and serene state of mind without any emotional disturbance. It is for others to interpret and explain them. Finally, I must declare that never, before or after October 13 [1917], have I observed similar atmospheric or solar phenomena.[87]

Less spectacular versions of this miracle have been reported at apparition sites throughout the world, including Necedah and Bayside. When I visited Flushing Meadows, many pilgrims claimed they saw the sun dance during a vigil to commemorate the forty-second anniversary of the apparition at Bayside. At 7 p.m. on June 16, over five hundred people were gathered to witness a procession of the statue of Mary to its place at the Vatican Pavilion monument. Not everyone present witnessed this miracle. At a banquet the following day, an organizer asked, "Who saw the sun dance yesterday?" Less than half of those in the room raised their hand. One woman asked me if I had seen the sun dance and when I told her I had not, she answered, "Don't worry. Our Lady said that one day everyone will see."[88]

Lueken's earliest descriptions of "The Ball" resemble the frightening aspects of the sun miracle at Fatima more than a comet. The first such message states only, "All must come to pass, and then the Ball of Redemption will be upon you."[89] At the next vigil, Mary explained that, "Many will die in the great flame of the Ball of Redemption!"[90] Over the next six months, more details are given about this "ball" but its exact nature remains mysterious. Consider this description from September 14, 1972:

> Oh, my goodness! I see—oh, coming down through the sky, a very large ball. It's—oh, it's spinning very fast, and oh, it's shooting out fire! It's like the sun falling. Oh, it's spinning and it's heading—oh, I can almost feel the heat. Oh, now it's passing by, but it's got a long, fiery tail. Oh![91]

This image of "the sun falling" and spinning resembles the sun miracle at Fatima. Mary herself never states that the ball is a comet and only the detail of a fiery tail suggests this interpretation.

On March 7, 1973, a new comet was sighted by Czech astronomer Lubos Kohoutek. Dubbed "Comet Kohoutek," it was expected to pass through the inner solar system, creating a bright display. The media quickly hyped Kohoutek as "the comet of the century." The Baysiders immediately interpreted the comet as the Fiery Ball of Redemption described in Lueken's prophecies. Lueken did too. On March 25, she described a vision she was receiving, "Now over to the left side, I see the comet streaking across the sky, and I see words written under it: 'MONTHS, DAYS, HOURS.' "[92] This was the first time the word "comet" had been used to describe the ball. For the next year, Lueken's followers pointed to Kohoutek to show both the validity and the immediacy of the prophecies.[93] In the end, Kohoutek failed to meet the expectations of the Baysiders or the media and quietly passed by. All of this further irritated Church authorities who were growing increasingly concerned by Lueken's movement. A letter to a nun from Chancellor King complained, "We were threatened with the comet Khoutek [sic], which would bring God's wrath to New York. Astronomers couldn't even find it with a telescope."[94]

However, pilgrims were hardly disappointed to have survived Kohoutek. On the contrary, they took responsibility for the Earth's salvation. On January 13, 1974, Lueken announced a revelation that the Chastisement had been delayed because heaven was pleased with the Baysiders' devotion. One Baysider later explained:

Astronomers were unable to explain the erratic behavior of the comet Kohoutec! Some Government sources said that the comet HAD CHANGED ITS COURSE! Publishers were asked not to print some of the Teletype news. Can anyone explain how, at Bayside, someone obtained a miraculous photograph with the words "K O H by sky" on it, months before the comet was discovered or named?[95]

The Ball of Redemption has remained the prevailing theme of the Bayside Prophecies. Eventually, Lueken received revelations suggesting that the Ball of Redemption was not a normal celestial object and could not be detected by scientists. In her last public locution, held on June 18, 1994, Lueken revealed that the ball was already in Earth's atmosphere. Mary told her, "I know what is in store for mankind. Several years ago I brought you the knowledge of the Ball of Redemption. Though you cannot see it now, it still hovers over the world."[96] A shrine worker for SMWA told me that he continues to monitor NASA data on "Near Earth Objects" or NEOs.

White Berets

Lueken began to spend more and more time in front of the statue at St. Robert Bellarmine's. In 1972, Mary ordered her to conduct a holy hour every Sunday in addition to honoring the feast days.[97] The holy hour prayers were for Catholic priests throughout the world to keep them strong in their faith. In December of that year, Lueken was diagnosed with carcinoma of the spine and was frequently seen in a wheelchair. Health problems did not keep her from the vigils, however. Instead, they only confirmed her charisma as a victim soul. While the small community that attended her vigils continued to grow, it remained a manageable size. Initially the vigils had attracted some curious onlookers, but by 1972 the novelty had worn off. Most vigils consisted only of Lueken and some of her companionable spirits, almost all of them women, who said the rosary in peace.

However, Lueken's messages had been disseminated across the country through networks of lay Catholics interested in apparitions. In 1973, pilgrims began to arrive from beyond Bayside Hills and the crowds grew considerably larger. By February Bayside Hills residents and parishioners at St. Robert Bellarmine's had begun to complain.[98] All over Long Island, flyers about Veronica Lueken were found in churches and on cars parked for Sunday services. Rumors began to spread that disabled people who had attended the vigils had been healed and had cast aside their crutches.[99] It was said that rosaries had miraculously turned to gold. During one vigil, a snake reportedly slithered up to the shrine, but just as it was about to bite someone it turned into a dove and flew away.[100] By May, the office of the Diocese of Brooklyn began to get calls from all around the country, many of them from monks and nuns, wanting to know about Veronica Lueken.[101] A vigil in August 1973 drew in 500–1,000 people, some of them from as far away as Oregon and Kansas.[102] In September, cars were sighted in Bayside Hills with plates from California, Texas, Massachusetts, and Pennsylvania.[103] The following month brought pilgrims in tour buses from Detroit, St. Louis, and Colorado.[104] Finally, on December 7, 1973, several buses arrived in Bayside bringing several hundred people from Canada.[105] These were the Pilgrims of Saint Michael and they had come to see the famous seer of Bayside.

The Pilgrims of Saint Michael were also called "the White Berets" for their distinctive uniforms. Their order was founded in 1939 by Louis Evan for advancing the economic principles of social credit. White Berets described themselves as "consecrated slaves of Jesus and Mary" and saw themselves as a spiritual elite preparing for the last days.[106] Their interest in social credit and monetary systems quickly led to conspiracy theories about international banking. Their literature combines apocalyptic scenarios that have been linked to Marian prophecy since the nineteenth century with twentieth-century conspiracy theories about banking cartels led by a satanic elite called the Illuminati.

It is unclear why, exactly, the White Berets decided to seek Lueken out. Lueken's friend, Grace Pera, had written them in 1970. Ann Ferguson mentioned in an interview that they had consulted another seer in Italy who had advised them to seek Lueken out.[107] Michael Cuneo suggests the group had been actively looking for a Marian seer to adopt for several years.[108] Whatever their reasons, the White Berets undertook a massive public relations campaign on behalf of the fledgling Baysider movement. They proclaimed Lueken the greatest seer of the age. All of her messages were printed in their French-language quarterly, *Vers Demain*, and its English equivalent, *Michael Fighting*. Together, these publications had a circulation of almost ninety thousand readers. The Pilgrims of St. Michael also sold books and audiotapes of Lueken's prophecies. Their support was instrumental in transforming Lueken into a global phenomenon. They also organized buses to take Canadian pilgrims to Bayside. The buses would come down as often as twice a month, bringing hundreds of people. Lueken eagerly accepted their help. On December 31, 1974, Lueken gave the following message from Mary, "We, My child, are much pleased with the speed and the assistance given to Our message by your brothers and sisters of the White Hats—berets. Yes, My child, the Father has a plan for unifying all of Our legions of souls to fight satan."[109]

I interviewed Kevin Farrelly, a resident who had grown up in Bayside. Farrelly had been a student at St. Robert Bellarmine's elementary school and was an undergraduate at Columbia when Lueken's group was forming. He watched the growing controversy over Lueken and later became president of the Bayside Hills Civic Association. Farrelly felt that the arrival of the White Berets had a profound effect on Lueken's movement. He told me that before their arrival, Lueken was widely perceived as a "neighborhood kook," whose activities were strange but harmless. After the arrival of the White Berets, she came to be seen as a threat to the social order of Bayside Hills. This was primarily because the small gatherings at St. Robert Bellarmine's had now turned into crowds of hundreds. Farrelly also said that the White Berets brought a sense of militancy with them and a puritanical streak that Lueken's followers had not previously expressed. They were known for chastising neighborhood girls whom they felt were dressed immodestly.[110]

Lueken also seems to have absorbed some of the conspiratorial worldview of the White Berets. After contact with this group, Lueken's messages frequently referenced the Illuminati, the United Nations, and other perennial villains of conspiracy theorists. One message stated that Franklin

Roosevelt, the father of the New Deal, was in hell and that his dark spirit was now entering "anew upon the earth from the abyss."[111] A similar pattern can be seen with Van Hoof, who seems to have been initiated into conspiracy discourse by her follower Henry Swan.[112] Church authorities, who had initially been dismissive of Lueken's visions, grew increasingly anxious about how her new supporters might influence her. In a letter to Lueken, Chancellor King warned her, "I am very fearful some people may be taking advantage of you."[113]

How People Become Seers

While many people report having mystical experiences, the early visions of Van Hoof and Lueken were exceptional in that they were profoundly frightening. A psychiatrist might interpret these experiences as "psychotic breaks." Both women were in poor health and under a great deal of personal stress when their anomalous experiences began. However, once they found a community of people who were supportive of them—Van Hoof's "Chosen Ones," Lueken's "companionable spirits"—their experiences were rendered intelligible. The visions ceased to manifest as intrusions into daily life, as when Lueken went shopping in 1968 and saw images so frightening she was forced to flee into a store to call her husband. Instead, the visions became, in a sense, "domesticated," generally manifesting only during times set aside by the community of believers for vigils and apparitions. Anthropologist I. M. Lewis describes indigenous cultures in which women who become "afflicted" with possession are not exorcised of the alien personality but inducted into a community of ecstatics where their relationship with the possessing entity can be rendered manageable. These women become shamans and their altered states of consciousness are believed to bestow prophecy and healing. This process is not necessarily "taking advantage" of these women as Chancellor King feared was happening to Lueken. Instead, it essentially repurposes the distressed person's affliction, turning it into a resource for the community. Lewis notes that cultures with a tradition of shamanism do have not have schizophrenics.[114]

This is not to engage in medical reductionism or pathologize the religious experiences of Van Hoof and Lueken. Rather, I propose that the tradition of Catholic seers serves a social function of repurposing the experiences of distressed individuals in a manner similar to the shamanic traditions described by Lewis. In Lueken's case it can be seen how the vernacular and ecclesiastical faces of Catholicism each played a role to effect her transformation into a seer. After Lueken's first mystical experience of smelling roses she went to confession to tell her parish priest. When her letter from Cardinal Cushing levitated across the room, she went to see her parish priests. But Lueken felt that her priests continually brushed her aside. Instead of making sense of her confusion and easing her distress, the response from clergy made her even more upset and her visions intensified. When lay Catholics began to support her, Church authorities responded with censure, making her feel increasingly alienated from her Church. We will never know what would have happened if, when Lueken first went to talk about her experiences, her parish priest had told her that she *had* experienced a genuine encounter with the supernatural, that she was a very special person, and that they were blessed to have her in their parish. Would this only have encouraged her? Or would such an affirmation have set her mind at ease, preventing the chain of events that led to her becoming the seer of Bayside? Chancellor James P. King once stated in an interview that almost every parish has a seer or a visionary.[115] If the initial reaction from Church authorities had gone differently, might Lueken have become merely a quirky parishioner who had an unusually intense relationship with St. Therese?[116]

In an interview given in 1977, Lueken explained that if Church authorities had taken her seriously, the Bayside Prophecies would have been "silenced." She remarked:

> Our Lady first started Her work with me, through me, in 1968 with St. Theresa. During that time, I approached many priests, trying to find a spiritual director, but it was not in the will of God, and later of course, I found out through Jesus that, He said, His very words, were "You will do better by yourself, My child. I will direct you, you will go further." I understand now why He said that. Experience has taught me that if I had been under a spiritual director, Our Lady's message would have been silenced a long time ago.[117]

But Lueken *did* have spiritual directors of sorts. In the absence of Church authorities, a number of interested parties stepped forward to affirm her visions and interpret their significance. These companionable spirits shared in her visions, gave her miraculous Polaroids to interpret, and created special robes for her to wear during vigils. In return, they wanted

Lueken to become something more than a housewife who had mystical experiences: They wanted her to become a Marian seer in the tradition of Lourdes, Fatima, and Garabandal. The White Berets lent even more support, in exchange for which they wanted Lueken to become the greatest seer of the age. Lueken did not disappoint them.

The Anomalous Experience of Vatican II

Sociologists argue that apparitional movements often form during periods of social unrest.[118] Of course, modern societies are always undergoing change and cultural stress, but Baysiders have consistently expressed that the world they grew up in has changed and that the traditions and values necessary for American Catholics to thrive have been lost. Just as a community of prophecy helped Lueken to interpret her anomalous experiences, she empowered the community to articulate their concerns and impose order onto their world. Her messages reflect Cold War anxieties, concerns about the youth culture of the 1960s, and general bewilderment at a world that seemed to have forsaken commonsense values for an ever-increasing array of modern philosophies and viewpoints. In her locutions, Lueken often warned of the dangers of "isms." A message from Mary given in 1981 explained, "The way to Heaven is a simple way. It cannot be compromised; it cannot be modernized; it cannot be cast aside or a new religion started. For your religion will be of man, of humanism, and modernism, and satanism, and all the 'isms' that destroy mankind in the end."[119] For Lueken's followers, her locutions validated their concerns and located them within a prophetic context that rendered them intelligible. The world was not changing by accident; these were the plans of Satan in the last days. Furthermore, the devotional culture that was forming around Lueken offered a form of embodied resistance. Through Lueken's vigils, Catholics who otherwise felt helpless in the face of a changing world could now engage in ritual battle for what they regarded as the core values of Catholic tradition.

Of all the issues that troubled Lueken and her community, the greatest was the Second Vatican Council, which was held from 1962 to 1965. The original purpose of the council was described as *aggiornamento* (updating). However, the reforms ended up being the most drastic in five hundred years. Pope John XXIII, who convened the council, explained that its purpose was to "open windows in the wall." As James Donahue, vice president and vigil coordinator for SWMA explained to me, "They said they were going to open up a window but they let in a tornado!"[120] John XXIII died in 1963 and the reforms were affirmed by his successor, Paul VI. The greatest change of the council was to replace the Latin mass with vernacular languages. Doctrinally, the council recognized other forms of Christianity as valid and even acknowledged the validity of other religions, provided they exhibit proper morality. Vatican II also re-emphasized a concept of "collegiality" in which the Church is understood to include the community of parishioners as well as clergy. This move loosened the hierarchy and distributed responsibility for governing the Church more widely between clergy and lay officials.

In the United States, there was not a coordinated national strategy to explain how the reforms of Vatican II should be interpreted. The documents were often vague and bishops possessed the sole authority to regulate changes to the liturgy. Because of this, reform occurred at different rates from region to region and from parish to parish. The response to these reforms from lay Catholics varied widely from excitement, to confusion and concern, to anger and even secession. Some Catholics had been calling for liturgical reform for decades. In 1964, The Christian Family Movement, a lay organization consisting primarily of middle-class Catholic couples, produced a document entitled, "How the 'People of God' Want to Worship." Based on surveys of their own members, it called for a vernacular mass in which the priest faced the congregation. Many nuns embraced the new definition of the Church as "the people of God" as a mandate to take on greater leadership roles within their parishes. Politically liberal Catholics embraced the encyclical *Pacem in Terris*, a Vatican II document on the Cold War and its threat to world peace, as an endorsement for Catholics to resist all dehumanizing social systems, including capitalism and militarism. Other Catholics raised concerns that tradition was being destroyed. In 1965, Father Gommar de Pauw of Baltimore published "The Catholic Traditionalist Manifesto." This was a twelve-point platform that de Pauw believed to represent "the majority of American Catholics." De Pauw's primary concern was that liturgical reform be understood as optional, not mandated, and that the traditional mass be allowed to co-exist with the modern mass. Point nine of the Manifesto specifies that devotion to Mary must be continued and encouraged.

Lueken and many lay Catholics like her shared de Pauw's concerns. On March 2, 1968, 150 people picketed Saint Patrick's Cathedral in New York City, carrying signs such as "Restore Our Latin Mass" and "Altar Yes, Table No." The authors of Vatican II were described as "liturgical beatniks" and

"hippies" who were "Protestantizing" the Church.[121] A more extreme response came from a number of separatist or "sedevacantist" movements.
These groups were Catholic secessionists, declaring that the Vatican had
lost its legitimacy as head of the Holy See. In many cases, the leaders of
such groups became "anti-popes," claiming that they, and not the pope
in Rome, were the true heirs to the Seat of Peter. Lueken and her followers were not about to abandon their Church in this fashion, but they
remained extremely critical of Vatican II.

For traditionalist Catholics the liturgical changes were the hardest to
bear. Baysiders constantly railed against the vernacular mass. They found
the practice of receiving communion in the hand, as opposed to having
the consecrated host placed directly onto the tongue, particularly upsetting. A letter to the editor of a parish bulletin from a Baysider demanded:

> Is the lay person so above the clergy that he can come directly from
> his home to Communion, from his morning toilet, without wash-
> ing his hands, to accept his Savior, his God? Can he, without guilt,
> accept his God in those soiled hands that have touched all sorts of
> contaminated articles during the intervening hours since he awoke
> this morning, and, the moment of Communion?[122]

Many Catholics also felt that their Church no longer valued the devotional practices of their youth. Vatican II never officially condemned
devotional practices, but local Church authorities often made an effort
to downplay them "in the spirit" of Vatican II. James Donovan, a writer
for the conservative Catholic magazine *Fidelity*, describes how after
Vatican II traditional devotions to Mary were seen as "a pre-Vatican II
aberrations belonging now to the Church's lunatic fringe." He continues, "Marian devotion is for old women, probably Italian immigrants,
dressed in black, wearing sad faces, and desperately clutching the rosary
in their hands while they should be attending Mass."[123] Marian devotees
were now keenly aware that their practices had been relegated to the
periphery. At a May Crowning in 2012, Michael Mangan, president of
SMWA, remarked on a graphic of two hands holding a rosary that was
being used to promote the forty-second anniversary of the Bayside apparitions. He pointed out that the hands holding the rosary were not those
of an old woman but strong hands, "mitts." The rosary, he explained,
was not an antiquated tradition but a supernatural weapon in a war
against evil.[124] Indeed, for Baysiders the absence of proper Catholic

ritual seems to lie at the heart of all the problems and "isms" that are now taking over the world.

Lueken seems to have been particularly horrified by the loss of Catholic devotions. Ronald Brown related a story that in the years after Vatican II, Lueken had driven a truck to the dumpsters behind churches, looking for statues of Mary and the saints that had been discarded by churches seeking to become more modern looking. Lueken would "rescue" these statues and take them home.[125] The provenance of this story is uncertain. It may be an apocryphal tale passed down by Baysiders. However, the story is consistent with a larger portrait of Lueken. Two of her most important early visions involved statues—those of Therese and Mary. For Lueken, the statues embodied the presence of these saints. She visited these statues and cared for them, maintaining a relationship with them as if they were flesh and blood people. To see churches discard unwanted statues in dumpsters may well have been intolerable for her.

Lueken urged her followers not to leave their parish churches, but she also became a voice of popular dissent against the changes of Vatican II. Many of her followers loved her for this. In an interview with Michael Cuneo, Ben Salomone, a former Baysider and bodyguard for Lueken, recalled why he followed her:

> I was forty years old and very confused and very disturbed over what was happening in the Church after Vatican II. And so were all of Veronica's followers. And Veronica gave us great stuff. The rosary at the vigils was absolutely beautiful. And there were the statues and the visions and the messages....We were so unhappy with the way the faith was being destroyed after the council, and Veronica came and filled the vacuum. We all loved her for this.[126]

Similarly, a letter from a Baysider to the Brooklyn Diocese explained that Lueken's vigils were more recognizable to him as Catholicism than the modern mass:

> As a Catholic who grew up in Brooklyn and was trained in many of the schools there, I am taking the liberty to write to you about one Veronica Lueken. I have recently read many of the things she has said, and truthfully I can find nothing in it that I wasn't taught as

a child ... Please let me know what the Church's stand is on all of this. I do not get any kind of answers here—perhaps we live in a different world? I can't see that what we were taught as "right" years ago should be "wrong" today. In fact, I really feel that today's Church does not stress most of this. The message seems to be one of loving your neighbor first and God comes in as almost second-best. Shouldn't God come first in any case?[127]

In the decades that followed, Baysiders developed a more nuanced critique of Vatican II. In 1975, Lueken famously claimed that Paul VI had been replaced by a communist agent. In 2011, David Martin, a Baysider organizer from Los Angeles published *Vatican II: A Historic Turning Point*, which critiqued the theology and legitimacy of Vatican II from a Baysider perspective. Martin explained that the modern mass was designed to distract from the supernatural significance of the ritual, presenting the Eucharist as symbolic rather than a literal manifestation of Christ's presence. He admits that the modern mass is still legitimate and efficacious for the salvation of souls. However, he compares it to a tree that vandals have festooned with toilet paper: The tree does not cease to be a tree just because it has been disrespected. In the same way, the modern mass does not show proper reverence for God but nevertheless remains a mass.[128] Nuanced arguments of this kind are not found in the Bayside Prophecies, which contain concise orders from heaven as well as cryptic messages and striking images. But the community that formed around Lueken did not want a theologian to give expression to their dissent. Numerous conservative and traditionalist priests had already stepped forward to do this. Baysiders wanted thaumaturgical authority—a figure that spoke for heaven and validated their concerns with revelations and miracles. Lueken gave them this validation and in return they validated her.

3

The Battle of Bayside

ON MARCH 31, 1971, Monsignor Emmet McDonald, pastor of St. Robert Bellarmine's Church, wrote Bishop Francis J. Mugavero about the problems he was having with "The Apparitions of Veronica." The matter was delegated to Chancellor James P. King, who responded to McDonald, "Perhaps at your convenience we might be able to work out a meeting to ascertain some reasonable way in which we might control the situation. It is difficult, of course, to prohibit a person like this from acting in this manner, but at the same time, certainly there should be some protection for the parish."[1] But as the crowds continued to grow and busloads of pilgrims arrived from throughout the United States and Canada, King found it increasingly difficult to find a "reasonable way" to control the situation. Added pressure was placed on the diocese by the Bayside Hills Civic Association (BHCA), which was incensed over what the crowds might do to property values. By 1975, the vigils were still occurring as often as eighty times a year and had grown larger than ever. The BHCA felt that both the diocese and the police were either unable or unwilling to control Lueken and her followers. Angry residents began to organize "counter-vigils" in front of St. Robert Bellarmine's in an attempt reclaim their neighborhood. These demonstrations led to heated confrontations that occasionally turned violent. As tensions heightened, as many as one hundred police officers would be present at vigils to keep the peace. The most brazen residents clashed with police leading to arrests and accusations of police brutality. Several state politicians became involved before the Supreme Court of New York finally issued an injunction banning the vigils from Bayside Hills. The "Battle of Bayside" became national news. *Newsweek* declared, "The real miracle of Bayside Hills may be that no one has been killed."[2]

The conflict in Bayside Hills was a defining event for the Baysider movement. The movement's struggle against the diocese and the BHCA to maintain control of their sacred space at St. Robert Bellarmine's became the model for future conflicts. Pilgrims attending vigils expressed surprise that diocesan authorities and the residents of Bayside Hills—whom they regarded as fellow Catholics—would show such hostility. This engendered a "fortress mentality" in which Baysiders saw themselves as opposed by authorities at every turn. Lueken's messages from heaven during this time describe diocesan officials and the leaders of the BHCA as being under demonic influence. Her followers, who generally prided themselves on their deference to Church authority, became increasingly angry with Bishop Mugavero and Chancellor King. Letters to Mugavero and King from Baysiders berate them for their perceived dishonesty and failure to follow proper procedure. One letter actually orders Mugavero to say the Hail Mary in atonement for his sins against the Virgin Mary.[3] Church authorities also underwent a process of alienation as they encountered a side of the laity they had never seen before. As the controversy wore on, Chancellor King, acting on behalf of the diocese, began to use authoritarian tactics that seemed at odds with the otherwise progressive stance of the Brooklyn diocese as well as the post-Vatican II concept of the Church as "the people of God." Throughout this process of escalation, the Baysiders never renounced their Church nor did King formally condemn Lueken as a heretic. Nevertheless, the Battle of Bayside left a wound between a Catholic movement and its Church. Nearly four decades later this wound is still felt by modern Baysiders.

Investigating the Seer

In Catholic tradition, it is always the duty of the bishop to assess matters of private revelation. Bishop Mugavero was first alerted to Lueken's activities in 1970, but it was nearly three years before any action was taken by the diocese. Mugavero's slow response is typical for bishops in his situation. Franciscan friar Benedict Groeschel notes in his book, *A Still Small Voice*, "It is generally seen as very bad news for officialdom when it is reported that Our Lady has appeared to someone."[4] Mugavero's biography suggests that investigating a Marian apparition was probably the last thing he wanted to do. The first Italian-American bishop of Brooklyn, he was known as a quietly progressive cleric who was interested in the social issues of his diocese. He was involved with the Nehemiah Housing

Project, which found homes for the poor in Brooklyn, and the Campaign for Human Development, which raised millions of dollars for the poor. In the 1980s, he allowed Dignity, an organization of gay Catholics, to use diocesan buildings. When the Vatican pressured him to stop, however, he immediately barred Dignity from his churches. He opposed abortion, but was unwilling to use the more aggressive and polarizing tactics of Cardinal O'Connor. He is also remembered as a pioneer in interfaith dialogue between Jews and Catholics. During Vatican II, Mugavero's model of interfaith dialogue influenced Paul VI's thinking about ecumenical issues.[5] He placed little value on tradition and formality. He was known for correcting people who addressed him by the honorific "Your Excellency," replying, "I'm not excellent."[6] A story in *The Bayside Times* covered Mugavero's visit to Saint Agnes High, a Catholic school for girls. An accompanying photograph depicted him casually playing cards with a group of students.[7] While assessing a Marian apparition was not something Mugavero had any desire to do, the situation in Bayside could no longer be ignored. So rather than dealing with Lueken directly, Mugavero delegated the matter almost entirely to Chancellor King.

By February of 1973, King had become concerned that Lueken and her followers were using the name "Robert Bellarmine's" in their literature and feared their activities were "bringing ridicule on the church."[8] In March, he wrote Lueken asking her to stop inviting people to her vigils. This letter did not deny Lueken's visions but warned of "the possibility of ridicule when private devotions suddenly become overly publicized."[9] In May, he wrote Mugavero, "It might be well for you to have a diocesan commission or group of priests look into this so that we might come up with an official diocesan position."[10]

The investigation of Marian seers has a long tradition both in Catholic theology and in the popular imagination of lay Catholics. For many lay Catholics, the interrogation of fourteen-year-old Bernadette Soubirous at Lourdes in 1848 provided a "script" for how an investigation ought to go: Soubirous was subjected to extensive and often humiliating interrogations by Church authorities, but in the end, her visions were affirmed. In 1942, Austrian-Bohemian writer Franz Werfel published his novel, *The Song of Bernadette*, about the apparition at Lourdes. The book was a wild success, spending more than a year on *The New York Times* bestseller list. In 1943, it was adapted into a film directed by Henry King. This adaptation was also popular, earning actress Jennifer Jones an Academy Award for her performance as Soubirous. The film emphasized Soubirous's persecution at the hands of Imperial Prosecutor Vital Dutour, played by Vincent Price. This film likely contributed to a wave of reported Marian apparitions that began in the second half of the twentieth century. Historian James Fisher describes how on November 5, 1945, twenty-five thousand people gathered at a vacant lot in the Bronx where a nine-year-old boy and his friends had constructed a crude shrine on the spot where he had seen an apparition of the Virgin Mary the previous week. The boy, Joseph Vitolo Jr., admitted that he had recently seen *The Song of Bernadette*, but insisted that the vision he saw was unlike the one in the film. Just as Lueken would do more than twenty years later, Vitolo predicted that a well like the one at Lourdes would spring forth at his sacred site.[11] Ray Doiron, a Marian seer from Belleville, Illinois, also recalled seeing this film as a child and began experiencing locutions after his own pilgrimage to Lourdes.[12] Ben Salomone, one of Lueken's bodyguards, recalled, "We were brought up on *The Song of Bernadette*. We grew up with stories like St. Anthony of Padua. Every Catholic would say, 'If I ever met a saint like that I would follow him to the ends of the earth.'"[13]

Because of the script established by Lourdes, contemporary apparitional movements often look forward to official investigations, viewing them as evidence of their significance and an opportunity to "prove" their validity. In the "Lourdes script," seers cannot really lose when investigated by a bishop because it is assumed that Church authorities will reject a true seer before they affirm them. For Marian movements, censure from Church authorities is paradoxically regarded as confirmation of the seer's authenticity. In fact, it is not uncommon for Marian movements to compare their critics to the scribes and Pharisees of the gospels, drawing a parallel between their persecuted seer and a persecuted Christ.

However, when Marian seers bring messages of millennial urgency— as was the case with Lueken—apparitional movements often argue that there is no time to wait for Church authorities to deliberate. As one Catholic explained on an Internet forum:

> If someone said a hurricane was coming, would you just sit there and read only approved books of the Church? Fatima took 30 years for approval, so should you have ignored those messages for 30 years?... What would be better is to COMPARE the current prophecies to the Church teachings to discern instead of ignoring them.[14]

Joseph Hunt, the self-described "Internet Advocate for Roman Catholic Visionaries," makes a similar argument. He explains that God "gave us scripture and the Church for the 'How to ... ' of our faith, but he also gives us private revelation for the 'When to ... ' of our faith in certain times of history. And we are in a very grave historical period right now."[15] In such arguments, millennialism supersedes the magisterium.

Church authorities have their own criteria for evaluating private revelations. Their approach is influenced by a different set of factors, the greatest of which are the political consequences of the seer's message and the risk of embarrassment to the Church. Where Marian movements are often driven by a sense of apocalyptic urgency, Church authorities usually take the long view, often thinking about the possible consequences in terms of centuries. Groeschel, considered an authority on private revelations, notes that it is much easier and less embarrassing for the Church to affirm a previously rejected revelation than to rescind its approval for an accepted revelation. For this reason, he argues that rejecting Marian apparitions is actually a "no-lose" situation for the Church. He writes, "The worst that can happen is that eventually the bishop may have to make some apologies to the Virgin Mary—but then we have it on the best authority that she is very benevolent and understanding."[16]

Without acknowledging it, Church authorities often employ a sort of double bind in evaluating the testimony of seers. If a seer's visions share too much similarity to previous apparitions such as Lourdes and Fatima, they are deemed false because they are derivative. On the other hand, if visions contain too many original elements, they are deemed false because they are unprecedented. Just as apparitional movements may interpret anything Church authorities say as affirmation of their seer (because a true seer will be rejected), so too Church authorities may interpret anything a seer says as evidence of delusion. When lay Catholics and Church authorities debate the merits of an alleged seer, the result is often a rhetorical deadlock.

Surprisingly, the Congregation for the Doctrine of Faith (CDF), the Vatican office charged with overseeing Catholic doctrine, had no official criteria for investigating private revelation in 1973.[17] Chancellor King later explained in an interview, "There is nothing in canon law to tell you what a canonical investigation is in a sense except if you are going in for Saints or Beatification, etc."[18] The CDF's omission was likely deliberate. Historically it has served the interests of the Church to let bishops resolve such cases on their own in accordance with the local needs of their community. Furthermore, in the modern era Marian movements have increasingly resorted to legalistic arguments; disseminating formal rules for investigating an apparition would empower them further. Despite Chancellor King's protests, however, there were more resources that he could have employed in his investigation of Lueken. Had he availed himself of them, the Baysider movement might have taken an entirely different direction.

In June 1973, King formed a committee of priests to investigate the apparitions. In addition to King, there were three "official" members of this committee. Monsignor McDonald was chosen because Lueken knew him personally. Father Vincent J. Powell was on the committee because he was vicar over the St. Robert Bellarmine's parish.[19] A Monsignor Fitzgibbon was selected because he was unfamiliar with the Bayside apparitions and could supposedly provide an objective viewpoint. Fitzgibbon had taught at St. Joseph's College and also lived near St. Robert Bellarmine's. Additionally, King asked two priests from St. Robert Bellarmine's, Father John McNulty and Father John Jurgensen, to be present because they had spoken to Lueken about her experiences.[20] In a 1979 interview, King implied that Father James P. Grace, a faculty member at the Immaculate Conception Seminary in Douglaston, New York, was present to advise as a theologian. However, a memorandum to Mugavero from the date of the investigation notes that Grace was on retreat and unable to serve on the committee.

King sent each committee member copies of all the literature he had received from Lueken's followers, including tapes and transcripts of her locutions. On June 29, 1973, the committee met in the rectory of St. Robert Bellarmine's. Later that day, a two-page report was sent to the bishop. King reported, "Everyone read much of the material that we have on file from this lady and all agree that it seems to be a rather rambling mish-mash of material gleaned from books about apparitions of Our Lady, especially at Fatima. Some indication from books about Garabandal is evident, but Fatima would seem to be the primary source." In essence, the committee dismissed Lueken's visions as derivative. Lueken herself was described as sincere and "a good-living woman who apparently is very good to her family." The committee conceded there was no proof that she was mentally disturbed. King also stressed the need for immediate action, explaining, "I believe the authority of the diocese would have to be used in order to discourage people coming here." The committee recommended that Mugavero approve a letter to Lueken explaining that a committee appointed by the bishop had found "nothing miraculous about the messages she was receiving" and requesting that she cease inviting people to attend her vigils. The committee also recommended contacting the United States Conference of Catholic Bishops (USCCB) to request its help in discouraging Catholics around the country from attending vigils at Bayside.[21]

The situation in Bayside had continued to deteriorate. In June 1974, King wrote James S. Rausch, secretary of the USCCB asking him to mention Bayside in the organization's bulletin. Specifically, King wanted it stated that the diocese had declared the vigils spurious and forbidden Catholics from attending them. He also explained, "Our investigation indicates that the alleged miracles are nothing but products of a fertile imagination."[22] The USCCB came to King's aid and bishops throughout the United States and Canada issued pastoral letters stating that the apparitions of Bayside were condemned.[23] The phrase "fertile imagination" became a watchword used by Lueken's detractors. In 2012, I interviewed ninety-four-year-old Adrian K. Cornell, a former vice president and chairman of the BHCA. Cornell is Catholic but believes that Lueken was definitely not seeing the Virgin Mary. I asked him what he thought was happening to Lueken during the vigils. He answered, "It's like the Church said, she had a fertile imagination."[24]

Lueken and her followers were incensed that Catholic bishops throughout North America were disparaging their movement based on an investigation that had never consulted Lueken or any of her followers. They wanted a lengthy interrogation as had happened at Lourdes and Necedah. In October 1974, Lueken sent a strongly worded letter to King and Mugavero arguing, "By your 'Judgment' you have set forces of Evil in action upon peoples who have a true Faith. Let us state a fact—I have never met you—or the Rev Bishop or anyone else who you claim to have found [me] to Have a 'Fertile Imagination.'"[25] In 1978, Anne Cillis, then a devoted Baysider from Ottawa, Canada, conducted her own investigation of King's investigation. She managed to get King on the telephone and launched into a surprise interview, the findings of which she published in her small print magazine *Sancta Maria*. According to Cillis, King admitted that his committee had never interviewed Lueken or any of her followers, had never listened to any of the tapes, and had not read all of the printed material available to them. Further, the committee had not investigated any claims of miraculous cures or conversions, nor had they done a serious investigation of any miraculous Polaroids. King responded to many of Cillis's questions that he simply did not remember, which was likely the truth. Cillis also argued that the committee only heard the perspective of parishioners from St. Robert Bellarmine's who had been inconvenienced by the vigils and were biased against Lueken. Most importantly, Cillis claimed that Bishop Mugavero had never been involved in the investigation. She concluded that the Diocese of Brooklyn had carried out a "monstrous deception."[26] Today, Baysiders continue to insist that, because Mugavero refused to investigate the apparitions personally, any declaration condemning Bayside remains null and void.

In 1976, King was replaced as chancellor by Anthony Bevilacqua, who would later become a cardinal and archbishop of Philadelphia. After the publication of Cillis's article, his office began to receive a stream of phone calls from interested Catholics demanding an explanation. This led Bevilacqua to interview King in order to prepare a response to Cillis's charges. King explained that he had attempted to interview Lueken but that she had an unlisted phone number and had not responded to any of his letters. This is likely true as Lueken had become increasingly reclusive. Furthermore, King said that he did not want to interrogate Lueken, out of compassion and a desire not to upset her. Similarly, the committee did not know who any of the vigil organizers were or how to contact them. The committee members had read all of the printed material and King had listened to some of the tapes. Claims of miraculous cures and conversions had not been investigated because the committee was unaware that any had been reported. Although Mugavero had not personally participated in the investigation, he had authorized King to conduct it and to form a committee, discussed the committee's conclusions, and approved its report. This, Bevilacqua argued, made the investigation canonically viable.[27]

In 1974 the diocese publicly described the work of King's committee as "a complete and thorough investigation." SMWA president Michael Mangan has since responded that if the diocese thinks this investigation was complete and thorough, then it is the diocese and not Lueken that possesses a fertile imagination.[28] The Baysiders' contention that the investigation was not thorough is warranted. Bevilacqua's defense—that the committee did not know what details to investigate or how to contact people worthy of investigation—hardly certifies King's findings as definitive. In fact, King's entire investigation appears to have consisted of a single, brief meeting in the church rectory. By contrast, in the 1950 investigation of Mary Ann Van Hoof, the priests interviewed the seer, attempted to reproduce alleged miracles, and even requested a week of medical tests at a hospital.

It seems that King's goal was never actually to determine whether Lueken's visions were authentic. As stated in his first letter proposing a committee, his goal was to see the situation in Bayside resolved. Groeschel advises those investigating apparitions to be "patient and gentle." But King's report after the committee meeting calls for immediate action. The true function of the investigation was simply to show that diocesan authorities had double-checked their assumptions before officially dismissing the apparitions as false.

Chancellor King cannot really be blamed for approaching the investigation in this way. There was an extent to which diocesan authorities were *incapable* of debating the evidence because to them the debate itself was absurd. Church authorities repeatedly described their verdict as self-evident. French theologian Rene Laurentin discusses the Bayside apparitions in a chapter of his *Apparitions of the Blessed Virgin Mary Today* entitled, "Apparitions without Credibility." He does not present extended arguments for *why* Bayside is not credible. He states that the messages contain "evident errors," but does not elaborate.[29] The only message cited in such assertions is the 1975 announcement that Paul VI was an imposter. To Church authorities this claim was evidence of rebellion against papal authority. But to Baysiders it was not a matter of doctrine at all. It was an observable fact. Many Baysiders claimed to have photographic evidence of an actor posing as Paul VI. In any case, Lueken had not yet made this accusation in 1973 when the investigation was conducted.

Bevilacqua commented, "Anybody who reads those visions must know this is not true. All you have to do is read any one of them. She has condemned everything. She has condemned priests, she has condemned Bishops, she has condemned nuns, she has condemned teachers, she has condemned the radio, she has condemned the telephone, she has condemned television."[30] But while the errors of the Bayside Prophecies may have been self-evident to Laurentin and Bevilacqua, they were not self-evident to thousands of Baysiders. In fact, the Baysiders said just the opposite: That the locutions must be true because they only confirmed what everyone already knew. One Baysider letter explained to Mugavero, "Much of the Bayside messages contain what any concerned Catholic might have already con-cluded [sic] regarding the condition of the world and the Church today."[31] This epistemological divide between Baysiders and Church authorities practically ensured that no investigation would be satisfactory. There was simply no common ground from which both parties could review the evidence.

In addition to the investigation itself, the delivery of the verdict also demonstrated a disconnect between Church authorities and the expectations of lay Catholics. King did not follow the Lourdes script. He had likely seen the *The Song of Bernadette* as well and did not want to play the role of a villainous inquisitor. In 1979, he said of his reasons for not interrogating Lueken, "We didn't want to upset an ordinary good woman. We didn't go after her like a district attorney or an examining attorney."[32] Similarly, although King wanted to produce an official statement from the diocese, he was reluctant to frame this statement in theological terms or even to dismiss Lueken's experiences entirely. After the investigation, the diocese drafted a form letter that was sent in response to inquiries about Lueken that were now coming from all over the country. It read in part:

> A thorough investigation was made and the conclusion was reached that there was no doubt that the alleged "apparitions" lacked complete authenticity. It is the official and firm position of the Diocese of Brooklyn that no credibility can be given to the so-called "visions" of Bayside.

As inquiries about Lueken continued to come in from all over the country, later drafts of this letter added another paragraph: "I would be grateful to you for any efforts that you may make in disseminating this official position of the Diocese of Brooklyn."[33] King's verdict that the apparitions "lack complete authenticity" is a far cry from branding them heretical. In fact, it leaves open the possibility that the visions may have an "incomplete authenticity"—whatever that might mean. This vague language reflected King's progressive views. Bevilacqua later explained the wording of this letter, "In pre-Vatican II days, the Church may have used the word 'condemned,' nowadays the Church simply says 'not authentic.' "[34] There was also a sense that an authoritarian tone might backfire and alienate lay Catholics. Father James LeBar explained the diocese's approach: "There is a concern that many of the people are good ordinary Catholic people, and if you threaten them with excommunication, it would do more harm than good."[35]

However, for Baysiders, King's attempts to take a progressive stance and to spare Lueken's feelings appeared inconclusive and confusing. They were tone-deaf to the nuanced message King was attempting to present and wanted the position of the diocese to be framed starkly in terms of sin and excommunication. Bevilacqua remarked:

They always ask us, "Well is it a sin for me to go there?" I don't want to put it on that level! Most of these people who go there are very good people. I'm not going to say you're committing a terrible sin. And that's what they ask us. "Is it a sin?" No, you can go any place and say the Rosary. But as far as do we approve of their going? We do not approve of it.

They want this former way of doing things—"We're going to condemn you." I don't like to use the word, because it sounds like everybody's evil. And it isn't that.[36]

But Baysiders were willing to risk condemnation if this meant Lueken would be taken seriously. Anne Cillis argued that if the diocese truly did not support the apparitions then they must impose an interdict against Lueken as they had done to Van Hoof.[37]

Lay Catholics who opposed the Baysiders also felt that the diocese's position was too vague and demanded that Church authorities provide some weapon to use against their opponents. Three months after King's committee met, the parish council of St. Robert Bellarmine's wrote Monsignor McDonald requesting a definitive investigation. They wrote, "While the Council is certainly cognizant to the possibility (considered to be most remote) that these alleged revelations and miraculous occurrences could be true, we consider it imperative that urgent action be taken to establish these matters or terminate Mrs. Lueken's activities."[38] Similarly, a woman from Michigan wrote the diocese seeking "official" documentation that Lueken's revelations were false:

I get very angry when persons actively participating in Bayside are constantly telling me I do not accept my Blessed Mother and that I am denying her if I do not participate and acknowledge Veronica. I stand my ground but they do make me feel very guilty. ... If it has been officially condemned by the church, could you please advise me where I could obtain a copy of the official condemnation document? It would stop the arguments I encounter every so often.[39]

A similar letter from a Byzantine Catholic in Pennsylvania asked for ammunition against a local Baysider, writing:

He claims that the end of the world will be in 1983, that Pope Paul VI was kidnapped, that the Catholic Bishops support abortion and so many other absurdities that I do not know how any can believe him but they do. Those of us who are loyal Catholic Christians have nothing to refute these lies.

He goes on to ask for the "history of Bayside's condemnation."[40]

Both the Baysiders and their lay Catholic opponents felt the diocese must either affirm that Lueken's visions were real or else condemn her utterly. No ambiguous position could be tolerated. Neither were efforts to spare Lueken's feelings appreciated. Finally, in 1986, Bishop Mugavero did promulgate a declaration that the Bayside Prophecies are false and contradict Catholic faith. But by this time, the Baysiders had already become a global movement. They were able to claim that the diocese had never conducted a "real" investigation and that Mugavero's statement was therefore without foundation.

The investigation of Lueken's visions was a moment in which the divide between Church authorities and Lueken's supporters was starkly revealed. Both sides appealed to what *anyone* ought to know. But appeals to "common sense" only work when both parties share a common worldview. King's initial attempt to resolve the problem in Bayside by invoking the authority of the diocese only angered Lueken's followers. Likewise, the Baysiders' letters and phone calls to the Chancery only further convinced King that the Catholics attending vigils were defiant and unreasonable. Instead of coming to an agreement, the two sides became increasingly estranged from each other.

Escalation

In the nineteenth century, the land that would one day become Bayside Hills was a 117-acre farm. The farm was sold and converted into a country club. Next it became the semi-public Queensboro Golf and Country Club before it was sold again to the Gross Morton company and finally developed into a subdivision in 1935.[41] Nine hundred and fifty new homes were constructed, selling for an average of $5,000. Today, many of these homes are worth more than half a million dollars. Homeowners founded the Bayside Hills Civic Association (BCHA) in 1936. The association was proud of the neighborhood and took its maintenance very seriously. Some of the streets in Bayside Hills contain grassy traffic islands or "malls." Maintenance of the malls fell to the New York Department of

Parks. When the city failed to properly mow the grass, BHCA president Al Falloni rented a small herd of goats and tethered them to the malls. He then invited the press to photograph his goats doing the job of the Parks Department. This effectively shamed the city into mowing the lawns until the publicity died down. After that, the BHCA purchased two mowers and took turns volunteering to mow the lawns. Finally, they pooled their resources and hired a landscaper. Al Falloni was a real estate agent and was considered a pillar of the community. By 1970 he had already been president of the BHCA for eight terms. Before going into real estate, he had been a manager for Italian-American heavy-weight boxing champion, Rocky Marciano.[42] If Falloni and the BHCA would not tolerate overgrown lawns on their streets, they were certainly not going to tolerate hundreds of pilgrims.

The BHCA members presented an ever-growing list of grievances against the vigils. They objected to the crowds, pilgrims taking all the parking spots, the sound of vigils that went until midnight, and the fumes emitted by tour buses. The crowds had also attracted curious onlookers. Kevin Farrelly recalled inviting friends to spend a Saturday night observing the spectacle of the vigils.[43] Growing crowds attracted vendors selling ice cream, hot dogs, and religious paraphernalia, as well as hecklers. All of these elements contributed to a raucous atmosphere. An editorial by BHCA board member William Caulfield described the situation:

> Bayside Hills has been invaded. The issue is as simple as that. Some of our neighbors have had the use of their property, and the right to its peaceful enjoyment, snatched away from them by a nomadic band. Garbage is strewn on their lawns and about the streets before and after every vigil. Urination and defecation on shrubs and lawns are common occurrences.[44]

Similar statements from BHCA members demonstrated that class tensions were very much present in the conflict in Bayside Hills. Lueken and her followers were described as invaders, nomads, and outsiders. The BHCA regarded the pilgrims as the antithesis of their own well-ordered community that was centered on homeownership. While Lueken lived only a mile from St. Robert Bellarmine's, she too was regarded as an outsider who lived in a rented apartment beyond the boundary of Bayside Hills. The BHCA was especially concerned about what the vigils would do to property values. A letter to the editor complained, "Our neighborhood is fast becoming a 'ghetto' and people are threatening to sell at their first offer."[45]

Another common accusation was that Lueken was exploiting her followers for money. Adrian Cornell claimed that at every vigil he saw a group of four men taking up a collection. In this story each man held the corner of a sheet that pilgrims flung money into.[46] I have found no evidence to corroborate this story and it appears to be apocryphal. While Baysiders encourage donations to fund their movement, they do not take up a collection during vigils. The idea that Lueken was a fraud motivated primarily by money was widespread. A manifesto demanded that elected officials use "all the resources of every level of government to expose Veronica's Vigil group as a fraud."[47] Chancellor King was persuaded by these claims, at least for a time. His letters express his suspicion that Lueken was sincere but that someone close to her was manipulating her visions for financial gain. In 1973, King noted that the Baysiders had begun distributing expensive full-color flyers that Lueken could not possibly have afforded to print. After publicly expressing his suspicion about the flyers, King received a letter from one Luis J. Montinola of Agana, Guam, explaining that he had freely donated $9,000 for printing and that nothing unethical was occurring.[48]

Letters from Baysiders to the diocese pushed back against the accusations of Bayside Hills residents. Lueken wrote Chancellor King claiming that there had never been trash left behind after the vigils and that four to ten people were always assigned to rake and sweep. "Why do you permit lies?" she demanded.[49] Some pilgrims blamed any disruptions on teenagers, who frequently heckled the vigils. A letter to Chancellor King signed "saddened father of the young" explained, "We do no wrong. The neighbors object to *undisciplined Catholic teenagers*."[50] Regarding the accusations of fraud, one irate Baysider wrote a letter insisting that no one had ever been encouraged to offer money. This letter actually reversed the charge of exploitation on the diocese claiming, "You have more wealth than any 20 people associated with Bayside."[51]

Homeowners became even more frantic when they heard about Lueken's plans to erect a national shrine in their neighborhood. There was a fear that if Lueken succeeded, the disruptions created by the vigils would never end.[52] David Chidester and Edward Linenthal suggest that conflict over sacred space arises in part because these spaces provide "symbolic surpluses" that can be appropriated toward a variety of ends.[53] The parish church of St. Robert Bellarmine had the potential to be either a symbol of a prosperous community of middle-class Catholics or the epicenter of a global apparitional movement.[54] The construction of a shrine would have allowed the pilgrims to permanently inscribe their own meaning onto a contested space. The BHCA understood that there was much more at stake than simply how a churchyard would be used. Control of St. Robert Bellarmine's meant the power to define numerous other definitional boundaries including who was practicing "true religion" as opposed to a cult, who was practicing "normal Catholicism" as opposed to superstition, and who "belonged" in Bayside Hills as opposed to being an invader or a nomad.

Faced with what they perceived as an existential threat, residents became increasingly aggressive toward the pilgrims. Some became regular hecklers during vigils. Adrian Cornell, who lived only a few hundred feet from the site of the vigils, recalled an incident in which a pilgrim had parked in front of a resident's driveway. Residents responded by double parking in front of the pilgrim's car and then calling the police. They told the police they would not move their vehicles and allow the pilgrim to leave until he had been issued a summons.[55]

By the summer of 1973 the pilgrims had begun to resist the pressure from homeowners. This was the beginning of the movement's struggle to control their sacred space. In June, Arthur Lueken sought a bullhorn permit from local police—presumably so that vigil organizers could be heard over the noise of the hecklers. Monsignor McDonald, the pastor of St. Robert Bellarmine's, convinced the police not to grant the permit.[56] In September, the pilgrims organized a letter-writing campaign requesting the use of the church itself. In the Archives of the Diocese of Brooklyn, I found a dozen copies of a form letter to Chancellor King signed by Lueken's supporters. The letter reads:

> We have been and presently are being subjected to derision, profanity as well as complaints from families in the area, during these devotions and prayers.... In view of the circumstances related I ask you please to consider granting permission for the use of St. Robert Bellarmine Church which is unused and directly behind our Blessed Mother's Shrine. We are willing to rent the church or whatever it takes, in order to be able to make use of it as a sanctuary.[57]

The church, however, was firmly on the side of the BHCA. In 1973, Bayside Hills was about 60 percent Catholic, with significant populations of Protestants and Jews.[58] Many of the influential members of the BHCA were also on the St. Robert Bellarmine's Parish Council. On September 9, the Council met to discuss the vigils. In a letter to Monsignor Emmett McDonald, Parish Council president Joseph E. Geoghan recommended that the diocese conduct a more definitive investigation and that the vigils be dealt with through a combination of civil remedies and criminal complaints.[59] The response of Church authorities to claims of private revelation is often determined by the local context, including political pressures. The day after receiving the Council's letter, McDonald sent a strongly worded letter to Mugavero calling for stronger measures to control Lueken. He wrote:

> I believe that Veronica Lueken is a charlatan and playing on the re-
> ligious feelings and beliefs of our Catholic people, some of whom
> do not appear to be entirely stable. I suspect that she herself is emo-
> tionally disturbed, but I do not have any medical proof of this as-
> sertion. I think that she is realizing a substantial financial return
> from these activities. She has not heeded in the slightest Monsignor
> King's admonition to cease inviting people to this Parish and has
> not accepted the advice of her Parish priests.

McDonald expressed total skepticism of the visions, not only because they seemed derivative but because the enormous cast of saints and angels Lueken claimed to see was unprecedented in other private revelations. He said of Lueken, "She seems to be the most privileged among the mys- tics I have read about." McDonald also described rumors that Lueken was receiving vast amounts of money at vigils and through the mail, including a check for $8,000 from someone in Florida. He concluded his letter by suggesting that the diocese adopt a more direct strategy and take any steps necessary to "terminate Mrs. Lueken's activities." He writes, "At first we had hoped that this activity would die a natural death, then we refrained from taking certain steps because of the notoriety and enhancement that it might give to Veronica's activities, but at this particular time in the situ- ation I think positive and vigorous action is called for."[60]

As it turned out, a criminal investigation of Lueken was already under- way before the Parish Council recommended such action. On August 10, the fraud bureau of the Queens District Attorney's Office sent nine of the Baysiders' miraculous Polaroids to the Polaroid Corporation for analysis. A senior corporate attorney at Polaroid responded with possible explana- tions of how the pictures could have been made through effects such as bending the film while withdrawing it, double exposures, or even placing fingers over the camera lens.[61] These findings were sent to the diocese. Although no charges were ever filed, this is perhaps the only case in which alleged miracles associated with a Marian apparition were the subject of a criminal investigation. Supernatural phenomena are generally beyond the purview of the legal system. Because the courts do not acknowledge the existence of miracles, it is almost impossible to convict someone for fraudulently offering a supernatural (and thus legally nonexistent) service. It is unknown how the District Attorney's Office acquired samples of miraculous Polaroids, but I suspect that these photographs were given by Baysiders to the diocese, which then submitted them to the authorities. In letters mentioning these tests, King always uses the passive voice, "These photographs have been submitted to experts."[62]

After McDonald and the Parish Council called for stronger action, Chancellor King wrote another letter to Lueken urging her to discontinue her vigils. He explained that they had become "a serious irritation to the people of the community." He again emphasized the possibility of embarrassment to the Church adding, "We [the Brooklyn Diocese] are a people dedicated to Our Lady. We are a people who love Our Lady, but we are also a people who do not wish and will do everything to prevent ridicule to Our Lady." This letter also came with an ultimatum: If the disruptions to the community did not cease, the diocese would remove the statue of Mary where Lueken held her vigils and build a fence around the church property to keep out trespassers.[63]

By November the crowds of pilgrims had only continued to grow. So far King had attempted to dissuade pilgrims from coming to Bayside; now he became more authoritarian. Monsignor Powell arrived at one of the vigils and began reading a letter from Chancellor King, "declaring once again that the church property is out of bounds for devotional use ... devotions to Our Lady will be conducted only in the parish church by priests authorized to do so by the pastor ... the meetings are contrary to diocesan authority and people should especially be discouraged from making any offerings of money or cooperating in money-gathering procedures."[64] This sort of tactic was unusual coming from a diocese with generally progressive leadership. King and Powell were likely unprepared for what the pilgrims did next: They simply ignored the vicar, saying the rosary louder to drown out his voice. The agent of the diocese was regarded as just another heckler. Powell returned at the next vigil and read the letter again, this time through a bullhorn. The pilgrims remained defiant.

Faced with what he saw as a "complete lack of cooperation," Chancellor King decided to carry out on his ultimatum and remove the statue of Mary from the grounds of St. Robert Bellarmine's—a move that the Parish Council supported in a vote of 21–1. King explained this decision in a letter:

> We have come to the very sorrowful conclusion that the only means left at our disposal is to direct that the statue of Our Lady be removed from church grounds at least until these people can be convinced that they must not assemble here.... They [the parishioners of St. Robert Bellarmine's] should not be deprived of their shrine and the use of their property in such a beautiful neighborhood because people from afar will not obey Church authority and will not accept the obvious that prayer to Our Lady is best offered in Church in the sacramental presence of her Divine Son.[65]

Monsignor McDonald expressed reluctance about this move. McDonald had himself visited the apparition sites at Lourdes and Fatima to celebrate the twenty-fifth anniversary of his ordination. He said of the diocese's increasingly forceful tactics, "You're in between—wanting on the one hand to promote devotion to Mary and on the other of stopping these demonstrations."[66] On November 27, 1973, the parish removed its statue of Mary, taking it to an undisclosed location. It is not entirely clear what the diocese hoped to accomplish by doing this. Perhaps this was simply a way to punish the pilgrims for their defiance. Or perhaps the diocese assumed that the movement would die if it could be separated from its statue.

Following the removal of the statue one Baysider remarked, "This is the place the Blessed Mother chose to bring her people. She asked Veronica to do this."[67] Once more, the pilgrims proved both resolute and resourceful. Almost immediately, pilgrims began to collect "holy dirt" from where the statue had stood. On December 2, Lueken arrived for the scheduled vigil bringing her own statue, made of fiberglass, which she set on a card table.[68] Carrying the statue to St. Robert Bellarmine's soon became a ritual that only added to the pageantry of the vigils. Farrelly recalls that pilgrims would arrive in buses that parked at Queensborough Community College, half a mile east of St. Robert Bellarmine's Church. They would then carry the fiberglass statue, now adorned with a blue cape and gold crown, in a procession to the church.[69] Farrelly added that the procession was an impressive sight, even for nonbelievers.

A Fortress Mentality

On January 29, 1974, Lueken's youngest son, Raymond, was shot and killed in a hunting accident while camping with friends in upstate New York near Callicoon. In an interview, Lueken described how Raymond's friend had thrown a block of wood in the air, hoping to impress Raymond by shooting it before it hit the ground. The shot missed its mark and hit Raymond in the heart.[70] The accident occurred one month after Raymond's sixteenth birthday. Raymond had been closest to Lueken among her children. Of all her family, only Raymond claimed to have shared in one of her visions.

Surprisingly, Lueken arrived for a vigil scheduled on the evening of February 1, traveling directly from the funeral parlor to St. Robert Bellarmine's. During this vigil she described a vision of her son among a host of blessed souls ascending directly to heaven on a golden stairway. In a locution, Mary stated, "I would have taken him on the loaded ladder sooner, My child, but I wanted you to see this and I wanted to give it to you as a special surprise."[71] Baysiders took pictures of Lueken delivering this message, her head wrapped in black rather than her usual white and blue. Due to the circumstances of Raymond's death, the funeral could not be held until February 4. It was an open casket funeral and Baysiders took Polaroids of Raymond's body. Some claimed to have pictures in which the coffin appeared empty and Raymond's spirit seemed to hover over the photograph, wrapped in a shroud.[72]

Within the Baysiders' community of prophecy, almost nothing happens by coincidence. Lueken described Raymond's death as a plan of Satan that God had allowed in order to test her faith.[73] Ann Ferguson described a miraculous Polaroid from November 1973 that appeared to depict a young man lying in a wooded area. She and Lueken came to interpret this image as an omen of Raymond's death.[74] But while Raymond's death may have been part of a supernatural plan, Lueken also looked to those she saw as Satan's agents on earth. In one of her letters to Chancellor King, Lueken wrote, "I am only doing what our Lady told me—and what my dear little son Raymond, who was shot to death January 29 'accidentally' a bullet in the heart by a gun in the hands of a 12 and 14-yr.-old boy—told me to do."[75] Placing the word "accidentally" in scare quotes implies a conspiracy to murder her son. Using this shorthand in a letter to King implies a connection between Raymond's death and her ongoing conflicts with the diocese.

The death of her son, along with the angry heckling from angry residents of Bayside Hills, caused Lueken to become concerned about plots on her life. She got an unlisted phone number, installed chicken wire on all of her windows, and set up an intercom system. Before this incident, her neighbors had described her as affable and gregarious. Now she spoke to almost no one. To make matters worse, stories about Lueken's vigils in the local paper often published her home address, encouraging a variety of strangers, friendly and hostile, to visit. A family who had travelled from Spain to present her with an ornate candelabra were told via intercom to leave it on the doorstep. A priest who had come from Chicago was turned away as were a group of mentally disabled children in wheelchairs who had been brought by nuns in search of a cure.

Lueken began to surround herself with bodyguards whenever she appeared in public. The White Berets apparently started the tradition of bodyguards, but Lueken would also handpick men from among her followers, who were mostly female, to serve as guards. Ben Salomone, a big man who weighed in at three hundred pounds, had been a regular attendee at the vigils. Lueken told him she had received a vision that she would be stabbed in the back and asked him to be her bodyguard. In an interview about this experience, Salomone recalled, "I couldn't wait to be martyred."[76] Eventually, she acquired over a dozen guards who formed a circle around her during vigils, often making it impossible for pilgrims to see her.

Michael Mangan reported that some people attending vigils had attempted to stick pins in Lueken during her locutions to see if she reacted. At Garabandal, the child seers were reportedly impervious to pain while in ecstasy. The circle of bodyguards made certain no such experiments were attempted on Lueken. Many Baysiders also believed that there was an active plot to kill Lueken. Shrine workers told me several anecdotes about foiled assassination plots. James Donahue recalled a possible assassin who had come to Flushing Meadows on a bus from New Jersey. In his bag, he brought a rifle that could be broken into parts for storage and transport. He was intercepted by police before he could use the rifle. Another worker told a story about a vigil in the mid-1980s where a woman flagged down a police officer and reported that a man in the audience had something in his lap concealed under a blanket. The officer looked under the blanket and found two .38 caliber handguns. Other workers could not recall the incident with the two handguns. However, everyone remembered an incident in Bayside Hills where a sniper was seen taking position on top of a house during a vigil. Before the sniper could take a shot at Lueken there was a sudden cloudburst that made aiming impossible.

Later I spoke with a pilgrim from California who had also heard the story of the sniper that was foiled by a miraculous downpour. In this version of the story, the sniper had been sent by "the Russians"—a perennial enemy in the Bayside Prophecies.

Lueken's experiences began after the assassination of Robert Kennedy, and stories of foiled assassination plots have become part of her hagiography. How were the Baysiders able to spot the sniper through the rain storm? Why did no one report the sniper incident to the police or the media? Such details might matter to a historian but not to the Baysiders. When Baysiders pass on such stories, they are not simply reporting data but rather sharing a sacred story about the life of a holy woman. These stories have even shaped the liturgy of modern vigils. Today, the Baysiders no longer have a seer to protect but SMWA still employs a circle of "shrine guards" that take positions around their statue of Mary during their vigil at Flushing Meadows.

Altercations

Pressure to drive the vigils out only caused the pilgrims to attach greater significance to their sacred space. Lueken's messages from this time emphasize both the significance of St. Robert Bellarmine's as a sacred site and the inability of human agencies to defy the pilgrims' divine mandate. On February 1, 1974, Lueken delivered the following message:

> Know well, man, that you cannot defy the Father, for it is in the will of the Father that this land be claimed for the salvation of souls. All who come to these hallowed grounds, My child, will receive graces in abundance, graces of cure and conversion. The crippled shall walk, the blind shall see. Those in darkness shall come forward into the light.[77]

The residents became more obstinate as well. The summer months seemed to draw larger crowds, which in turn drew more vendors selling hot dogs and cold drinks. In June 1974, Al Falloni wrote Bishop Mugavero describing the situation:

> The vigils held on Sunday afternoons and on the eve of holy days, has [sic] taken on a carnivale [sic] atmosphere in our residential area. We do not believe this is the type of devotion sanctioned by the

Church toward the Virgin Mary. The residents of our community are suffering the brunt of these repeated vigils. The police have been notified of the civil infractions namely, pollution of the air from numerous buses which arrive each time from other states, empty food containers, candy wrappers, and empty beer and soda cans which are left as the people leave. Due to lack of public facilities, people are seen voiding in the area, between cars, in the bushes on the adjacent properties and thereby esposing [sic] themselves indecently.[78]

Heightened tensions between pilgrims and residents sometimes erupted into violence. On June 15th, 1974, seventeen-year-old Daniel Slane got into a heated argument with a pilgrim. While walking back to his car, he was stabbed twice in the back. The assailant was described as a white male between fifty and fifty-five. Slane recovered after being taken to Flushing Hospital. A letter from King to James Rausch of the USCCB describes this incident and claims that the assailant had been one of the Pilgrims of Saint Michael who boarded a tour bus back to Montreal and successfully crossed the border to Canada without being arrested. Three days after this incident, the fourth anniversary of the vigils brought two thousand pilgrims to Bayside. They were met by 150 picketers from the BHCA.[79]

In July and August, the BHCA and parish authorities began meeting with police to discuss a solution to the situation in Bayside.[80] King wrote to the diocese of Rougemont, Quebec, where the Pilgrims of Saint Michael were headquartered, to ask for their assistance in discouraging pilgrimages to Bayside.[81] Attorney Donald Kiley was hired to represent both the BHCA and the Parish Council. One of Kiley's first recommendations was to always address Lueken as "Mrs. Lueken" and never "Veronica." Calling her by her first name, he warned, would play into her growing persona as a saint.[82] In September 1974, a meeting was held at St. Robert Bellarmine's between Lueken's followers, the BHCA, and the parish council to see if some agreement could be reached. Lueken did not attend, explaining that she had wanted to but that Our Lady had forbidden it.[83] The position of the pilgrims was that if holding their vigils in public was a problem, they should be allowed to use the church gymnasium. However, the parish council found this proposal unacceptable. Allowing Lueken and her followers to use church facilities was tantamount to giving formal approval to her movement. Furthermore, many members of the parish council were also members of the BHCA. They wanted Lueken and her followers out of Bayside Hills.

Negotiations broke down. The meeting became another moment of alienation when Church authorities and pilgrims realized that they saw the world in very different ways. Monsignor McDonald reflected on the meetings: "Our response that the Parish and Diocese are legal corporations and have a right to determine the use of their properties had little effect."[84] Lueken eventually asked Chancellor King, "What do you mean that the church is private property? ... Has the church become a *business*? We can't pray there?"[85] For Lueken and her followers, the church belonged to God, not the quotidian bureaucracies present at the meeting. What were the wishes of homeowners and the parish council compared to a direct command from the Virgin Mary? Furthermore, the pilgrims argued that their movement represented thousands of Catholics and, as such, they should have a say in how Catholic resources were allocated.

The meeting also affirmed Lueken's suspicion that Church authorities and the BHCA were conspiring against her, furthering the movement's fortress mentality. The following month she wrote in a letter to Chancellor King and Bishop Mugavero, "Getting the Civic Associations etc. on your side avails you all nothing. God will take care of them too. Of course we all pray that the light will come their way." This letter also stated, "And if you or the Rev Cardinal or Bishop think that you shall stop the good prayers by getting rid of me—you are mistaken. Others will carry on the Mission. We fear no man."[86]

This passage reflects Lueken's belief that parishioners had proposed hiring a hitman at the September meeting. She later told an interviewer:

> At that meeting, we have a witness, Mrs. Caroline Stevens. She was there as witness and others too, and I believe a whole taping was made of this meeting; it was done secretly but it was made! And right at that meeting, one of the parishioners of St. Robert's jumped up and said, I can't quote her exact words, but the words that are important, she stated, "We can end all this! Two men came to my house and said they would be willing to shoot Veronica." I guess for a price, is what she meant, but actually this was getting terrible.[87]

For Baysiders, the proposed hitman became another testament to the extent of Lueken's persecution. When I met with Michael Mangan, he also mentioned that the BHCA had suggested hiring an assassin.

A little over a week after the meeting in September, Chancellor King issued the following statement:

As a result of a complete and thorough investigation and hopeful of inspiring only true devotion to Our Lady, the ecclesiastical authority of the Diocese of Brooklyn hereby gives notice that all Catholics are directed to refrain from frequenting this site and any devotions not authorized by the priests of St. Robert Bellarmine Parish are un-authorized and forbidden.[88]

The statement was distributed in both English and French, so that pilgrims from Quebec would be able to read it as well. For Chancellor King, invok-ing the authority of the diocese to tell Catholics how they could pray was a drastic step. If such a move had been made earlier, or if Bishop Mugavero had acted directly, the diocese might have been able to stop Lueken's mo-mentum. During the height of the Van Hoof apparitions in 1950, Cardinal Samuel Stritch, Archbishop of Chicago, ordered Catholics not to attend. As a result, charter buses from Chicago were cancelled and the crowd shrank con-siderably.[89] However, the Baysiders had been gathering momentum for four years and reached a kind of critical mass. The situation continued to escalate.

On October 6, 1974, Lueken delivered a message from Mary request-ing a basilica at St. Robert Bellarmine's. This message was typed up and disseminated through the movement's network, which now extended throughout the United States, Canada, and beyond. As a result, the dio-cese received numerous letters as late as 1979 demanding that a basilica be built at St. Robert Bellarmine's. Most of these letters were from people living in other states who had never seen St. Robert Bellarmine's and had no idea how small the available space was. A few of the letters contained donations of five dollars, all of which the diocese returned along with a standard form letter dismissing the Bayside apparitions as inauthentic.[90]

In November, the parish council erected a three-hundred-foot-long snow fence with a "No Trespassing" sign, effectively barring the pilgrims from accessing their sacred site.[91] The pilgrims, however, would not be deterred by a fence. Instead of trespassing, the vigils were moved to the grassy malls that adorned the middle of 56th Avenue, which runs roughly east-west past the north side of the church grounds. The malls were each a block long but only about ten feet wide with traffic on either side. To accom-modate all of the pilgrims, it was sometimes necessary to use five blocks worth of malls between 211th Street and Bell Boulevard. Loudspeakers and other devices allowed vigil leaders to communicate with pilgrims who were standing blocks away.[92] In the first locution given on the lawns, Lueken announced, "Know, My child, that I will be with you. I will be here at the sacred grounds up to the coming of My Son. No fence shall be high enough to shut out the light. No man can go above his God."[93] These were the very malls that Al Falloni and the BHCA had previously waged a long and expensive campaign to keep manicured and pristine. For Bayside Hills residents, having Lueken and her followers on the malls was even more intolerable than having her on the church grounds.

Vigils continued on the malls for months until this practice became the new standard. The BCHA implored the police to intervene, claiming that holding religious rituals on public property violated the separation of church and state. However, Police Commissioner Michael J. Codd took just the opposite view—that the pilgrims were exercising their First Amendment right to the free exercise of religion. In response, Falloni told the *New York Post* that the BHCA was hoping to prove that the vigils were *not* an expression of religion.[94] The BHCA repeatedly described the vigils as "quasi-religious," implying that they might resemble Catholicism but were neither true Catholicism nor worthy of constitutional protection. William Caulfield, who was both a BHCA board member and member of the parish council, wrote in an editorial:

> I know that many of our Catholic friends have opinions about the religious aspect of the vigils. That is within the scope of their religious beliefs, however, and is not a suitable subject for a civic association to deal with. But it is also true that, in innumerable ways, the activities which take place on the corner of 56th Avenue and 214th Street are not religious issues. They affect the whole society, and it is to this aspect of the issue that this editorial is addressed.[95]

Caulfield's argument invokes a long-held assumption in America that religion is a private matter and that public expressions of faith are not really religious. Isaac Weiner traces the tacit distinctions between "true religion" and "noisy religion" to liberal Protestant and post-Enlightenment assumptions that acceptable modes of piety must be "individualized, internalized, and intellectualized." None other than Thomas Paine opined, "Religion does not unite itself to show and noise. True religion is without either."[96] This criterion of "real religion" made a convenient bookend to the claim that the vigils violated the establishment clause. The BHCA tried to have it both ways: As far as religious liberties were concerned, the vigils were not religious, but if holding religious ceremonies on public property was unconstitutional, then the vigils were definitely religious.

The police repeatedly explained to residents that this was a civil matter and not a criminal one. Eugene Biegel, captain of the Bayside police
precinct, told the residents, "Give me a piece of paper signed by a judge
and you will see action."[97] Residents found this response unhelpful and
became frustrated with police. Adrian Cornell recalled speaking to a police
officer at a vigil who said, "I don't think you like me very much." Cornell
responded, "I do you like you. I think you're a decent guy. I just don't think
you're doing your job well."[98] Indeed, the sympathies of the police often
did seem to lie more with the pilgrims, possibly because they identified
with the working-class piety of the pilgrims more than the interests of
middle-class homeowners. After giving a paper on these events for the
American Historical Association, I was approached by a man whose father
had been an officer deployed to keep the peace in Bayside Hills. His father
had said that many officers were themselves working-class Catholics. To
them, the devotional practices of the pilgrims did not seem unreasonable
but reminded them of their own mothers. Ann Ferguson said of the police,
"I must say Captain 'B' and his men were very kind to us."[99] The police
also advised residents that until they obtained a court order, the community could instead focus on curtailing the rowdiness, vandalism, and
harassment that resulted from clashes between residents and pilgrims.
Monsignor McDonald responded to this proposal, "I am very strong
behind you to move [Mrs. Lueken] out. There is no substitute for it."[100]
Both the BHCA and the diocese were distressed by what they perceived as
Codd's lack of cooperation. King sent Codd a telegram reprimanding him
for not taking a more active stance against the pilgrims.[101] Falloni threatened to picket Codd's office. At one BCHA meeting, residents voted to sue
the police department, although a lawsuit was never actually filed.

The BHCA felt that the rule of law had failed them. Some called for
the National Guard. This led to a period that saw increasingly aggressive
tactics from residents. Some went to picket the house of Lueken's confidante, Ann Ferguson, whom they suspected as being the mastermind
behind the vigils.[102] Residents also began organizing counter-vigils, which
were held on the malls at the same time as Lueken's vigils. These events
were sometimes described as "bicentennial celebrations," although their
purpose was clearly not to celebrate the anniversary of American indepen-
dence, which was still a year away. The counter-demonstrations turned
the area around St. Robert Bellarmine's into a battlefield where residents
and pilgrims vied for territory and symbolic dominance. While the pilgrims said the rosary, homeowners would sing patriotic songs or run their

lawnmowers to drown out their voices. They handed out copies of King's statement condemning the vigils and held up signs reading, "Your Bishop forbids you to be here" and "Her visions are spurious. A product of a fertile imagination."[103] An increasingly larger police presence was needed to maintain public order. Wooden police barriers were set up along the malls.

As the BHCA's tactics became more aggressive, William Caulfield distinguished himself as one of the group's most zealous members. Caulfield was a tall man and a good orator. He had been an English teacher before pursuing a career in politics. He firmly believed that the presence of the pilgrims on the public malls was a violation of the establishment clause. At a counter-vigil on March 22, 1975, Caulfield got into a confrontation with a police officer and was arrested for disorderly conduct. He told reporters, "Apparently shouting your prayers out loud, chanting at night, lighting hundreds of candles in a quasi-religious ceremony, spraying people with holy water, and shoving a camera in somebody's face isn't disorderly conduct."[104] That night a crowd of Bayside Hills residents went to the police precinct and signed civilian complaints regarding his arrest.[105]

Even after this incident, Caulfield continued manning the front lines against the pilgrims. On April 5, 1975, the BHCA planned a "bicentennial concert" to be held on the same mall in front of the church where the pilgrims were planning to hold their vigil. The *Bayside Times* reported, "It's simply a case of who gets there first, the worshippers or the concert-goers. Each will only be exercising their right to freedom of assembly."[106] Caulfield and a few others volunteered to spend the night in a tent in order to give the pilgrims no chance of staking a claim on their mall.[107] Obviously, a ten-foot-wide traffic island is not a safe campsite, but Caulfield was undaunted.

The night of April 5 was unusually cold. The date fell on a Saturday, leaving more people free to attend both the vigil and the BHCA's "concert." One hundred police officers were present to keep the peace. Two hundred and fifty pilgrims arrived, only to find their mall was already occupied. They still set up their card table and fiberglass Mary statue and began to pray. Police took the position that the contested mall had already been claimed by another party and asked the pilgrims to break up their vigil and move elsewhere. While the police were speaking with the pilgrims, an altercation broke out between forty-year-old James O'Connor, a Bayside Hills homeowner, and Lieutenant John Karcich, a tactical patrol force officer. According to

Karcich, he felt a fist bounce off his shoulder and when he turned around, O'Connor struck him in the jaw. Karcich retaliated by striking O'Connor across the head with his baton, inflicting a wound that required eight stitches. Caulfield had a different version of the story, declaring, "We were hit with a flying wedge of cops. Absolutely nothing provoked it." After this incident, BHCA members filed fifty complaints against Karcich. Queens District Attorney Nicholas Ferraro asked to impanel a special grand jury to investigate charges that the police overreacted. Meanwhile, vigil organizers filed thirty-five complaints against the BHCA for harassment, criminal mischief, and abuse. Following this incident, police declared that no one could occupy the mall directly in front of the church between 213th and 214th streets.[108] This was to be a sort of "no man's land" separating pilgrims and residents.

That night, when Lueken was finally able to carry on with her vigil, she delivered a locution equating Bayside residents with the forces of Satan and predicting their imminent demise:

> Satan never sleeps, My child. He has many agents now upon the grounds, My child. I have often cautioned you to remember the message from My Son: Beware of an evil force that surrounds a shrine of purity.... Remember, My child, they turned away and did not listen to the message of the prophets of old. Nineveh fell, Sodom and Gomorrah, and so will your country and your city.

Divine retribution would also fall on the neighborhood teens, whom the pilgrims saw as the shock troops of the BHCA. Lueken added, "The children are the true victims of their elders. The example given to them is poor. Many children shall be removed from the world, my child. It will be necessary for the salvation of their souls."[109]

After this vigil, Ferguson wrote Captain Biegel to complain that Caulfield had "incited young minors to shout abuses." She added that one young girl had shouted, "Let's shoot Veronica." The following month, Caulfield led a demonstration in front of Lueken's apartment. In open meetings of the BHCA, some residents had suggested turning the tables on the pilgrims by picketing in front of Lueken's home. Lueken wrote Chancellor King to complain that Caulfield had been outside her house threatening to shoot her. She later told a reporter from *Rolling Stone* that a small mob had gathered outside the apartment chanting, "Kill Veronica! Kill Veronica!" Years after this event, Lueken said of Caulfield, "Mr. William Caulfield, the poor soul, directed by satan, I have to say the truth—satan used him as an individual."[110] By contrast, the BCHA still honors residents who demonstrate exceptional service to the neighborhood by bestowing upon them the William H. Caulfield award.

Following the chaos of April 5, the BHCA adopted a new tactic and attempted to take the moral high ground. On April 13, an event was organized called "Cool Sunday." The event emphasized removing Lueken through legal means rather than open aggression. A number of state politicians had become involved in the conflict and spoke at the event, including State Senator Frank Padavan (R-Jamaica), City Council Member Matt Troy (D-Queens Village), and Assembly Member Vincent Nicholosi (D-Bayside). Seventy-five police officers were present and Queens Police Commissioner Joseph Veyvoda had closed the malls and streets to all parties. However, the parish council allowed the BHCA to hold their event on the church lawn. When Lueken and 150 of her followers arrived for their Sunday holy hour, they found there was nowhere to go and so they filed into St. Robert Bellarmine's for Sunday mass.[111] The pilgrims sat in the back snapping Polaroids. After the service, Lueken went into an ecstatic trance and her followers began to chant the rosary. Monsignor McDonald had several baptisms to perform that afternoon and asked the pilgrims to be silent, exclaiming, "You are profaning the Church." King, who was also present, told the pilgrims, "The Blessed Mother Mary is not pleased with what you are doing. Pray in silence. We are about to baptize children."[112] The pilgrims ignored his pleas for quiet and the baptisms had to be rescheduled. Monsignor McDonald filed a detailed report with police commissioner Codd. Lueken later claimed that, while in prayer, she tunes out the world and is essentially deaf. As a result, she simply failed to notice McDonald waving his arms and yelling at her to cease.[113]

Adrian Cornell describes a similar Sunday holy hour in which pilgrims entered St. Robert Bellarmine's, apparently separate from the incident on April 13. In this account, Lueken was not present but her "lieutenants" occupied the pulpit and began addressing pilgrims sitting in the pews. Cornell began taking pictures of the pilgrims. Some turned away or attempted to cover their faces when confronted with Cornell's camera. He countered this by pretending to aim in a different direction and then turning suddenly on the pilgrims before snapping a photograph. Cornell took twenty pictures that were later used in court proceedings—an accomplishment that Cornell remains proud of to this day.[114]

Resolution

The Battle of Bayside finally reached its conclusion in the spring of 1975. A petition signed by Bayside Hills residents called on the diocese to issue strong religious sanctions instead of "reading position papers."[115] On May 5, 1975, Bishop Frederick Freking of La Crosse, Wisconsin, placed Mary Ann Van Hoof under an interdict—a lesser form of excommunication. Freking was quoted in *The Bayside Times*, "I was rather quiet about the matter for a few years and said nothing. But they interpreted my silence as tacit approval and I had to do something."[116] In Brooklyn, some saw Freking's action as evidence that their diocese did have the power to control the pilgrims if it would frame their censure in terms of religious error rather than social disruption. However, it was the courts and not the authority of the church that finally evicted the pilgrims from Bayside.

After the incident in April when baptisms had to be rescheduled, Frank Padavan asked the state attorney general to begin a full-scale investigation into the legality of the vigils.[117] St. Robert Bellarmine's finally took legal action against Lueken and one judge Hymann signed an order requiring Lueken to show cause for her public demonstrations. He also issued a preliminary injunction barring Lueken from the vigil site. However, serving Lueken and her followers with court summonses proved difficult. News travelled quickly in Bayside and Lueken and her followers were alerted that process servers were looking for them. Lueken, already reclusive, simply did not answer her door. However, when someone accidentally hit her car, Lueken came running out of her apartment, giving the process server a chance to serve her with papers.[118] Similarly, Ann Ferguson described receiving a visit one Saturday from a "Mr. C"—probably William Caulfield—who was accompanied by a police car. Ferguson's husband answered the door whereupon Mr. C presented him with two court summonses, one for Ann and one for their daughter, Maureen, who was also active in the vigils. Mr. Ferguson simply refused to accept them. The next day, Ann and Maureen attended mass in a different parish, fearing that Mr. C would know to expect them at St. Robert Bellarmine's. However, at the next vigil, Senator Padavan arrived in person and issued summonses to Ann, Maureen, and several other workers.[119]

The court summons convinced Lueken to meet with Church authorities, something she had avoided for the past five years. She later stated in an interview, "And then, as time went on we were going to be summoned to court, and I felt this was a horror. So I called, first I called Fr. McDonald on the telephone, and that's the first time I really, we ever even spoke to each other about this."[120] McDonald advised her to speak with Chancellor King. On April 29, Lueken called Chancellor King's office and left a message with a receptionist. She was apparently livid. The message said, "She will no longer treat you as a priest—but on the level of just another human being. Intends to bring you to court—and start a real legal battle."[121] Lueken and her husband decided to show up at the Brooklyn Chancery unannounced. This was the first time Lueken and King ever spoke face to face. Lueken later claimed that prior to this visit she received a locution in which Mary told her, "Have pity on them, My child, because you are going to face the red serpent." The phrase "red serpent" indicated that Lueken was not only confronting demonic forces, but communist ones as well. King, in his version of events, returned from lunch to find the Luekens waiting for him. He brought them into his office where they talked for about an hour. In his interview with Anthony Bevilacqua, King recalled:

All I could say was that if ever I was convinced the lady was not having miraculous visions, I was convinced by having a two-minute talk with her ... I simply told her, "I am not convinced." The more I told her that I didn't believe what she was saying, well I shouldn't say she got more hysterical, but the more heated she seemed to get. But we left as good friends.[122]

Bevilacqua, who was working in the chancery that day, recalled that from his office he could hear Lueken shouting. King said that he never formally condemned Lueken during this meeting; however, his claim that they left as "good friends" is dubious. Lueken recalled this encounter differently. She explained, "Somewhere I felt in my heart, there was like a glass between us, that he couldn't look through, and I couldn't go through. And I knew it was obedience, he had his orders, and he had no other choice, his hands were tied, I don't—he could listen, but he couldn't even, uh, he could listen and not listen, if you know what I mean."[123] This image of an invisible barrier is a powerful metaphor for the growing disconnect between Lueken and Church authorities.

As the pilgrims prepared for their day in court, Lueken revealed a new form of spiritual protection for her followers. At a vigil, she described a vision of Mary who asked her to hold a long-stemmed rose and extend it toward heaven. Lueken did this and saw Mary kiss the rose. She then gave a blessed rose petal to everyone who would appear in court. Today, blessed rose petals are an important sacramental used by Baysiders. They are distributed at every vigil and used especially for healing. This episode demonstrates how some of the Baysiders' most cherished traditions are rooted in their trials in Bayside Hills.[124]

The vigil organizers filed their own legal action against the BHCA. Lueken and her allies were asked to appear in court on May 8, 15, 16, 20, and 22. During these proceedings, the police, who seem to have had a better rapport with Lueken than anyone else outside of her movement, suggested she relocate her vigils to nearby Cunningham Park. Lueken initially resisted this suggestion.[125] The last vigil in Bayside occurred on Pentecost, May 17, 1975, in defiance of Judge Hymann's injunction. Two thousand pilgrims arrived from as far away as Nebraska. Residents offered heavy resistance, attempting to drown out the locution with lawnmowers. Others bore placards proclaiming, "Veronica is a hoax." One agitator organized a call-and-response chant of, "Who's a naughty girl? Who's a you-know-what?" To each question the crowd would shout, "Veronica!"[126]

The following evening, Mary and Jesus reportedly appeared in Lueken's apartment. They were visible not only to Veronica but also her husband Artie and a third individual named only as "Mr. N.S." The apparitions gave a message, which Mr. N.S. wrote down and Lueken later read to her followers:

> My child, you have passed the test and have given complete obedience to the Eternal Father. Now is the time for a small change. The numbers of the faithful are reaching too and [sic] far in excess of what can be accommodated. Therefore, you will tell the Bishop: "You will be given a sign by the Eternal Father." He (the Bishop) will find this sign unquestionable. You will, My child, receive the message from Me on the eve of all feast days as in the past. The peoples of the world will continue to go to the Shrine in great numbers—that will not consist of crowds—until the basilica is opened by the sign given to your Bishop. The peoples must continue to pray. Accept the offer of the Department of Police, and I will do the rest. There is a time for everything, My child, even for change.[127]

With this message, the Baysiders were able to yield control over their sacred site without admitting defeat. The message also lent some stability to the Baysiders' deteriorating relationship with Church authorities. A supernatural sign would one day vindicate the Baysiders, at which point Church authorities would admit they had been wrong. This prophecy signified that the conflict between pilgrims and their bishop—no matter how bitter it seemed—was ultimately temporary.

On May 20, a lawyer representing the pilgrims indicated that they would accept an offer from the Parks Department to find a new location for the vigils.[128] On May 22, Lueken met for three hours with representatives from the BHCA in the office of Justice Joseph Kuzeman of the New York Supreme Court. Kuzeman worked out a settlement in which Lueken would cease holding her vigils at St. Robert Bellarmine's. Instead, the pilgrims would move to an appropriate public space and obtain proper permits. If any pilgrims did continue to gather in Bayside Hills, police were authorized to disperse them. In return, the BHCA agreed not to harass Lueken if she visited St. Robert Bellarmine's alone. On reaching the agreement Kuzeman declared, "Here nobody lost and both sides won because they both approached the problem sincerely. I hope they all go back to the community and realize that what has been done today has been done in the best interests of all. Both sides deserve to be commended."[129] Lueken emerged on the steps of the courthouse where many of her followers and reporters stood waiting. She announced, "The way of the cross will persist. The Lord works in mysterious ways, but we will prevail. His will be done."[130] So ended the Battle of Bayside.

Although several parks had been suggested, Lueken and her followers ended up relocating to Flushing Meadows; they wanted to use the monument commemorating the former site of the Vatican Pavilion during the 1964 World's Fair. Michelangelo's Pieta had been displayed here during the Fair. This history provided a form of symbolic capital that helped to compensate for the loss of St. Robert Bellarmine's. Baysiders noted that one of Lueken's first poem-messages from Saint Therese had been called "Pieta." On May 26, the Baysiders held their first vigil in their new home. At least twenty-five pilgrims, unaware of the change of venue, showed up in Bayside Hills.[131]

The Battle of Bayside had a lasting effect on the community of Bayside Hills. On June 14, 1975, the BHCA organized a neighborhood "Jubilation Day" celebrating their victory over the pilgrims. A thanksgiving mass and an interfaith service were held at St. Robert Bellarmine's, followed by a history in slides and home movies of the vigil battle. At 1 p.m. celebrants were invited to "report in work clothes to the mall at 56th Avenue and 214th

Street, to mow, clean, rake, and spruce up the mall in a gesture of thanks-giving and dedication." Watermelon, balloons, and lemonade were avail-able for children in the church parking lot. The St. Robert's parish band spent the afternoon parading from mall to mall, playing patriotic songs. An evening dance for adults featured more music and included soda, beer, and cocktails in the price of admissions.[132] In a sense, the BHCA also regarded the malls as a sacred space. They were a collective symbol of their community and their prosperity. Chidester and Linenthal suggest that one way space is sacralized is through the "politics of exclusion." That is, space is marked as sacred in part by who is kept out. The act of parad-ing and gardening on the malls was a sort of exorcism in which the BHCA ritually reclaimed their space and reestablished their authority.[133]

The Civic Association's victory over Lueken came to be an important part of the neighborhood's cultural memory and heritage. In 1995, Kevin J. Farrelly—who had become BHCA president—organized another event to commemorate the Battle of Bayside. Farrelly showed a silent film of the vigils that had been created by David Oates, an editor for the *Queens Tribune*. For Farrelly, this was not an expression of enmity toward Lueken but a commemoration of an important moment in the community's history. The event was covered in a *New York Times* article entitled, "A Cherished Memory: Banishing Veronica," which appeared only two months before Lueken's death.[134] In 1999, the *Queens Tribune* ran an article entitled, "Dirty Thirty: The Borough's Most Notorious." Veronica Lueken was number seventeen on a list of the worst people ever to have lived in Queens, right below a man who shot and killed two police officers and above an individual dubbed "The ATM Rapist." This degree of con-tempt can only be explained with an understanding of what was really at stake in the Battle of Bayside. Lueken was neither violent nor a criminal, but her movement had threatened the very categories by which the resi-dents of Bayside Hills organized their existence. In this way, the pilgrims had inspired more dread than a rapist or a murderer.

Today, few people in Bayside Hills remember Lueken or her vigils. However, some enmity remains. A pilgrim from California described vis-iting St. Robert Bellarmine's and claimed that a resident emerged from his home and threatened to sic his dog on him. When I called St. Robert Bellarmine's, I started to explain to a receptionist that I was writing a book about Veronica Lueken. The receptionist cut me off, "She's not recognized here!" Once I was able to explain myself, she told me that she had received dozens of calls from Baysiders in her time at St. Robert Bellarmine's.

Monsignor Martin Geraghty, the current pastor, told me that no one had called about Lueken in the last five years.

For the Baysiders, the battle for the grounds of St. Robert Bellarmine's was a crucible that defined their movement. It became a story that Baysiders live by. Baysiders feel that they were harassed, slandered, and assaulted simply for saying the rosary on the grounds of a Catholic church. The fact that Church authorities sided with the BHCA and state politicians engendered further feelings of confusion and betrayal. The narrative through which Baysiders made sense of all this was twofold. First, they were not ordinary Catholics but a spiritual elite whose prayers have a powerful and global influence in a supernatural battle now unfolding in the last days. Second, their work was so important that the forces of Satan, acting through the BHCA, media, politicians, and Church authorities, would attempt to stop them by any means possible—even hiring a hitman to murder their seer. Within this narrative, to be a Baysider is to be persecuted and persecution is evidence of performing powerful spiritual work. As one Baysider put it to Michael Cuneo, "We are the most despised group in America. The media, religious leaders, the so-called intelligentsia—everyone laughs at us and holds us in contempt. Why? They should be thanking us. We're the only group that's warning the country of the horrible catastrophes that lie ahead."[135]

The Battle of Bayside also shaped Baysider ritual. Many of the Baysiders' devotional innovations, such as giving out blessed rose petals and employing a circle of guards during vigils, have their origins in this conflict. Through their struggle against the parish council and the BHCA, the Baysiders developed their technologies of power. They learned how to occupy sacred space in the face of legal and physical opposition. They also learned how to assert their ritual presence using the sound of their prayers to counter hostile sounds such as Monsignor Powell with his bullhorn or the BHCA with their lawnmowers. In future confrontations, the Baysiders would return to the repertoire of techniques developed in Bayside Hills. Shortly after arriving in Flushing Meadows, Lueken delivered the following message from Mary, "I give you this lesson of reality, My children: the demons cannot stay with the sound of prayer ringing in the air."[136] Several subsequent locutions reiterate that Satan is repelled by the sound of prayer, establishing the relationship between sacred sound, sacred space, and spiritual combat.

Finally, the Battle of Bayside crystalized the complex and painful relationship between Baysiders and their Church. The parish priests that

Lueken had first come to with her visions were now seen as adversaries. It seems that at least some of Lueken's early followers lobbied for a sede-vacantist position that rejected the entire Catholic hierarchy as corrupt and illegitimate. Many of Lueken's messages specifically address this and call on Baysiders to remain loyal to the Church. Ann Ferguson recalls being in court on May 15, 1975, where a number of Baysiders were present as well as Chancellor King. Ferguson approached King to ask when he would perform a proper investigation of Lueken. A group of White Berets from Canada saw her speaking with a man in a clerical collar and told her, "You are talking to the enemy and that is wrong."[137] But for most Baysiders, including Lueken, priests were not "the enemy." Instead, the Battle of Bayside convinced Lueken that well-meaning priests are rigidly locked into a hierarchy that has been taken over by evil forces who would destroy the Church under the guise of progress.

In 1973, Lueken stated that she could not hold anything against the local clergy because "Rome makes all the decisions."[138] In a more exasper-ated letter to Bishop Mugavero, she wrote, "I have reached the conclusion by your actions that you all don't think for yourselves, but follow orders—caring more for your worldly position than the Truth of God. That is truly sad."[139] Later in her career, she delivered several locutions urging her fol-lowers to remain obedient to the Church, no matter how much it seems to have lost its way. A message from Mary in 1979 advocated "cleansing" the Church rather than abandoning it:

> What do you do, My children, when your house has been infested by rodents or vermin? You clean out your house. You do not abandon it, for it has taken much love and much labor to build the walls. You do not abandon it, but you work and pray, and use every means to clean out My Son's House, His Church.[140]

Another message from 1989 stated, "Remember, My child and My chil-dren, no matter how rough the road gets, you will stay within your parish church. And by good example and many prayers you will bring the priest-hood back into the light."[141] By defying the will of the diocese but pledging loyalty to the Church as a whole, the Baysiders offered a middle course between yielding to the spirit of Vatican II and sedevacantism that many traditional Catholics found appealing.

After the Battle of Bayside, Baysiders began to scrutinize their Church with increasing attention. Before becoming estranged from

Church authorities, Lueken and many of her followers had been highly deferential to clergy. They rarely questioned parish priests or gave much thought to the Church's chain of command. After their battle with the diocese, Baysiders began to study the structure of the Church and canon law seeking justification for actions that they felt to be right. This blend of fierce devotion to the Church tempered by legalistic scrutiny of the Church's orders became part of the ethos of the Baysider movement. At a speech in 2007, Michael Mangan explained, "Normally, you wouldn't dare think of defying legitimate Church authority. But there's a difference between intelligent obedience and mindless obedience. You being informed and educated, you realize—you come to realize—the utter travesty of justice committed against Our Lady's mission here."[142] If parish priests and even diocesan authorities opposed the Baysiders because they were "just following orders," the question now became where in the hierarchy these destructive orders originated. Who was really responsible for what Baysiders perceived as radical changes in their Church? Lueken discovered an answer to this question shortly after arriving in Flushing Meadows.

4

Baysiders as Homo Faber

FLUSHING MEADOWS PARK was once known as the Corona Ash Dumps. In the early twentieth century, it was used to pile ashes from coal burning furnaces, as well as horse manure and other garbage. It was a dismal place immortalized in F. Scott Fitzgerald's *The Great Gatsby* as "the valley of ashes." In 1939, it was transformed into Flushing Meadows Park to prepare for the 1939/1940 World's Fair. The landscape changed again for the 1964 World's Fair, which brought such features as the Unisphere and the New York State Pavilion. The official name of the park was also changed in 1964 to Flushing Meadows-Corona Park. Councilman Edward Sadowsky explained that the new name was meant to correct an injustice: The people of Corona, Queens, had long had their name associated with ashes and garbage, only to have it erased when the dumping grounds were transformed into something beautiful.[1]

The Baysiders' new vigil site is also near La Guardia airport and recordings of Lueken delivering messages during vigils are sometimes marred by the sound of jet engines. On one occasion, Lueken described the Queen of Heaven's irritation at having to share the sky with the airplanes.[2] But regardless of this nuisance, the Baysiders were finally free to congregate in large numbers. Flushing Meadows soon became a secondary sacred site. One of Lueken's messages from Mary and Jesus explained:

We are not leaving; My Son and I will be upon the grounds until the last person leaves. And should anyone come here to pray during the weekdays, before the vigils or the Holy Hours, We will come .... Yes, My child, one day these grounds, also, will be renown. These grounds shall be a holy place of visitation, as shall also be the Shrine at Bayside.[3]

J. Z. Smith famously noted that *homo religiosus* is first and foremost *homo faber* and that religion is often an ongoing project to create a meaningful world to inhabit. Consecrating a sacred space through ritual repetition is a particularly important part of this project because it allows further "mapping" of the sacred and the profane.[4] After moving to Flushing Meadows, the Baysiders began to construct a distinct worldview that accounted for the significance of Lueken's visions and the movement's problematic relationship with the Church. The emerging Baysider worldview served to interpret a wide variety of discourses and world events that were important to Lueken's followers by incorporating them into a unified prophetic vision. The move to Flushing Meadows also brought other forms of routinization such as an organizational structure for promoting Lueken's messages and a liturgical structure for vigils. These developments gave the Baysiders their distinctive character and ultimately made it possible for the movement to continue after Lueken's death in 1995.

Baysider Bricolage: Inclusion and Exclusion

To outsiders, the Baysider worldview can seem completely incomprehensible and other. This is particularly the case if one attempts to understand the Baysiders by opening the Bayside Prophecies to a random page. Consider the following message from May 1973:

NOW OUR LADY SAYS: "Watch, My child, what else is exiting from the hole."
VERONICA: Oh, my goodness! There are things that look like bright lights, but they're like dome-like on the top. And they don't have any windows; they're just great lights. And Our Lady now is standing at the edge of this hole and She's pointing, and She's saying:
OUR LADY: "Man will not accept the truth. These are transports of hell."
VERONICA: Oh, Our Lady's referring to these things that are being seen on earth.
OUR LADY: "Make it known, My child, that the false miracles of the end time are now at hand. Satan seeks to confuse you. Make it known, My child, that there is no life beyond your earth as you know it. Man will go out into space; better that he uses these efforts to find his way back to God."[5]

This is one of several messages in which Lueken describes flying demonic craft that emerge from under the earth and that the public has misinterpreted as extra-terrestrial spaceships. Critics often ridicule the Bayside Prophecies because they are replete with "subjugated discourses"—ideas and beliefs that mainstream society stigmatizes or is unwilling to talk about.[6] In addition to such elements as planet-destroying comets and miraculous Polaroids, the Bayside Prophecies discuss elaborate conspiracy theories, UFOs, and the Rapture—a theological concept that is generally regarded as Protestant. There are even some messages that allude to zombies, vampires, and Soviets armed with futuristic death rays. Despite the Baysiders' cultural conservatism, there is an element of eclecticism in this worldview that to outsiders can resemble New Age spirituality more than strict traditional Catholicism.

To understand the eclecticism of the Baysider prophecies, it is necessary to shift focus from the institutional boundaries maintained by Church authorities to the daily project of meaning-making undertaken by individuals. Meredith McGuire has suggested that there is much to learn by studying religion as "an ever changing, multifaceted, often messy—even contradictory—amalgam of beliefs and practices that are not necessarily those religious institutions consider important."[7] The imagined boundary between "Catholic" and "non-Catholic" discourses is simply not a factor in how some lay Catholics understand the world. For instance, Lueken's contemporary, Jeane Dixon, who delivered prophecies, used a crystal ball, and was one of the astrologers consulted by Nancy Reagan, also considered herself a devout Catholic and believed her gift for prophecy came from God. This strategy, which Catherine Albanese calls "combinativeness," is especially common in Marian lore.[8] Scholars have noted that searching for information on Marian apparitions online invariably leads the seeker to material on UFOs, Bigfoot, spontaneous human combustion, and other "paranormal topics."[9] E. Ann Matter suggests that tabloids, despite their sensationalism, appear to understand these porous definitional boundaries better than scholars and Church authorities.[10] Tabloid publications that juxtapose such topics as Mary, the end of the world, and extraterrestrials demonstrate an awareness of how their readers approach these topics. Significantly, the Baysiders eventually advertised their movement in the tabloid *Weekly World News*.

Lueken's prophecies and the numerous interpretations that surround them do not represent a creedal position to which all Baysiders are expected to subscribe. Instead, they offer an evolving and dynamic framework into which individual Baysiders can incorporate a variety of discourses. The modern Catholic Church does not have an official position as to whether there is life on other planets, whether a cure for AIDS will be discovered, or why the attack on the World Trade Center occurred. Lueken's visions not only provided answers to these questions, but a means of incorporating nearly any discourse into a unified model of how the world works. In this sense, the project of interpreting the Bayside Prophecies resembles Levi-Strauss's model of bricolage, in which material is selected from a finite range of signs and then repurposed to form a "myth"—that is, a narrative that makes sense of the world.[11] Like a clever tinkerer, the "bricoleur" solves a particular problem by taking whatever is lying around and repurposing it into something useful.

Through their project of meaning-making, Baysiders supplemented traditional Marian lore with ideas and language from a variety of sources including secular conspiracy theories, popular dispensationalist literature such as Hal Lindsey's *The Late, Great Planet Earth,* and metaphysical traditions. However, as the Baysider movement became organized, its leadership imposed its own set of definitional boundaries. As Baysider leaders sought to distinguish themselves from similar movements and appear legitimate to Catholic Church authorities, they developed their own criteria for what topics may be brought into the Baysider worldview. This has produced a countervailing force to combinativeness. Ideally this works as a strategy of inclusion and exclusion: the inclusion of new discourses can solve new problems and attract new members, while the exclusion of other discourses can help to secure a coherent and enduring identity as a distinct movement. As Baysider leaders continue their efforts to be taken seriously by Church authorities, there has been an ongoing process of contraction whereby some of the more exotic elements of Lueken's messages are downplayed or even redacted from the messages. While modern Baysiders continue to emphasize such topics as the coming Chastisement, today they rarely talk about UFOs or other topics that might appear in tabloid stories.

Inclusion

Of all the elements discussed in the Bayside Prophecies, Lueken's messages about UFOs are perhaps the most controversial. Catholic critics of the Baysiders have argued that Mary would never discuss UFOs and that their very mention in the context of Marian prophecy is worthy of ridicule. But such critiques overlook the historical and cultural context in which these messages were delivered. The modern UFO phenomenon is widely considered to have begun with a sighting made by Kenneth Arnold on June 24, 1947. Christian Williams notes that a wave of Marian apparitions occurred throughout Europe in June and July of that year. He suggests that both phenomena may reflect anxieties and millennial hopes associated with the Cold War.[12] By 1973—the year in which Lueken first began delivering messages about UFOs—95 percent of Americans had heard of UFOs.[13] Stories of UFO sightings were picked up by the Associated Press and frequently made the front page. In an interview, Lueken described a UFO sighting over New York's Shea Stadium that had been reported in the local papers.[14] Nor was Lueken the only religious leader commenting on the phenomenon. A number of new religious movements discussed UFOs during the 1970s, as did evangelical Protestants like Hal Lindsey.[15] Even Billy Graham occasionally mentioned UFOs, suggesting that they might be angels.[16] More established religious institutions ignored the UFO phenomenon, however. Certainly the Catholic hierarchy was silent on the matter.

Many Baysiders not only read about UFOs in the papers but reported actually seeing them. Ann Ferguson described an encounter with a UFO on her way to a vigil. She and her daughter Maureen were terrified and prayed to St. Michael until the strange object disappeared.[17] Lueken claimed to have seen UFOs on the grounds of Robert Bellarmine's as early as 1969. Even Philip Nobile, a former seminarian and reporter for *New York Magazine*, described seeing "five luminous disks" in the sky while attending a vigil in 1978. He reported, "I had no explanation for what I had seen with my own eyes." Nobile even contacted the Port Authority at La Guardia to see if there had been any other UFO reports that night.[18]

Unlike Church authorities, Lueken was willing to speak with authority on the religious significance of UFOs. For Catholics who were interested in UFOs, this was an important service that the hierarchy did not provide. Lueken located UFOs within a larger worldview of millennialism and spiritual warfare. In an interview she explained, "These scientists, they call them humanoids. Well, that's a good name, but I, but they're just plain demons. And they're the false miracles, and that's why the world is in such a state. The abyss is open and we are approaching the Second Coming of Jesus."[19]

Hal Lindsey also regarded UFOs as demonic and a sign of the end times. However, Lueken took this further and integrated UFOs with Baysider ideas about the importance of sacramentals. Several of her messages discuss an "unholy ray" that is fired from the UFOs. The exact nature of this ray is unclear, but it appears to cause demonic possession, as demons "ride" the ray into its target. In some cases, the rays appear to actually disintegrate people. The demons who pilot these craft particularly seek to use this ray against children. In 1973, Lueken explained, "I know of several instances there have been absolutely disappearance of children. They are taken aboard actually and disintegrated, or they just seem to evaporate into thin air. Well, this has happened in many, many places and it's going to become more prevalent [*sic*]."[20] The way to protect children from the unholy ray was to have them avoid being in a state of sin and to always wear Catholic sacramentals such as the St. Benedict medal and the scapular.

During the Battle of Bayside, Lueken even integrated UFO sightings into her ongoing conflicts with the diocese. She explained:

> Now they are congregating, these flying saucers, on the roof of the gym [the old St. Robert Bellarmine Church]. There is only one manner in which this can be done, is because the building itself will have to be reblessed. Obviously, there is sports or some evidence of some nature contrary to the will of God taking place within that edifice. That is why the demons are congregating on the roof by means of these miracles, these transports [*sic*].[21]

Here UFO sightings at St. Robert Bellarmine's function as an indictment of Church authorities (and possibly the parish council), whose activities as poor stewards of the church effectively created a staging ground from which demons may attack the parish.

By bringing UFOs into a traditionalist Catholic worldview, Lueken's messages offered something that Church authorities could not and attracted a wider range of people to the Baysider movement. But Lueken did more than provide a Catholic understanding of UFO sightings. She used them to reinforce the worldview of traditional Catholics. UFOs were not only demonic, they were another reason why children should avoid lives of sin and wear sacramentals. Their arrival was also evidence that the media and scientific authorities were easily deceived (believing the UFOs to be of extraterrestrial origin) and that Church authorities are in error and unable to fulfill their duties as spiritual guardians. This strategic use of UFOs demonstrates the kind of meaningful worldview that a skilled bricoleur can make from a subjugated discourse.

Another discourse that was incorporated into the Baysider worldview is a belief in the Rapture, more or less as espoused by the Protestant dispensationalist John Nelson Darby. In 1974, Lueken delivered the following message from Mary, "In the great Chastisement many of My children will be removed, some without going into the deep sleep."[22] In other words, pious Catholics would be transported physically to heaven and spared the coming disasters. By 1977, Lueken was explicitly referring to this event as "the Rapture."[23] Catholic authorities reject the doctrine of the Rapture, arguing that it lacks sufficient basis in scripture. However, this idea has saturated American culture through media such as the writings of Hal Lindsey and Tim LaHaye and Jerry Jenkins's best-selling dispensationalist novels, the *Left Behind* series. Survey data suggests that roughly a third of Americans now believe in the Rapture, including many Catholics.[24]

It is understandable that many Catholics found Lueken's talk about the Rapture appealing and reassuring. However, for strict Catholics this material presents a problem. In Bayside, I asked the shrine workers whether the Bayside Prophecies describe the Rapture. I received two different responses. One shrine worker explained that the Rapture *was* a Catholic doctrine, that the Protestants had stolen it from the Catholics, and that this idea had been suppressed during Vatican II. Another shrine worker explained that there would be a Rapture but not as described by Protestant dispensationalists. "All the Rapture is," he explained, "is God's going to pick you up before the Chastisement and put you back down afterwards. Otherwise he would have to create the human race all over again. God could do that, of course, but fortunately He's chosen not to."[25] These strategies of accounting for the Rapture in Lueken's messages demonstrate how the inclusion of new discourses provides both a resource for Baysiders and a potential obstacle for Baysider apologists.

Exclusion

While many elements were incorporated into the Baysider worldview, many others were excluded or condemned. Discussion of popular practices such as astrology, tarot cards, and Ouija boards were condemned as occult and demonic. So too was the charismatic Catholic movement, which arose, like the Baysiders, in the aftermath of Vatican II. The origin of this movement is usually traced to the so-called Duquesne Weekend, a retreat for Catholic theologians held by Duquesne University in Pittsburgh in February 1967.[26] Catholic charismatics borrowed elements from Pentecostalism, namely belief in the gifts of prophecy, exorcism, healing, and speaking in tongues. An estimated eight million to ten million people became charismatic Catholics between 1967 and 1984.[27] Philip Jenkins speculates that, in the long run, the Catholic charismatic movement may prove to be one of the most influential changes in the history of the Church, as it continues to gain numerous converts throughout the Global South.[28] Not surprisingly, the resurgence of Marian piety after Vatican II and the charismatic Catholic movement have been closely linked. Many apparition sites are attended by Catholic charismatics. The apparitions at Medjugorje, arguably the most famous to occur in the late-twentieth century, were preceded by a charismatic renewal conference held in Italy in 1979 in which a priest received a prophecy of a coming Marian apparition to children in Medjugorje.

One might assume that the Baysiders, whose practice also emphasizes religious ecstasy, miracles, and healing, would see charismatic Catholics as allies. Nothing could be further from the truth. Lueken's messages repeatedly condemn Pentecostalism and the charismatic movement, claiming that "many have fallen into the web of Satan" due to these practices.[29] The same shrine worker who felt that the Rapture was originally a Catholic idea also explained that the term "charismatic Catholic" was an oxymoron, because Pentecostalism is an inherently Protestant phenomenon. Baysiders have also condemned the apparitions of Medjugorje, which many of them regard as false and inspired by Satan.

How is it that charismatic Catholicism is rejected as a Protestant-inspired innovation but the doctrine of the Rapture is endorsed? One possible explanation is that by condemning charismatic Catholics or the apparition of Medjugorje as demonic, Baysiders help to preserve their own unique identity. That is, these movements are condemned as demonic deceptions precisely because they appear so similar to Baysider practices. This principle also applies to the Baysider condemnation of occult practices. While many conservative Christian groups warn of the dangers of the occult, Baysiders have actually been accused of occultism themselves. Their Catholic critics have compared miraculous Polaroids to tarot cards, locutions to séances, and even described stories of rosaries turning to gold as "Satanic alchemy."[30] By soundly condemning occultism, Baysiders try to preempt these comparisons. The principle by which seemingly similar elements are excluded from the Baysider worldview recalls Freud's notion of "the narcissism of small differences," according to which social groups are most threatened by those they are most closely related to.

Baysider leaders have also moved to block the inclusion of certain discourses that might embarrass the movement or undermine the notion that Baysiders are traditional Catholics. One shrine leader conceded that the vigils attracted "some real weirdoes."[31] In 1978, a reporter for *New York Magazine* described meeting a pilgrim named "Katy," a twenty-three-year-old painter. Katy explained to the reporter, "At my highest potential, I am an incarnation of the Blessed Mother. I was told that by my higher mind." Katy was soon led away by a man in a white beret who explained, "Some people are fanatics."[32] The problem was not that Katy was fanatical (Baysiders have never objected to zeal), but that she had embarrassed the movement in front of the press.

Some elements, such as UFOs, were suppressed almost completely. Interest in reports of UFOs has declined since the 1970s and mention of UFOs is now more of a liability than an asset. When I visited Flushing Meadows, no one was interested in the subject and I felt a little silly even asking about UFOs. In 1991, a Baysider group published a book entitled *The Incredible Bayside Prophecies on the United States and Canada*. This is a sort of digest of the Bayside Prophecies. It critiques Vatican II and describes a global conspiracy, but it omits any mention of UFOs, vampires, Soviet death rays, and similarly controversial elements. The content of the Bayside Prophecies is narrowed to manageable parameters. This process of contraction is found in the history of many other communities with a sacred text, which likewise come to emphasize some passages while downplaying others.

While individual elements of the Baysider worldview may change as new discourses arise and then lose favor, there is a more permanent structure underneath. In the 1970s the Baysiders developed a grammar that allowed them to rapidly integrate new developments and locate their significance within a larger Baysider worldview. Although Lueken died in 1995, it is now possible for Baysiders to incorporate almost any news story or idea into a prophetic context, identifying its significance within a previously existing pattern. The website "These Last Days Ministries" does just this, presenting daily news items juxtaposed with passages from the Bayside Prophecies. There are two aspects to this grammar. The first is conspiracy theory, which assembles new social and political threats into a monolithic pattern of spiritual warfare. The second is a theology of history, which locates dates and other temporal developments within a prophetic understanding of history. Together, these two aspects of the Baysider worldview describe the two sides of a supernatural battle between good and evil. The conspiracy theory defines the enemies in this battle while the theology of history provides clues as to when the battle will conclude. Both dimensions of this narrative leave room for new material and new discoveries. The machinations of Satan and the forces arrayed against the saints are not fully defined. Similarly, while the broad strokes of God's divine plan are known, it continues to reveal itself through history.

This worldview provides the security of knowing that there is a divine plan and that almost nothing happens by coincidence. At the same time, it provides a facile apparatus for interpreting and integrating new data into a familiar pattern. Finally, it provides Baysiders with a great deal of agency to become their own bricoleurs. Lueken almost never presented a dogmatic end-times scenario. Most of her messages deliver visions of future events with little context or clue as to how they might fit together. The task of assembling all of these elements into something meaningful is left to others. Thus every Baysider has the opportunity to discover further details about God's divine plan. Heaven has hidden clues within the Bayside Prophecies, miraculous Polaroids, and even in the dates of history itself. This means that Baysiders do not engage in blind deference to authority or dogma, as outsiders might imagine. On the contrary, almost all Baysiders are engaged in an active and individual process of analysis, weaving diverse data points into an increasingly detailed pattern of meaning. There seems to be an inherent pleasure and excitement in making these discoveries that, for some, is likely part of the movement's appeal.

Conspiracy Theories

Lueken had already adopted a conspiratorial worldview to explain the increasing hostility of Church authorities and the BHCA, as well as the death of her son. Her later prophecies began to describe a single, grand conspiracy that she sometimes referred to as "the octopus of evil." After they were driven from Bayside Hills, conspiracy theory became the tool by means of which the Baysiders defined their new relationship with their Church. At the first locution given from Flushing Meadows, on May 28, 1975, Lueken described the following vision:

> I see a large dome, and I know it's Rome. Oh, and standing on a balcony ... There's a large window, and over to the left I can see

Pope Paul, and he's waving. He has on a white robe, and I can see a very large cross suspended from his neck on a chain, a golden cross. And he's waving now. And standing behind him are two men. I know they're cardinals. But oh, they're not nice to look at. Oh, my! These two men, cardinals, don't look like they're graced. Oh, they look evil. And now, written above on the—it's right on the stones above Pope Paul's head, and arrows pointing to the two cardinals. There are words: "A CONSPIRACY OF EVIL AGAINST THE PAPACY." Oh, my goodness! A conspiracy of evil against the papacy. Oh, dear![33]

This vision resolved the cognitive dissonance that arose from openly defying diocesan officials. The Baysiders were not in rebellion against Pope Paul VI or their parish priests. Instead, they understood themselves to be resisting corruption that began just below the pope with a number of treacherous cardinals.

On September 27, 1975, Lueken revealed the full nature of this conspiracy: Vatican II had been hijacked by a cabal of traitorous cardinals and their reforms had been affirmed by an imposter masquerading as Pope Paul VI. At a gathering for the Feast of the Archangel Michael, Lueken delivered this message from Mary:

My child, I bring to you a sad truth, one that must be made known to mankind. In doing this, My child, you must proceed without fear. It must be made known to mankind. Our dear beloved Vicar, Pope Paul VI, he suffers much at the hands of those he trusts. My child, shout it from the rooftops. He is not able to do his mission. They have laid him low, My child. He is ill, he is very ill. Now there is one who is ruling in his place, an impostor, created from the minds of the agents of satan. Plastic surgery, My child—the best of surgeons were used to create this impostor. Shout from the rooftops! He must be exposed and removed.... My child, make it known at this time that you must go back in the immediate years and bring the knowledge to mankind that these changes, the changes that have given bad fruits, have not been given to you through the Holy Spirit and through your Vicar, Pope Paul VI. It is the web of satan reaching out.[34]

This conspiracy theory, which the Bayside Prophecies refer to as "the deception of the century," facilitated the Baysiders' seemingly paradoxical relationship with the Church, simultaneously loyal and defiant. A papal doppelganger meant that Baysiders could legitimately question the pope while still identifying as loyal Catholics. The theory that Paul VI was an imposter became a wedge issue that defined the Baysiders as distinct from mainstream Catholics. It also distinguished the Baysiders from more radical, sedevacantist groups, which had formally broken with Rome and openly criticized the pope. However, Lueken was not the first person to make this claim about Paul VI. There is, in fact, a long genealogy to this claim among traditionalist Catholics responding to the reforms of Vatican II.

The Paul VI Conspiracy Theory

Today, a Google search for the words "Paul VI" and "imposter" reveals dozens of websites, many of them created by Baysider groups, which claim that the true Paul VI was regularly drugged by communists, Freemasons, Satanists, or other conspirators and replaced by an imposter created by means of plastic surgery. Some conspiracy theorists support this claim with photographs from different points in Paul VI's career and sonograms comparing the voice of Paul VI with that of the alleged imposter. To skeptics, this evidence is not compelling and the pope simply appears to be aging over time. For believers, the merit of this theory is not really derived from empirical evidence but a network of Marian seers all of whom have received revelations of a papal imposter.

The original provenance of the theory is unknown and it is impossible to say if it began with a single seer and was borrowed by others, or if multiple seers arrived at this claim independently. The earliest iteration of this theory I have found comes from a Mexican nun named Maria Concepcion Zuniga Lopez. Lopez received messages from heaven that were published and attributed to her pseudonym "Portavoz." On January 21, 1970, Portavoz delivered a message from Jesus announcing, "Paul VI suffers! Do not leave him alone in his prison. Go in search of him, take him to a safe place where he can speak freely." In 1975, Clemente Dominguez Gomez, a seer in Palmar de Troy, Spain, declared that the man claiming to be Paul VI was an imposter and that the true pope was imprisoned. A few months later Lueken outlined a similar conspiracy theory in a locution given before her followers. Lueken's prophecy quickly spread back across the Atlantic. In 1976, Chancellor Anthony Bevilacqua received a clipping about Lueken from an Italian tabloid article entitled, "Allarmi! Satana ha preso un osttaggio. Papa Falso" (Warning! Satan has taken a hostage. False Pope).[35]

In 1977, Theodor Kolberg, a German follower of the traditionalist archbishop Marcel Lefebvre published a pamphlet entitled, *Der Betrug des Jahrhunderts* (The Deception of the Century), which also alleged that Paul VI was an imposter and cited the Bayside Prophecies as evidence. Kolberg's work appears to draw from Lueken or at least to share a common milieu of conspiratorial lore. The term "deception of the century" was first used by Lueken in 1975. Kolberg also claimed that, in 1975, Cardinals Villot, Casaroli, and Benelli had carried out a plot to discredit Lefebvre. Lueken gave these same three names in a locution in 1976.[36]

The imposter pope theory appeared again in a text by Jean Marty entitled *Avertissements de l'Au-delà à l'Église Contemporaine—Aveux de l'Enfer* (*Warnings from Beyond to the Modern Church: Confessions from Hell*). This is allegedly a transcript from a series of exorcisms performed on a woman in Switzerland from 1975 to 1978. This text was circulated through small Catholic presses and has been translated into both German and English. Structurally, the possessed acts as a sort of backwards seer to reveal a Satanic conspiracy. Rather than fighting the exorcist, the demons (identified as Beelzebub, Judas Iscariot, Akabor, Allida, and Veroba) are surprisingly cooperative. They describe the horrors of hell, the saving power of the Virgin Mary, and the fallen state of the Catholic Church. Hell, it seems, has exactly the same message as heaven.[37] In an exorcism on January 16, 1976, the demon Veroba revealed that Paul VI was an imposter and beseeched the exorcists to publish this fact in their book.

In a subsequent exorcism, the exorcists ask the demons whether Theodor Kolberg's book is correct. Beelzebub responds, "Kolberg tells the truth in his book. He has only a few small things that are not completely correct; but that is not very important."[38] It is ultimately irrelevant whether *Warnings from Beyond* is based on exorcisms that were actually conducted or is simply a hoax. The Baysiders endorsed the text as confirmation of Lueken's messages. Several letters from Baysiders at the Archives of the Diocese of Brooklyn refer to the testimony of the Swiss exorcisms.[39] Each new version of the imposter pope theory worked to affirm the others, forming a global web of allied seers and conspiracy theorists. In 1978, the comparatively mainstream author Malachi Martin published *The Final Conclave*, which also outlined a plot to elect a pope that would serve the agenda of a communist-dominated one-world government.

Like UFOs, the imposter pope theory was incorporated into the Baysider worldview to fulfill a specific function, namely, explaining rejection from Church authorities. Notably, other traditionalist groups that endorsed the same theory did not employ it toward the same purpose. Gomez in Spain eventually declared himself pope, taking the title Gregory XVII. He claimed the true Paul VI had appeared to him from his prison in the Vatican using the saintly power of bilocation in order to express his wish that Gomez succeed him. Portavoz used the conspiracy theory to justify her separatist group, the Franciscan Minims of Mexico City. A Canadian group called "The Apostles of Infinite Love" also claimed that Paul VI had been a Freemason and their leader Michel Colin declared himself pope. Father Lucian Pulvermacher of Springdale, Montana, argued that Paul VI's predecessor, John XXIII, had defected to Freemasonry during a secret ceremony held in Turkey in 1935. On October 24, 1994, Pulvermacher was "elected" pope by a conclave consisting primarily of his own family and held in rural Montana.[40]

By contrast, the Baysiders did not use the imposter pope theory to turn their backs on Rome or to establish an anti-pope. Instead they used it to resolve the tension of being loyal Catholics who are at odds with Church authority. Baysiders did not use the conspiracy theory to indict Paul VI as a conspirator but rather to exonerate him of supporting the changes that followed Vatican II. Baysider Anne Cillis remarked, "Our Lady tells us that he is not personally behind many of the changes in the Church, and that he is a suffering victim."[41] When Cillis eventually left the Baysiders she renounced the imposter pope theory. She reflected on her former belief, "I suppose some of us believed it because it seemed to make sense. I mean how could Paul VI be doing all this stuff. Well, the answer was that he wasn't. You see what I mean?"[42]

The conspiracy theory allowed for a kind of selective loyalty, in which Baysiders could show unquestioned fealty to the pope while also asserting their own moral autonomy. In many Baysider versions of the Paul VI conspiracy theory, the true pope and the doppelganger occupied the Vatican at the same time—meaning that some of Paul VI's public statements were legitimate and others were not. Only by thinking critically about the pope's statements could Catholics discern whether the man making them was the genuine pope. Furthermore, Lueken assured her followers that this situation was only temporary, and that Catholics would soon be able to place full trust in their Church again. As Mary says in one of Lueken's messages, "The Church of My Son, that is being stripped of all holiness, shall emerge with the world and the world's leaders to be directed for a short time by satan."[43]

It seems unlikely that all Baysiders take these claims about Paul VI literally. Some of those I spoke with certainly did. One pair told me that Satanic rituals had been held inside the Vatican, a claim that was put forward by Malachi Martin.[44] However, SMWA leaders never spoke to me about Paul VI being an imposter. Baysider David Martin's book, *Vatican II: A Historic Turning Point*, incorporates many aspects of the conspiracy theory including photographic evidence, the work of Theodor Kolberg, *Warnings from Beyond*, and, of course, the Bayside Prophecies. For Martin, the theory accounts for apparent inconsistencies in Paul VI's public statements. He writes:

> The reign of an impostor pope would explain the many discrepancies that had confused the faithful concerning Pope Paul VI, for instance why he would condemn the Charismatic Movement in 1969, and why he would embrace it in 1975; or why he would denounce Communion in the hand in May of 1969, and why then he would sanction it from 1975 on. Having an impostor in Rome made it easier for modernists to get on with *their* reform which up to that point had been hampered by the Holy Father's resistance.[45]

Martin's critique of Vatican II is not dependent on acceptance of the Paul VI conspiracy theory. He also offers a less fantastic account of how Vatican II was hijacked by "arch-progressives," some of whom were allegedly Freemasons. At a banquet in honor of the forty-second anniversary of the Bayside apparitions, Martin gave a short lecture on the findings of his book. The audience was very responsive and seemed primed for a revelation of conspiracy. There were audible gasps when Martin claimed, for instance, that Cardinal Annibale Bugnini, who oversaw the liturgical reforms of Vatican II, had been a Freemason.[46] This response demonstrated the ease with which new elements can be introduced into a conspiratorial worldview.

While not all Baysiders appear to share the same beliefs about Vatican II, conspiracy theories remain an important part of the Baysider worldview. Evil, for the Baysiders, is inherently monolithic. Rumors of sinister international bankers, communists, subversive media, and local Satanic cults are all understood to be tentacles of "the octopus of evil." Here too, the Baysiders perform bricolage, incorporating elements from previous conspiracy theories. Consider the following message from the Archangel Michael given on September 13, 1974:

ST. MICHAEL "There is a man who hides behind the mask ruling your
    country! He will soon approach and reveal himself. He is the man who
    compromises your country for the love of power. "He has affiliated
    A-L-L of the money powers of the world, joined them for unity in a
    one-world-government.
    "Step down and reveal yourself, the leader..."
VERONICA—Oh, my goodness! Oh my goodness! The man behind the
    mask, Mr. Rockefeller. The man behind the mask!
OUR LADY—"There sits in your country masters of great magnitude!
    Recognize the Grand Masters in control! As it was in the time of My
    Son, they now control your country. A synagogue of Satan is covering
    your land."[47]

Folklorist Bill Ellis, in his book on Satanic conspiracy theories, explains that "Mr. Rockefeller" refers to then vice president Nelson Rockefeller, a man who became vice president without being elected. Rockefeller was previously implicated as being near the pinnacle of a Satanic conspiracy in such sources as Canadian Catholic William Guy Carr's *Pawns in the Game* (1958).[48] Lueken was likely exposed to Carr's ideas by the Pilgrims of Saint Michael. An article in the group's publication, *Michael Journal*, describes *Pawns in the Game* as "the best single work available on the evil conspiracy that has been responsible for the devastating wars and continuing conflicts of the past century, and which is now close to its ultimate goal of total world domination through a dictatorial One World Government."[49] Carr's theories also resonated with the anti-communist zeal shared by many American Catholics in the 1950s. Robert Welch, the founder of the John Birch Society, was particularly impressed with Carr's theories. He paraphrased Carr's ideas about the Illuminati in *American Opinion*, the society's magazine. According to Welch, half the members of the John Birch Society were Catholic.[50] Thus, the inclusion of Nelson Rockefeller alongside the imposter pope in an emerging pattern of the octopus of evil represents a further process of assembling diverse elements into a coherent whole.

Stalking the Son of Sam

Lueken's involvement with the investigation of the Son of Sam murders in 1977 is a particularly interesting chapter of Baysider history. Between July 1976 and July 1977, serial killer David Berkowitz, "the Son of Sam," perpetrated eight shooting incidents across New York City, killing six people and wounding seven more. Berkowitz taunted police and media with a series of cryptic and lurid letters. Both during the killing spree and after his arrest the media spoke of little else. There remains a widespread conspiracy theory that Berkowitz had not acted alone but was part of a network of criminal Satanists. At one point Berkowitz confessed to this narrative, but in a 2013 interview he explained that he had never had an accomplice or been part of a cult.[51] It now seems that Baysiders had a significant role in advancing and legitimizing the theory that Berkowitz did not act alone.

A Bronx homicide detective named Henry "Hank" Cinotti is credited with sparking speculation that Berkowitz had an accomplice. Cinotti was not only a Baysider, but served as one of Lueken's bodyguards for ten years.[52] In 1979, a photographer named Walter Karling from the *North Queens Observer* attended a vigil in Flushing Meadows. In an attempt to get a better shot of Lueken, he climbed over a rope set up around the monument by shrine guards. This led to a brief physical altercation with bodyguards, apparently led by Cinotti. Karling and his editor, Rick Moran, threatened to take the group to court for infringing on their freedom of the press. Moran published a series of negative articles about the Baysiders and claimed that this led to retaliation in the form of phone calls threatening the lives of his family members. He also alleged that several police and firemen were zealous Baysiders and that they had formed a nationwide "intelligence network" for Lueken's security.[53] Presumably, this network included Cinotti.

In 1980, the New York Police Department called a hearing regarding Cinotti's investigation into Berkowitz's possible involvement in Satanism. Cinotti was placed on clerical assignment as punishment for what the department considered to be an embarrassing waste of resources. While reporters and detectives were seeking evidence of a criminal Satanic network, Lueken offered tips to some of the investigators and even implicated one of her neighbors in the murders. This episode shows how Baysiders collaborated to rapidly incorporate new developments into an existing narrative of conspiracy and spiritual warfare. It is also an early example of law enforcement becoming entangled in conspiracy theories advanced by conservative Christian groups—a phenomenon that became increasingly common throughout the 1980s.[54]

As the murders were happening, Lueken described the Son of Sam as a manifestation of supernatural evil. A locution on February 10, 1977, stated, "My children, the man you call 'Sam' is satan in a human body. He has powers beyond what most human beings could understand."[55] In the 1970s and 1980s, many Americans believed in an organized network of criminal Satanism. Lueken frequently referred to the threat of Satanic cults. In fact, one of her earliest public locutions given in August 1970 mentioned Satanic cults conducting human sacrifices.[56] A locution delivered in 1985 reported that no fewer than thirteen Satanic covens were active on Long Island within a sixty mile radius of each other and practicing human sacrifice.[57] These cults represented one more tentacle of the octopus of evil.

For Baysiders, the threat of Satanists was linked to the liturgical changes of the modern mass. The Baysider "Blue Book" contains an article, "Satanists Seek Holy Eucharist to Defile It." The article concerns Mike Warnke, an evangelical minister whose book *The Satan Seller* (1972) describes how he was once a high priest in command of some 1,500 devil worshippers in Southern California before his conversion to Christianity. In 1992, Warnke's claims of involvement with Satanism were debunked as fiction by the evangelical magazine *Cornerstone.*[58] But for twenty years *The Satan Seller* was a seminal text for a national panic over Satanism. Warnke identified as an evangelical Protestant but explained that the new Catholic practice of communion in the hand was a gift for Satanists. He explained, "One thing that Catholics and devil worshippers have in common: they both believe that Jesus Christ is really and truly present in the Holy Eucharist." Warnke described how during his days as a high priest of Satan, he would regularly send Satanists to attend Catholic mass in order to steal consecrated communion wafers, "Then we step on It to desecrate It, and pass It around while drinking blood or whatever.... If the Bishops approve Communion in the hand, it will be even easier to palm the Wafer. I don't think Communion in the hand is a good idea."[59]

Several of Lueken's messages also warn that communion received in the hand facilitates desecration of the host by Satanists. More recently, David Martin described communion in the hand as "the greatest thing that ever happened" to Satanists. These rumors are actually a revival of medieval stories about host desecration in which Jews, rather than Satanists, sought to acquire and desecrate holy wafers.[60] In their modern incarnation, host desecration stories serve to integrate such diverse elements as Catholic liturgical reform, youth counterculture, and stories of Satanic serial killers, into a single coherent narrative.

Maury Terry was an investigative reporter working with the Queens police force. After Berkowitz was arrested, Terry became convinced that there was a national Satanic organization to which both Berkowitz and Charles Manson had connections. His search for evidence brought him into contact with many people making dubious allegations about criminal Satanism. In his book, *The Ultimate Evil*, he describes how Steve Dunleavy, a columnist for the *New York Post*, was regularly receiving anonymous phone calls and letters from a woman who provided detailed accounts of a Satanic cult to which Berkowitz had allegedly belonged. The calls continued for five months and provided some very specific information about the most recent murders. The source also named the cult's leader, an accountant who maintained two addresses: one in Forest Hills, where two of the murders had occurred, and one at 583 Van Duzer Street in Staten Island. The Staten Island address was described as a "major cult safe house" where black masses were conducted. In one phone call the mystery source mentioned she was leaving town for fear of her life. With no other leads, Terry and his associates decided to investigate these claims. Only after investing substantial time and energy on this lead did Terry discover that the mystery caller was Lueken, who at that time was living on 577 Van Duzer Street, in a room rented from one Erna Wagner.[61]

Jim Mitteager, a journalist who had previously worked for the New York City Police Department, drove past the alleged cult safe house and ran the license plate numbers of any cars that visited. Eventually, Terry and Mitteager met a bartender named Jim Duffy, who, in an astounding coincidence, had rented a room at 583 Van Duzer Street while he attended Wagner College in Staten Island. He identified the owner of the house as John Meehan. Duffy agreed to accompany the journalists to the house and get them inside. The alleged cult safe house turned out to be home to a normal middle-aged couple and their son. When Terry asked if they had ever had any trouble with neighbors, John Meehan described a "strange woman" in a long robe who had regularly come by to stare at the house. At one point she had stopped their son, saying, "I know who you are and what you're involved with. Don't think you're going to get away with it."[62] The strange woman—who turned out to be Lueken—had moved out of the neighborhood a few months prior.

This tip led Terry and Mitteager to Wagner's home, where Arthur and Veronica had recently been living in a rented room. Terry noted that the home "was filled with statues of various saints and the Blessed Virgin." Wagner gave the investigators a letter from her former tenant, who was once again living in Bayside. Terry described the letter as "rife with crosses and symbols." It outlined an elaborate plot connecting the Son of Sam to a cult on Van Duzer Street. Lueken also described being on a "secret mission" for the police.[63] This claim had some basis in truth, as Lueken did have several friends in law enforcement, including detective Cinotti. She was working "with" police, but not in an official capacity.

Terry and Mitteager next went to Lueken's house in Bayside, using the return address on the letter they had examined. Veronica would not leave her bedroom, but Arthur let the reporters in and answered some questions. Terry quotes Dunleavy after learning his mystery caller was Lueken, "The whole thing is Lueken's hallucination. . . . She sounded believable; she really did." Terry answered, "To her, it probably *seems* real. That's why she was so convincing." This was not the end of Terry's dealings with Lueken. In 1979, Terry was still seeking evidence for his theory that Berkowitz had been part of an organized Satanic cult. One day, he received an anonymous call providing the same details that had been given to Dunleavy a year before about an accountant who was really a Satanic cult leader, etc. Terry cut her off declaring, "Cut it out, Veronica. I know just who you are. I was at your house last year, but you ducked under the bed." Lueken hung up, but later called back and apologized, explaining that she had "made a mistake." Lueken had surveilled the Meehans' house and had gotten a friend of the Meehans' son confused with the accountant that she claimed was Berkowitz's accomplice. Arthur picked up the phone to support Veronica's explanation.

It is difficult to discern how exactly Lueken came to believe that her neighbor was involved in the Son of Sam murders. Significantly, Lueken never claimed to have received this information through revelation. Instead she felt she had detected a Satanic criminal through her own investigation and by speaking with her sizable network of contacts. She explained to Terry, "People come to me, they confide in me. That's how I know about the cult." Lueken also directed Terry to Cinotti, who she said could vouch for her story. Cinotti defended Lueken's observations and theories as credible. He explained Lueken's behavior to Terry, "She's eccentric and she was scared."[64]

Terry continued to work with Cinotti, even though his fellow journalists found the detective's behavior disconcerting. Terry was particularly perturbed by a meeting where a group of journalists and law enforcement agents acting independently agreed to do a late night stake out in a park, hoping to witness a Satanic cult meeting. Cinotti arrived accompanied by two friends armed with baseball bats. He then distributed holy medals to everyone and delivered a lecture on demonology. But despite Terry's skepticism about Cinotti, his book draws heavily on his theories. *The Ultimate Evil* was wildly popular and went through several editions. Meanwhile Cinotti, after being reprimanded by the police department, went on to discuss his conspiracy theory on *Unsolved Mysteries* and in other popular media. The conspiracy theory has persisted to this day.

In 1980, reporter Roberta Grant managed to get an interview with Lueken, who told her, "That David Berkowitz, he's *not* the real Son of Sam! He's an imposter, part of a conspiracy. He's covering up for the real murderer." She added that there were witch covens all over Staten Island.[65] Today, media and law enforcement are far more skeptical of stories about criminal Satanists. However, the SMWA shrine leaders I spoke with were still very much concerned about the threat of Satanic cults. One explained to me that several Baysiders are police officers who work in or around New York City. They believe there are still Satanists active on Long Island but have been instructed by their superiors not to discuss the threat of cults with the public. He also mentioned that Baysiders had been involved in the Son of Sam investigation.

Lueken's adventure demonstrates a degree of self-aggrandizement: In a city of seven million people, she felt that she alone could solve a series of high-profile murders. This may seem narcissistic, but it also demonstrates the powerful sense of agency that can be experienced through conspiracy theory. Finally, it is significant that Lueken did not form her theory about Berkowitz alone. She incorporated information she received from a variety of sources and "companionable spirits," including police officers. Much of the Baysider worldview reflects a similar collaborative project in which diverse elements are assembled into a pattern that, while frightening, holds great personal meaning.

Baysiders still believe they are threatened by a global conspiracy that has many branches and takes many forms but is ultimately Satanic in nature. Today, they are more likely to refer to this entity as "the New World Order," a term that has become increasingly popular in conspiracy theory discourse. Baysiders explained to me that the New World Order seeks to establish a one-world government that will enslave the population and demand adherence to a single religion. The nebulous term "New World

Order" provides a useful grammar onto which new threats can be grafted. Some Baysiders regarded the immolation of the Branch Davidian compound in 1993 as an attack on Christians by the forces of the New World Order. The bombing of the Oklahoma City Federal Building the following year was regarded as a "false flag" attack carried out by federal agencies in order provide an excuse for further persecuting conservative groups.[66] A shrine worker from SMWA described a meeting in which they had gone through documents from FEMA's website that discuss the suspension of normal government in the aftermath of a catastrophic emergency. In June 2012, the HHS Mandate of the Obama healthcare plan was also seen through a conspiratorial worldview. Shrine director Michael Mangan described the mandate as one step closer to the "reign of antichrist."[67] For Baysiders, the pattern continues to emerge with each new development.

A *Theology of History*

While conspiracy theory allowed Baysiders to find patterns in social and political developments, a Marian theology of history allowed them to discover patterns in time, connecting current events to both the past and the future. In Flushing Meadows, Baysiders began to develop techniques for discerning prophetic significance in dates and events. This became a tool through which Baysiders could locate new developments within an unfolding divine plan, culminating in the return of Christ. The connection between Marian piety and millennial expectations was firmly established in the seventeenth century by French missionary Louis-Marie Grignion de Montfort (1673–1716). Montfort founded two Marian religious orders, the Montfort Fathers and the Daughters of Wisdom. His book, *Treatise on the True Devotion to the Blessed Virgin Mary*, was discovered by a priest in 1842 at the bottom of a chest in a house on Saint Laurent-sur-Sevre. The manuscript had reportedly been lying there for over a century.[68] Once published, it immediately became a French devotional bestseller, going through fourteen editions by 1895. In this text, Montfort predicted that an "Age of Mary" would precede the return of Christ, during which there would be revelations of the glories of Mary. This prediction built on the writings of medieval apocalypticist Joachim of Fiore (1135–1202), who believed that the millennium would be heralded by an "Age of the Holy Spirit." Montfort also emphasized spiritual warfare. He prophesied a battle between Mary and the forces of Satan in which Mary would be aided by a special elite who would become the greatest saints in the history of Christianity. This is precisely how the Baysiders came to see themselves. The Baysiders regarded Montfort's prophecies as accurate and at one vigil Lueken announced that Mary had ordered her to read aloud from Montfort's treatise.[69] Many Marian devotees also believe that an apocalyptic battle between Mary and Satan is prefigured in Genesis 3:15, where God declares that Eve shall crush the head of the serpent.[70] Thus the entire pageant of human history begins and ends with Eve/Mary defeating the forces of Satan.

In the twentieth century, American Catholics built on Montfort's work by locating the conflict between the United States and the Soviet Union within this dispensationalist model. In 1952, Don Sharkey published *A Woman Shall Conquer*, which draws heavily on Montfort's work. The book begins with a chapter entitled "Mary Needs Our Help" that explains the communist revolution in terms of Marian piety. Sharkey attributes the ideas of Karl Marx to the rejection of Catholicism in favor of Enlightenment values during the nineteenth century. He notes that Vladimir Lenin and Leon Trotsky met in Petrograd, Russia, on April 17, 1917, to plan the Communist Revolution. The revolution itself occurred seven months later on November 7. He equates communism with the forces of Satan: "'First Russia, and then the world,' was the motto of the godless, religion-hating communists." Holding this connection together is the Marian significance of these dates: It was during these seven months in 1917 that the apparitions at Fatima occurred.[71] Looking for these sorts of patterns—historic events that coincided with Marian apparitions and events that occurred on the anniversary of important Marian dates—has become an important means by which Marian groups discern God's plan unfolding in history.

Seers could also contribute to this understanding of history through revelation. Mary Ann Van Hoof located the history of the United States within a theology of history. She described how Mary had appeared to George Washington shortly after the Revolutionary War. The "Madonna Maria" had warned Washington about the future of the nation he had founded and had told him that this nation would have to withstand four great sieges: The American Revolution, the Civil War, and World Wars I and II. After these four conflicts, the Virgin said, there would be a long period of corruption and bloodshed in which people would offend God. This would lead to the fifth and most terrible period of all, in which blood would flow all over the globe. There would be "man-powered flying machines" dropping great destruction from the sky, and all nations on earth would be involved.[72] Once again, this vision unites the past with the future while locating American Catholics at a pivotal turning point as spiritual warriors of the last days.

The Baysiders became adept at applying this Marian hermeneutic to new developments, in part because making these connections was necessary to demonstrate that Lueken's messages from heaven contained accurate prophecies about future events. In the first few years that Baysiders convened in Flushing Meadows, the movement was able to capitalize on a number of disastrous events in order to demonstrate the prophetic abilities of their seer. In 1977, a major blackout darkened the city. Then 1978 became "the year of three popes" in which both Paul VI and his immediate successor, John Paul I, died. Finally, there was the attempted assassination of John Paul II in 1981. The Baysiders set to work interpreting each of these developments. In *Disaster and the Millennium*, Michael Barkun argues that millennial movements not only benefit from the social anxiety created by disasters but are always resisting a return to life as normal and require an ongoing sequence of disasters to maintain their membership.[73] This model applies to the Baysiders who frame almost every disaster and misfortune within the context of the Bayside Prophecies. Thus there was a reciprocal relationship between the performance of Lueken's charisma as a seer and the development of a Marian theology of history.

In 1977, a lightning strike was the cause of a blackout that darkened most of New York City from July 13 to July 14. The reaction to the blackout was aggravated by several factors including a heat wave and a prolonged economic recession. Thousands of stores were looted and arsonists set 1,037 fires. Although it was essentially a natural disaster, journalists regarded the blackout as an index of the state of society. *Time* magazine wrote a sort of jeremiad, viewing the event as a sign of a declining nation and describing the looting as "illuminating in a perverse way twelve years of change in the character of the city, and perhaps of the country."[74] The Baysiders used several techniques to locate the blackout within the context of Marian prophecy including a direct revelation from Lueken, finding a correspondence between the date of the blackout and previous Marian events, and locating passages in Lueken's previous prophecies that appeared to predict the blackout. The day after the blackout was the Eve of Our Lady of Mount Carmel and Lueken gave the following message: "You understand, My children, I hope, the lesson given to you in the past night of how man in his sin will become as an animal. I sent onto your city, My child, three warnings. Now the next shall be a terrible cross for many."[75]

A Baysider from Florida wrote to Bishop Mugavero and pointed out that July 13, 1977, was the sixtieth anniversary of the day the children of Fatima saw a vision of hell.[76] Others pointed out that on June 18, Lueken had described seeing a map of the United States in which a black cross hovered over Manhattan and Long Island.[77] The blackout was seen as the fulfillment of this prophecy.

Pope Paul VI died on August 6, 1978. One might expect that the Baysiders would rejoice, as they regarded Paul VI as an imposter who had affirmed the hated reforms of Vatican II. However, this was not the case. Within Lueken's worldview, the imposter and the true pope apparently died at the same time. On August 14, Lueken delivered the following message, "I bring you the glad news, My child and My children; I give you this knowledge from the Eternal Father, that your Vicar this day is with Us in Heaven."[78] John Paul I became the next pope on August 26. On September 28, he was found dead in his bed, having suffered an apparent heart attack in his sleep. His reign was one of the shortest in papal history. John Paul I had only been sixty-six and many were suspicious that he had been poisoned or otherwise murdered in his sleep. Philip Nobile was told by Baysiders that John Paul I had been poisoned with curare—a neurotoxin derived from South American plants.[79] Once again, Baysiders found evidence that Lueken had foretold the pope's untimely death. On September 13 she had delivered a message to pray for the pope because "there is a foul plan afoot against him."[80] This prediction was all the more impressive considering that the Baysiders only held three vigils during John Paul I's short reign.

John Paul I was succeeded by John Paul II on October 16, 1978. On May 13, 1981, twenty-three-year-old Turkish gunman Mehmet Ali Agca shot Pope John Paul II in St. Peter's Square. The attempted papal assassination was highly significant not only for the Baysiders, but for all Catholics interested in Marian prophecy. Since the apparitions at La Salette in 1846 there had been numerous prophecies about the violent death of a pope. Now they were all apparently proven correct. Marian devotee David Michael Lindsey wrote of the assassination, "He was to be the suffering pope of Fatima and La Salette!"[81] The shooting even occurred on the anniversary of the first appearance of Our Lady of Fatima in 1914. In 1979, not long after John Paul I's death, Lueken had made an equally dire prophecy for his successor, explaining that "the enemy has set forth a plan to crucify your Vicar." Lueken then proceeded to give a lurid description of an apparent assassination (complete with onomatopoeia to represent machine gun fire):

Oh, I hear, I hear a great commotion. I hear the stomping of feet, and I hear people screaming. And I hear "rat-a-ta-ta-ta-ta-ta-tat!" Like ... something, I don't know—it's like pellets or machine-gun fire. I hear screams, and the voice of a woman saying "Oh, no-o-oh!" Oh![82]

The assassin did not have a machine gun, but he did have an automatic pistol that fired multiple shots. The assassination attempt also occurred in a highly public place. To her followers, it appeared that Lueken had predicted the event perfectly. The Baysiders moved quickly to capitalize on the situation. Shortly after the assassination attempt, they distributed a copy of their newsletter featuring a reprint of the locution from 1979. Hastily penned onto the newsletter before photocopying were the words "God's Message Before Pope Shot!" as well as the time and location of the next vigil.[83]

Today, Baysiders have found precedent in the Bayside Prophecies for numerous disasters including the terrorist attacks of September 11, 2001, sexual abuse by priests, and the financial collapse of 2008. Baysider websites such as These Last Days Ministries continue to assemble links to breaking news stories, each of which is seen as confirmation of the Bayside Prophecies and the immanence of a divine chastisement. Initially, making these kinds of connections was necessary to maintain Lueken's charisma and further the momentum of the Baysider movement. However, the Marian theology of history has become an end to itself. This is partly because there is an intellectual pleasure in discovering meaningful patterns in history. The Marian hermeneutic also provides a form of agency. Along with miraculous Polaroids and conspiracy theories, reading history in light of prophecy is one more technology that empowers Baysiders to discover new sources of meaning and to reorder the world. This interpretive framework is certainly one key to the movement's success.

Organizational Structure

The mid-1970s was also a time during which the Baysider movement underwent a period of routinization, developing an organizational structure with its own traditions and hierarchy. The sheer momentum of the movement virtually required this. Large vigils continued to attract

thousands of visitors and with a secure site the vigils could go on indefinitely. Money was being sent in from all over the world, making it possible to establish a full-time mission to promote the Bayside Prophecies.
At vigils Lueken was now surrounded by so many bodyguards that the
crowd could no longer see or hear her.[84] A lighting system was designed
to give attendees in the back some idea of what was happening. A flashing
blue light signaled the arrival of Mary, red indicated the presence of Jesus.
The audience could also not hear Lueken speaking and so shrine workers
began recording her visions and then replaying them at the end of the vigil
using a loudspeaker.[85]

All of this success put a strain on Lueken's relationship with her allies,
the Pilgrims of Saint Michael. In 1977, the White Berets withdrew their
support. The exact reasons for this are unclear, but it seems that they
felt they could no longer control their seer and that her charisma threatened to usurp leadership of their own organization. As James Donahue
explained to me, "They [The Pilgrims of Saint Michael] got too big for their
britches."[86] In 1974, Lueken's messages began to prescribe uniforms for
her followers: "The men of the United States will wear the white berets.
The women of the United States will wear the blue berets, and wear, as My
direction, the prayer shawl. White berets for the men, blue for the women
of the United States."[87] Somehow, this command for women to wear blue
berets instead of white berets became the official reason for the split. In
most accounts of the "the beret fiasco," the Pilgrims of Saint Michael left
because their women had always worn white berets and did not want to
don blue berets.[88] Donahue suggested that the color of the berets did not
really matter—Lueken was testing them to see if they cared more about
the mission or the color of their uniforms.

On closer reading of Lueken's messages, it seems the divisive issue
was not the color of the berets, but what they symbolized. In the 1974
locution announcing the blue berets, Lueken added, "Our Lady said that
the women are not women; they are men. And they must be returned to
their role as women and mothers. Therefore, they will wear the blue cap in
signification of their honor to their husbands.... They will wear the blue
berets, for they will not be above their husbands."[89] The Pilgrims of Saint
Michael may have regarded this as an indictment that they were unable to
maintain traditional gender roles.

In the messages from 1974 to 1977, there is some evidence that
Lueken attempted damage control over the issue of the berets. She always mentions that the prescribed uniforms are only for her followers

in the United States. Consider the following message from 1976: "The Message from Heaven is reaching to all corners of the world, the earth. I bless Our children, your neighbors, your brothers of the north who wear the white berets. I bless those in your country, My child, the United States, who wear the white berets and the blue berets."[90] The symbolism of the blue berets also changes in this message: "I understand, My child, there is confusion. The blue berets will be worn only by the ladies who are in the circle of light. They are signatures and signify the placement within the circle of light. This message of the blue berets was a personal one, My child, and not to be adopted universally. I repeat: all will wear the white berets, all but the ladies of the inner circle."[91] In 1978, a year after the split, a reporter asked a Baysider why they wear blue and white berets. He answered, "There is a reason for it, but we don't know why."[92]

The Pilgrims of Saint Michael continued to affirm that all of Lueken's messages were true, but they ceased to organize bus tours from Canada or to support her in *Vers Demain*. The departure of the Pilgrims of Saint Michael only encouraged Lueken's followers to demonstrate more of their own initiative in promoting their seer. By the end of the 1970s, Lueken's followers had created a formal organization called "Our Lady of the Roses Shrine." The same year that the Pilgrims of Saint Michael left, Baysiders created a group called the Lay Order of Saint Michael. These were full-time male shrine workers who had dedicated their lives to promoting the Bayside Prophecies. The Shrine also began printing their own newsletter called *Roses* (later *Rose Notes*).

The Shrine rented two apartments in the Bronx that eventually housed twelve full-time workers who handled mail, printed shrine materials, and stuffed envelopes. Details are sketchy, but it appears that each apartment was referred to as a "workshop" and that men lived in one and women in the other. A locution from 1988 refers to "the workrooms of the White Berets and the Blue Berets."[93] This arrangement meant that full-time shrine workers could not live with spouses and were usually celibate. One description of the shrine headquarters refers to "the workshop" as a facility operated by single men between eighteen and fifty-five who printed and disseminated her messages.[94]

By the 1980s, Our Lady of the Roses Shrine had an operating budget of about $50,000 a month. This was enough to fund missionaries to spread the word of Lueken's prophecies. In 1984, a full-time worker named Arthur Becker toured thirty-seven cities to disseminate the Bayside message.

Baysiders were also able to host a show via UHF television, allowing viewers in the New York area to watch the processions and vigils in Flushing Meadows. Soon a hierarchy emerged. At the top were Lueken and her husband Arthur. Immediately below them were Ann Ferguson, Lueken's confidante, and Frank Albas, a former Pilgrim of Saint Michael, who stayed with Lueken and served as shrine director. Next came those who lived in the communal housing, known as shrine workers. Finally there were individuals abroad called "organizers."[95]

Around 1980, the Luekens purchased a new home in Terryville, Long Island, for $89,000. They were now able to afford vacations every year.[96] The residents of Bayside Hills had regarded Lueken as an outsider in part because she was not a homeowner. Now that she had become a seer the Luekens could finally enjoy a middle-class lifestyle. With the success of the Baysider movement in the 1980s, Lueken's opponents again began to claim that the movement was a hoax perpetrated for financial gain. I have found no evidence that the Baysider movement has ever been motivated primarily by a desire for donations. The most obvious problem with the fraud narrative is that no attempt is made at vigils to take up a collection. A box is normally present at vigils for prayer petitions and attendees have occasionally placed money in this box. But if the purpose of the vigils was to collect money, they fell far short of their potential. With crowds numbering in the thousands, Lueken's movement could have easily raised a small fortune by simply passing a collection plate. In all the vigils I attended, neither SMWA nor OLR ever asked for donations. Nor did they seem to have any apparatus in place to accept donations during vigils, such as a designated collection box. Instead, every vigil appeared to represent a net loss of resources. I returned from each vigil with an expensive long stemmed rose, sometimes two. In addition, my pockets would be laden with rosaries, crucifixes, scapulars, and other sacramentals that had been given to me. The first such object I received was a plastic rosary given to me by James Donahue. I thanked him and asked if he required a donation for the rosary. He shook his head solemnly and answered, "Absolutely not."[97] At a vigil for the anniversary of the first apparition at Bayside, SMWA did set up a card table where visitors could purchase holy medals, books, rosaries, and other religious paraphernalia. But even this appeared to be an attempt to distribute sacramentals rather than a financial venture. Rosaries sold for $3, holy medals sold literally for a few pennies. Similarly, OLR features an online store where visitors can purchase books about the Bayside Prophecies.

A disclaimer at the top of the site reads: "In accordance with the wishes of Our Lady and Our Lord, no person will be refused the urgent messages from heaven due to financial circumstances. If any person wishes to obtain the messages from Heaven and is unable to afford them due to personal financial circumstances please write the Shrine explaining the situation and we will make every effort to accommodate that person with the messages within reasonable means."[98] My overall impression was that Baysider leaders regard money as a means to proselytizing. Contrary to the narrative of a greedy religious fraud living a life of luxury on the donations of believers, current Baysider leaders seem quite willing to lower their standard of living in order to free up more resources for the promotion of their shrine.

The Vigil Liturgy

In addition to a prophetic worldview and an organizational structure, the third institution developed in Flushing Meadows was a dedicated liturgy for vigils. Newspaper accounts of Baysider vigils often emphasize the sheer number of people while giving little description of what actually occurs at a vigil. Vigils are depicted as mob events rather than religious ceremonies. However, freed from the constant heckling they experienced in Bayside, the vigils began to develop a distinct liturgical structure. Today, both Baysider groups employ a similar liturgy that was developed in the 1970s. The liturgy draws on Catholic devotional culture and incorporates hymns and prayers associated with other Marian sites such as Lourdes and Fatima. It also includes new devotional practices that are unique to the Baysider tradition.

On a June evening, I went to the former site of the Vatican pavilion to attend a vigil held by OLR. When the Baysiders split into two groups in 1998, OLR was able to retain the original name chosen by Lueken but became the smaller group. This particular evening was one of the rare occasions when only one of the two groups was present in the park. When I arrived unannounced for a 7 p.m. vigil, there were only two people present: A middle-aged white woman and an older white man with a white mustache and a heavy Irish accent. They both wore berets, blue and white, respectively. They were just finishing setting up for the vigil. A nearby van had been used to bring all of the needed materials, including their statue of Mary, a portable microphone and loudspeaker, and a stack of folding chairs.

The monument that is currently the locus of the Baysider movement is a modest architectural structure known as an exedra. It is elevated on a round dais of three steps and consists of a semicircular concrete wall with an attached bench. The wall is designed to resemble a scroll with rolls of parchment at either end. It bears the following inscription:

This the site of the Vatican Pavilion was /authorized by Pope John XXIII /visited on October 4, 1965 by /Pope Paul VI / during his mission of peace to/ the United Nations/ The building exhibited Michelangelo's Pieta and/ other art treasures. It symbolized the brotherhood /of man, the spirit of ecumenism and the theme/ of the New York World's Fair 1964–1965/—Peace through understanding.

The surrounding trees provide shade, and bushes behind the monument create a certain feeling of intimacy.

A fiberglass statue of Mary was set upon a small table in the center of the dais. OLR possesses the original statue used by Lueken after the parish council removed the statue from Robert Bellarmine's. To the statue's left was an American flag. To its right was the flag of the Vatican. In front of the statue was a blue wooden box for petitions. A slot in the box allowed pilgrims to leave petitions, asking for Mary's intercession on behalf of friends and loved ones. On top of the box was placed a small replica of Michelangelo's "Pieta." To the right of the altar was a microphone on a stand connected to a portable speaker. When I arrived, the man in the white beret was splashing holy water around the perimeter of the dais.

The woman leading the vigil seemed nonplussed by my presence. After explaining that her organization does not give interviews, she added that I could stay for the vigil and offered me a seat. The man in the white beret stepped up to the microphone and began to say a rosary. I pulled my own rosary out of my pocket and followed along. When the man finished, he stepped down and the woman took his place at the microphone. Normally, the rosary is divided into five sets of ten beads known as "decades," each separated by larger beads. The rosary is recited by saying a "Hail Mary" prayer for each of the small beads of the decade and a prayer called "Glory be to the Father" for each of the larger beads. Many devotional groups build on this basic structure by adding additional prayers. When Baysiders say the rosary, they insert two additional prayers after "Glory be to the Father." The first is the "Prayer to Saint Michael":

Saint Michael the Archangel
defend us in battle;
be our protection against the wickedness and snares of the devil.
May God rebuke him, we humbly pray:
and do thou, O Prince of the heavenly host,
by the power of God, thrust into hell Satan and all the evil spirits
  who prowl about the world seeking the ruin of souls. Amen.

This is followed by the so-called Fatima Prayer: "O my Jesus, forgive us our sins, save us from the fires of hell, lead all souls to Heaven, especially those who have most need of your mercy."

The way Baysiders say the rosary demonstrates their connection to a rich tradition of apparitional and traditionalist lore as well as spiritual warfare. The Fatima Prayer was introduced to Catholic tradition by Lucia Dos Santos, one of the child seers of the apparitions at Fatima. She reported that the Virgin Mary had requested a new prayer to be inserted into the rosary. The Prayer to Saint Michael is one of the "Leonine Prayers" that were introduced by Pope Leo XIII at the end of the nineteenth century and suppressed after Vatican II. When the nation of Italy came into being in 1861, anti-clerical forces moved to annex the papal states, depriving the pope of worldly or "temporal" power. Pope Leo XIII ordered that a series of prayers be said after Catholic masses throughout the world to pray for a solution to the problem in Italy. In 1929, Vatican City was created as a sovereign state, eliminating the purpose of the Leonine Prayers. The following year, Pope Pius XI found a new purpose for these prayers: That the people of Russia be granted the freedom to practice their faith. Dos Santos wrote her memoirs between 1935 and 1941, in which she explained how Mary had requested that Russia be consecrated to her Immaculate Heart. These further revelations about Fatima served to reinforce the connection between the Leonine Prayers, Marian devotional culture, Russia, and prophetic expectation.

For traditionalist Catholics, there is an additional piece of lore associated with the Prayer to Saint Michael. Leo XIII was supposedly inspired to create this prayer by something he experienced on October 13, 1884—exactly thirty-three years before the dancing sun miracle at Fatima. In this story, Leo had just finished celebrating mass in his private Vatican chapel, when he began staring intently at something no one else could see. He continued staring for ten minutes and his face turned white with dread. He went immediately to write the Prayer to Saint Michael. Later, when asked about his vision, Leo XIII explained that he could hear two voices, one kind and gentle, the other guttural and demonic.

The guttural voice declared, "I can destroy your church."
The gentle voice answered, "You can? Then go ahead and do so."
"To do so, I need more time and more power."
"How much time? How much power?"
"75 to 100 years, and greater power over those who will give themselves
    over to my service."
"You have the time, you will have the power. Do with them what you will."

Traditionalist Catholics note that seventy-five years after 1884 would have been 1959—the year in which the second Vatican Council was summoned.[99] By augmenting the rosary with these two prayers, Baysiders are not just being thorough in their prayers, they are also enacting their faith in the apparitions of Fatima and a belief that Vatican II had weakened the spiritual defenses of the Church.

After the second rosary, the woman approached me. "Would you like to say a rosary?" she asked. Then she added, "Are you Catholic?" I realized that there were still only three people at the vigil and that I was the only one who had not yet said a rosary.

"I am Catholic," I explained, "But…"
"That's alright," she said, "Most people don't lead a rosary their first
    time."

As an ethnographer it seemed inappropriate to lead a ritual that I had come to study. I was also not familiar with the idiosyncrasies of the Baysider rosary, such as the Fatima Prayer. In addition, all of the rosary payers, when said in English, have slight regional variations. For instance, I noticed that the Baysiders consistently said "Holy Ghost" during rosary prayers and not "Holy Spirit."

As we started the third rosary, I began to notice some of the other activity going on in the park. Birds and squirrels sported around the shrine. Summer mosquitos were also out. I noticed several people who approached the microphone wearing sandals would discretely stand on one foot, using their toes to scratch bites on their opposite ankle. My clothing covered most of my body, but on the subway home I later realized I had no fewer than six bites on my hands. In 2010 the Maloof Skate Park was created near the vigil site and I could hear the crashing of skateboards over the sound of the rosary. I could also hear the faint sound of traffic on the Long Island Expressway. But despite these distractions it was a peaceful way to spend a summer evening. There seemed to be an aura of sanctity in this quiet outdoor ceremony that is rarely found inside a crowded, air-conditioned church. As the sun set, the light that filtered through the trees would hit the statue at different angles, causing Mary's face to seem alive. Near dark, fireflies emerged and hovered around the grove.

In addition to leading the rosaries, volunteers would also lead litanies. These were longer prayers in which the audience would intone a response after each verse. The woman presented a book and asked me if I would like to recite a litany. Having already turned down her offer to say a rosary, I agreed to step up to the microphone and read the Litany of the Most Blessed Sacrament. The woman was patient showing me where to stand in front of the microphone and explaining that everyone already knew the proper responses. I read from the book and the audience (which had now grown to four people) gave the appropriate response after every line. The litany went something like this:

"Jesus, Bread of Life"
"Have mercy on us."
"Jesus, Bread of Angels"
"Have mercy on us."

There were about fifty verses. In middle school I had been an altar server at my parish church and I had experience being in front of a Catholic congregation. Still, as a lay Catholic it felt strange to me to lead such a ritual. When I reached the end of the text, I was asked to say a blessing in the name of the trinity. This was awkward because I no longer had a script and I was not sure exactly what I was expected to say. Instinctively, I said, "In the name of the Father, the Son, and the Holy Spirit." I immediately realized that Baysiders usually say "Holy Ghost," and I sensed that they were not pleased with my variation on their liturgy.

After forty-five minutes, more people began to arrive for the vigil. In total, I counted twelve visitors in addition to myself. A Latino couple arrived who looked to be in their mid-twenties. I spotted a wedding ring on the woman's finger. The couple's appearance contradicted the rhetoric about dress commonly raised by traditionalist Catholics. The man was wearing cargo shorts and a T-shirt. I spotted tattoos on all four limbs, including one of a rosary coiled around his forearm. The woman was heavily made up. She wore a miniskirt and sandals that displayed her hot pink toenails. Several of Lueken's messages warn against women wearing immodest clothing; however, no one seemed to object to the couple's presence. Two Asian women came next and took a seat behind me. An African-American woman in a blue beret arrived—clearly a leader. She took turns leading the rosary. An Indian couple arrived who I later learned were from Goa, a former Portuguese colony with a high population of Catholics. They were followed by another Asian woman wearing hospital scrubs. There was another white woman who seemed to be new to the vigils and had not brought a rosary. Finally, an African-American man arrived shortly before 10 p.m. when the vigil ended. All of the Baysider events I attended at Flushing Meadows showed a similar level of diversity.

I also noticed that those who attended were free to enjoy the vigil as they pleased. They could stand, sit, or kneel as they chose. For those who wished to kneel, OLR had brought a number of things that could be used to cushion the knees, including carpet samples and foam pads. At subsequent vigils I noticed that some visitors eschewed any such comfort while kneeling. At crowded vigils, the most hardy visitors would kneel on asphalt for up to twenty minutes at a time. Some neither knelt nor sat but preferred to pace around the shrine as they said the rosary, even walking behind the statue. Others would kneel so low that they were nearly prostrate with their heads on the grass in front of them. Naturally, some people snapped pictures. On one occasion a white dove perched in a tree over the monument and I watched a woman get up from saying the rosary and move to photograph the bird. This freedom was very different from a modern Catholic mass in which everyone is expected to stand, sit, and kneel at the same time.

As the sun set, more and more lights were brought out to illuminate the statue. A row of lanterns was placed around the edge of the dais. As the light grew dimmer, a large flashlight was set pointed at the statue's face. Then more candles were placed along the circular bench behind the statue. Then another flashlight, aimed at the statue's torso. When all the lights were lit, the woman leading the service asked everyone who was able to kneel to do so and to hold up their rosaries so that Mary and Jesus could bless them. Everyone knelt and held their rosaries over their heads toward the statue. A woman to my right held up two rosaries, presumably so that both of them would receive the blessing. No one spoke and by this time the park was largely empty and silent. We stayed like this for what seemed like a very long time.

The blessing of the rosaries was the most intimate moment of the vigil. It was also a profound example of what Robert Orsi calls "sacred presence." When Lueken led the vigils, she would describe the physical presence of Mary and Jesus. Pilgrims who could not hear her could still see red or blue lights indicating that these heavenly personages were present. The blessing of the rosaries suggests that Baysiders still have a strong sense of Mary's physical presence at Flushing Meadows. The liturgical leaders said and did nothing during the blessing because it was understood that no earthly leader was presiding over this part of the service: *Mary herself was.* This represented a direct encounter with the supernatural that was made all the more intense by the absence of music, prayers, or other earthly rituals. There was only the statue, the candles, and the raw experience of Mary's presence. Orsi argues that of all aspects of religious tradition, sacred presence is the least tolerable to modern societies and the one most often branded as "superstition."[100] Baysiders often accuse the modern Church of reducing Catholic ritual to a symbol rather than a supernatural manifestation of the sacred. Here in the park was a radical rejection of modern notions about religion.

The blessing of the rosaries was followed by additional rosary prayers and litanies. Finally, everyone was given a long-stemmed rose and a small candle. Roses are purchased by volunteers and distributed during every vigil and holy hour. It is not uncommon to see people at Baysider vigils juggling to handle a rose, a lighted candle, and a rosary simultaneously. More experienced attendees know how to set some of these objects down as required for the ceremony. By this time, it was so dark that the candle was necessary to read a photocopy I was handed with hymns printed in English and Spanish. The group sang "Immaculate Mary," a common hymn at Baysider vigils. "Immaculate Mary" is sung to a traditional French tune and was composed by Abbé Gaignet to be used for the shrine at Lourdes. Like the Fatima prayer said during the rosary, this hymn serves to locate the Baysider vigil within a global web of Marian apparitions.

At the culmination of the ritual everyone raised their candle at arm's length above their head and said, "Mary, light of the world, pray for us." The candles were then lowered until they were even with the face and the group said, "Our Lady of the Roses, pray for us." The candles were lowered again until they were level with the heart and the group said, "Mary, Help of Mothers, pray for us." This was repeated seven or so times with the candles being raised and lowered. This is a ritual that has gone on since the vigils were held in Bayside.[101]

Unlike the candle, the roses have no designated ritual purpose and pilgrims are free to do with them what they want. They are always distributed at vigils and are considered to be blessed objects. Shrine organizers affix the petals to cardstock and laminate them to be distributed all over the world.[102] Laminated rose petals can be purchased online for less than a dollar. I was given at least three of them by friendly Baysiders. The petals are said to bring "healings and conversions." Baysider literature features countless testimonials from people who feel they have experienced a miraculous cure after being given such a petal. The website for These Last Days Ministries contains an archive of testimonials sorted by disease. Cures of everything from cancer to diabetes to paralysis have been attributed to sacred rose petals. Many of these testimonials are from Latinos. In 2007, an article on Latino Baysiders appeared in *El Diario La Prensa*, the largest and oldest Spanish-language newspaper in New York City. The article described a network of Latino Americans not only in New York City but as far away as Detroit dedicated to "las Virgen de las Rosas." Curiously, the article makes no mention of Veronica Lueken, but attributes thousands of healings to Baysider rose petals. For the Latino community, Our Lady of the Roses may resonate especially with the story of Our Lady of Guadalupe, in which roses were miraculously imprinted onto the cloak of Juan Diego, an indigenous Mexican.[103]

At a Sunday holy hour for SMWA, I learned that some Baysiders eat rose petals. I was given a great many sacramentals meant to confer supernatural protection by a woman who combined the sarcasm of a jaded New Yorker with a sincere sense of millennial urgency. She plucked a handful of petals from her rose, popped them in her mouth, winked and me, and said, "Breakfast of champions!"[104] There seemed to be no specific beliefs about the effects of eating blessed rose petals. For Baysiders who attended multiple vigils a week, this seemed to be simply an efficient and respectful way of disposing of a surplus of holy rose petals.

After the ceremony of raising the candles, the vigil ended. Those in attendance took time to chat and catch up with each other while shrine leaders began to dismantle the shrine and load everything into their van. I made small talk with the couple from Goa. The woman leading the service still seemed distrustful of me. She was very dubious that my degree was not from a Catholic university and told me, matter-of-factly, that all of my knowledge about Catholicism was wrong. She explained that I had been indoctrinated by modernists who were in error. I am still not certain how she decided all of this about me. Was it because I was an academic? Or because I had said "Holy Spirit" instead of "Holy Ghost?" Or was it simply because I was under forty?

The African-American woman in the blue beret was friendlier and offered to give me a ride to the subway. She explained that in the 1980s, some Baysiders had been attacked walking through the park after vigils. Her car was covered with bumper stickers about Mary and the saints. She explained that before becoming a Baysider she had been a Baptist. She became disillusioned with Protestantism after learning its history. She was particularly bothered by the story of King Henry VIII creating the Church of England so that he could annul his own marriage. As a Catholic, she continued to get into arguments with her parish priest, who disapproved of her kneeling and taking communion on the tongue. When she explained to her priest that this was the proper way to receive communion, he responded, "Who do you think you are? The Pope?" It was 11 p.m. when she dropped me off at the subway and midnight by the time I reached home. Eight hours later I was back on the subway to Flushing Meadows for Sunday morning holy hour. When I arrived, the van from OLR was again parked in front of the monument. The woman who had led last night's vigil had already set up the statue and folding chairs for another ritual.

Weeks later, in a conversation about my research, a shrine worker from SMWA asked me, "Do you believe that Jesus and Mary are appearing in Flushing Meadows?" This was the only time I was directly asked about what I believed. It is the sort of question that ethnographers dread, particularly after having worked so hard to negotiate entry. I wanted to give an answer that was honest and not misleading but would also not close down dialogue.

"I believe *something* is happening in Flushing Meadows," I answered.
The shrine worker seemed surprised.
"You *do* believe something is happening in Flushing Meadows?"

I described my impressions of attending vigils and the sense that there was an aura of sanctity during them. I added that I am still theologically agnostic as to *why* the vigils in Flushing Meadows produce these unique feelings. The truth is that I did not share the beliefs of the shrine workers and was very much an outsider. But I wanted to show that I had come to understand the Baysiders in a way that most outsiders do not. In Robert Orsi's words, I was trying to understand them in such a way that "difference is not otherness."[105]

I understand the Baysiders well enough to sense what was at stake in this question. While individual Baysiders may subscribe to a wide variety of conspiracy theories and unusual beliefs, it is the shared praxis of the vigils that unites them as a religious community. Baysiders do not have to believe that Paul VI was an imposter or even in the prophecy of a coming Chastisement. They may come to vigils to stave off the coming Chastisement through prayer, nostalgia for pre-Vatican II devotional culture, a desire to heal a sick loved one or to free a family member from purgatory, or simply out of curiosity. Ultimately, Baysiders are those who either come to Flushing Meadows to say the rosary or believe that it is worthwhile to do so. To believe that Flushing Meadows is a sacred space is, in a very important way, the whole of the Baysider catechism. The vigils that mark Flushing Meadows as holy ground are the heart of the Baysider movement and its most important technology of power in its ongoing struggle for legitimacy. If the Baysiders gain acceptance within the larger Catholic culture it will not be through devising new interpretations of canon law, finding further evidence of a conspiracy, or even a disaster that confirms Lueken's prophecies. For Baysiders, their greatest claim to legitimacy is their continued ability to organize vigils in Flushing Meadows Park, gently asserting their existence in the public sphere with a quiet dignity.

FIGURE 1 Veronica Lueken in her Army Red Cross uniform. Photo courtesy of Jeremy Lueken.

FIGURE 2 Veronica and Arthur on their wedding day. Photo courtesy of Jeremy Lueken.

FIGURE 3 Veronica Lueken at a vigil in Flushing Meadows. Photo courtesy of Jeremy Lueken.

FIGURE 4 Arthur Lueken in front of the Unisphere at Flushing Meadows. Photo courtesy of Jeremy Lueken.

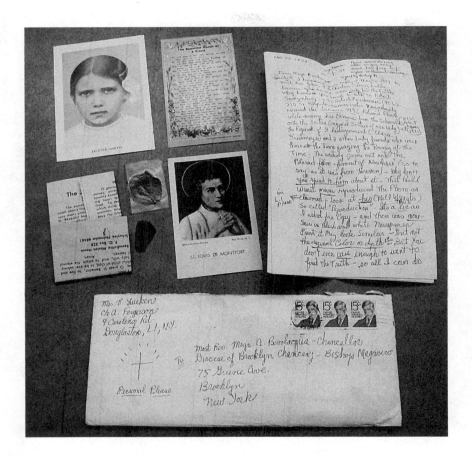

FIGURE 5 Religious paraphernalia accompanying a letter from Veronica Lueken to the Diocese of Brooklyn. From left to right: A photograph of Jacinta Marto, an old prayer card with a poem entitled "The Beautiful Hands of a Priest," literature from the Benedictine Mission House in Schuyler, Nebraska, blessed rose petals (one encased in plastic), a saint card of St. Louis de Montfort. Photo taken by the author at the archives of the Diocese of Brooklyn.

FIGURE 6 A procession of Baysiders in white berets taken at Flushing Meadows on July 13, 1978. The anomalous streaks resembling beads of light are common in Baysider miraculous Polaroids. Photo courtesy of the archives of the Diocese of Brooklyn.

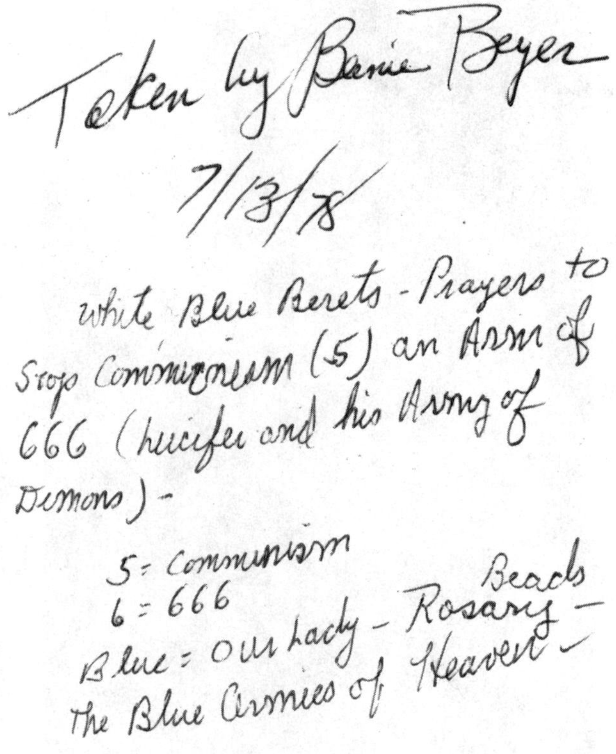

Taken by Bernie Beyer
7/13/78

White Blue Berets - Prayers to
Stop Communism (5) an Arm of
666 (Lucifer and his Army of
Demons) -

5 = Communism
6 = 666
Blue = Our Lady - Rosary Beads -
The Blue Armies of Heaven -

FIGURE 7 An interpretation of the anomalies in the photograph by Bernie Beyer. Beyer interprets the color of the streaks and their shape, in which he discerns the numbers "5" and "6." Photo courtesy of the archives of the Diocese of Brooklyn.

FIGURE 8 A vigil held in front of the Excedra in Flushing Meadows park. Lueken is delivering a locution from Jesus in the bottom left. The woman to the right holds a recording device to her face. An anomalous ray of light appears to descend from heaven and shine on Lueken. Photo courtesy of the archives of the Diocese of Brooklyn.

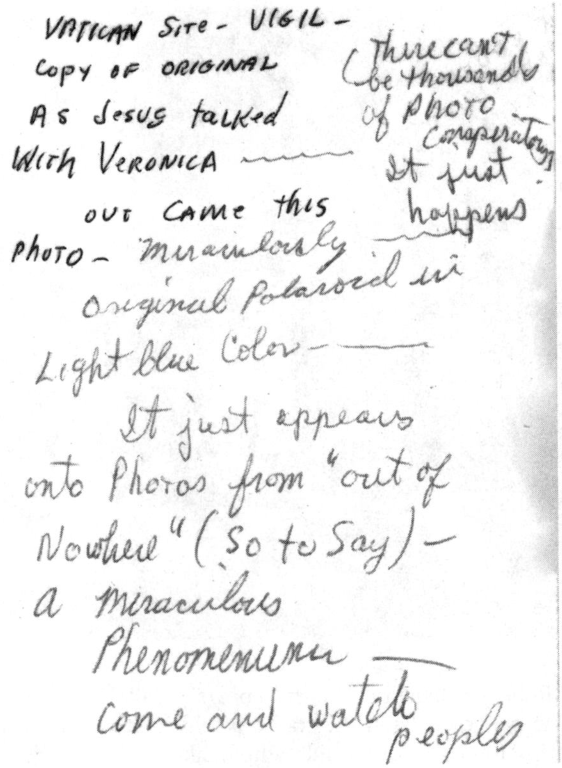

VATICAN Site - VIGIL -
COPY OF ORIGINAL
As Jesus talked
With VERONICA
OUT CAME this
PHOTO - Miraculously
Original Polaroid in
Light blue Color
It just appears
onto Photos from "out of
Nowhere" (So to Say) -
a Miraculous
Phenomenum
Come and watch peoples
(There can't be thousands of photo conspiratory
It just happens

FIGURE 9 Interpretation of the preceding photograph. The text reads, "There can't be thousands of photo conspiratory [*sic*]! It just happens. Vatican Site – VIGIL – Copy of Original as Jesus talked with Veronica. Out came this photo – Miraculously. Original Polaroid in light blue color. It just appears onto photos from 'out of nowhere' (so to say) – a miraculous phenomenon – come and watch peoples." Photo courtesy of the archives of the Diocese of Brooklyn.

FIGURE 10 St. Robert Bellarmine's as it appears today. Note the houses in the background. The police declared the traffic island in front of the church a "no man's land" during the Battle of Bayside. Photo taken by the author.

FIGURE 11 The malls of Bayside Hills are only about ten feet wide. Photo taken by the author.

FIGURE 12 The Exedra monument in Flushing Meadows Park marks the site of the Vatican Pavilion during the 1964–1965 World's Fair. It serves as a bench and resembles a scroll. Photo taken by the author.

FIGURE 13 Veronica Lueken's grave in Queens. Veronica, Arthur, and Raymond Lueken are all buried here. This photo was taken in early January and a Christmas wreath still adorns the grave. Photo taken by the author.

5

The Consequences of Growth

ONE OF THE paradoxical features of apparitional movements is that while they are intimately tied to a sacred space, they are often global in scope. While scholars and journalists sometimes frame the Baysiders as an isolated phenomenon local to Queens, Baysiders have been a global network since the early 1970s when Lueken began receiving institutional support from Canada and financial support from Guam. In the Archives of the Diocese of Brooklyn, I found evidence of Baysider activity on every inhabited continent. When I attended the anniversary of the apparition in 2012, families had travelled to Flushing Meadows from as far away as Malaysia and Mumbai. This international presence problematizes claims that the Baysiders represent a "vernacular" form of Catholicism.

The Baysider movement experienced rapid growth throughout the 1980s and 1990s. In 1995, Our Lady of the Roses Shrine maintained a mailing list with 35,000 names in the United States and another 55,000 worldwide. According to shrine officials, 30 percent of these people were giving money to the shrine and 60 percent of donors were women. Baysiders began taking out full-page ads in *The Boston Globe* and *The Los Angeles Times*. On December 13, 1994, an ad appeared in the tabloid *Weekly World News*. According to shrine literature, this ad elicited 5,000 phone calls and 1,500 written responses. In 1995, the shrine launched its hotline: 1-800-345-MARY. Callers heard a recording explaining that Jesus and Mary have been appearing in Bayside and have an urgent message for the world. To hear the message, callers need only leave a name and address. The number appeared on billboards as far away as Spokane, Washington, and even in the Mojave Desert.[1] The Baysiders' global reach demonstrated their success in contesting the definitional boundaries of Catholic tradition. From the beginning, Church authorities had hoped that Lueken's movement would "die a natural death." But by the 1980s, letters continued to pour into the diocese from all over the world. The hierarchy's apparatus for responding to claims of private revelation was not developed to deal with a highly mobile population. Baysiders armed with plane tickets and the Internet proved impossible to control.

Our Lady of the Roses Shrine began to create a network of shrine coordinators in cities across the United States and abroad. Coordinators disseminated literature and organized pilgrimages to Flushing Meadows, usually by charter bus. Today, SMWA maintains a directory of shrine coordinators in sixty-six cities throughout the United States as well as cities in Canada, Germany, Guatemala, India, Malaysia, and the Philippines. Shrine leaders explained that coordinators are vetted to ensure they can properly represent their movement. However, around the country groups sprang up that were entirely independent of leadership in New York. In 1985, three people in Fort Lauderdale, Florida, began holding public vigils in hotel conference rooms. The group called itself "The Circle of Light" and wore blue berets and uniforms as specified in Lueken's messages. Other groups formed with names like "Roses of Our Lady of Mount Carmel" in Spokane, Washington; "These Last Days Ministries" in Grand Rapids, Michigan; "The Apostles of Our Lady" in Lansing, Michigan; "Our Lady's Workers" in Los Angeles; "Mary's Children of the Desert" in Arizona; and "Our Lady's Children of Maryland" in Millersville, Maryland.[2]

As the Baysider movement grew in the decades following the move to Flushing Meadows, it too became an "imagined community" as defined by Benedict Anderson. Thousands of people who had never met Lueken or been to Flushing Meadows nevertheless felt deeply connected to the movement and set about advancing the message of the Bayside Prophecies as they saw fit. In East Hartford, Connecticut, a group of Baysiders called "The Blue Berets" formed a political organization called Connecticut Citizens for Decency. As "the political arm" of the Blue Berets, their group succeeded in passing tough anti-smut laws in East Hartford. When Hartford resident Curtis Heinz was charged with four counts of promoting an obscene performance after presenting exotic dancers at his club, the Venus Lounge, a key witness was Mary Ann Pressamarita, founder of the Connecticut Citizens for Decency. The defense attempted to cross-examine Pressamarita about her affiliation with the Baysider movement in an attempt to prove that her standards of decency were abnormal. The defense was particularly keen to ask Pressamarita about her interest in miraculous Polaroids and other subjugated discourses. The prosecution blocked this line of questioning, arguing that witnesses should not be required to discuss their religious affiliations.[3]

In 2006, Saint Mary's by the Sea Roman Catholic Church in Huntington Beach, California, drew national attention when pastor Martin Tran insisted that the congregation stand rather than kneel during the consecration of communion. This is a debate between traditionalists and modernists that has divided several parishes. Like the Baysider movement itself, arguments about when it is proper to kneel represent a struggle over who gets to define Catholic tradition. At Saint Mary's by the Sea the conflict became particularly ugly, with a large contingent of parishioners continuing to kneel against the direct orders of their pastor. Tran responded in the parish bulletin with fiery pronouncements that kneeling during the consecration was defiance of church authority and a mortal sin. Fifty-five members of the parish received letters from Tran inviting them to leave the parish. Lita Farag, one of the traditionalist lay Catholics who remained obstinate against Tran, had been a Baysider for many years.[4]

It is likely that small groups of Baysiders have exerted similar effects on their parishes and communities all over the United States. Some of these Baysider cells acted in ways that the New York leadership found objectionable. Some made headlines when they engaged in disruptive or even illegal activity in the name of the movement. Others decided that Lueken did not properly represent the values of traditionalist Catholicism and became apostates. Some of these even became seers in their own right. Robert Orsi notes that religious meanings are "volatile" and often defy the expectations of authorities.[5] In some ways, the Baysider movement became a victim of its own success. Just as Lueken's conflict with Church authorities represented a disagreement over where the definitional boundaries of Catholicism lay, the leaders of Our Lady of the Roses Shrine found themselves attempting to police Baysiders whose activities were a liability to the movement. Ironically, shrine leaders were no more able to control these individuals than the Diocese of Brooklyn had been able to control Lueken. In this sense, the growth of the Baysider movement is an interesting case study in what Rodney Stark and Roger Finke call "the sect-church process," a sociological model of religious groups in which sectarian movements are constantly forming, growing larger, and then spawning new sectarian movements.[6]

Outflanking the Hierarchy

As the Baysider movement spread, it became a global problem for the Catholic hierarchy rather than a local one. At the Archives of the Diocese of Brooklyn, I found letters describing local Baysiders from forty-one states.[7] Many of these were from clergy who had Baysiders in their flock and sought resources for dealing with stories of world-ending comets and imposter popes. A Carmelite nun in Jefferson City, Missouri, wrote Bishop Mugavero about a novice who had become preoccupied with the Bayside Prophecies.[8] A chaplain from Monroe High School in Fairbanks, Alaska, complained of a student who was disseminating Lueken's prophecies to classmates.[9] A letter from Mrs. Palma Lionetti, a CCD teacher in Stony Point, New York, described with dismay how her students continued to bring up Lueken.[10]

I also found numerous letters from beyond the United States. There were reports of Baysiders from Canada, Haiti, Guatemala, Panama, Germany, France, England, Ireland, Italy, Switzerland, Nigeria, India, Guam, Oceania, the Philippines, Japan, and Korea. A letter from Jaime Cardinal Sin, the Archbishop of Manila, complained of being "swamped with periodicals" about the Baysiders. Similar letters had been sent in by Lolesio Fuahea, Bishop of Ille Wallis in Oceania. William J. McNaughton, the Bishop of Inchon, Korea, described an "increasing flow" of Bayside messages being distributed through his diocese in Korean.[11] An American priest returning from the Philippines reported that "practically every bishop there (as well as in Korea) complained of being bothered by Bayside materials."[12] A Dominican friar doing missionary work in Nigeria wrote with alarm that copies of the Pilgrims of Saint Michael newsletter, *Michael Fighting*, were circulating among his flock and that many had begun to believe that Paul VI was an imposter.[13] All of these letters beseeched the Brooklyn Diocese for resources to discredit Lueken's prophecies.

If the Diocese of Brooklyn struggled to control the Baysiders when they were gathered primarily in Bayside, they had even less ability to control them now. The Catholic hierarchy functions through a global grid of dioceses and parishes. The Church's apparatus for evaluating claims of private revelation was never very systematic and developed during the early modern period when lay Catholics rarely ventured beyond their own parish. In that context, delegating the evaluation of private revelation to the bishop served the interests of the Church well. If an apparition in a particular region might be an asset to the Church, as was the apparition of Fatima that appeared during an anticlerical regime in Portugal, it could be approved fairly quickly and declared "worthy of belief."[14] On the other hand, if a bishop felt an apparition might leave the Church vulnerable to charges of superstition or alienate Catholics with modern sensibilities, as was the case with the apparitions of Necedah and Bayside, they could reject it. But regardless of the bishop's decision, Rome remained above the fray. No one could accuse the Mother Church of being overly credulous or overly skeptical because the decision was not hers to make. This system worked well until the mid-twentieth century. Before modern times, it was almost impossible for lay Catholics to contact Church authorities outside of their own diocese or seek out a "second opinion" regarding an apparition. The Baysiders, however, were inventive and had an unprecedented reach.

In the file boxes of mail regarding Lueken, I found several letters from Baysiders addressed to the pope. These had been returned, unopened, to the diocese from which they originated. For most of the Church's history, a lay Catholic could not hope to gain an audience with the pope, especially if they were separated from Rome by an ocean. Today, the pope has an e-mail address and even a Twitter account. More importantly, anyone can purchase a plane ticket to Rome. October 24, 1979, an enterprising Baysider named Vincent McDonnell managed to approach John Paul II at a public gathering at St. Peter's Basilica. He handed him a package containing a rosary blessed during an apparition at Bayside and copies of some of Lueken's messages. Upon receiving the package, the pope reportedly said, "I know about it [the Bayside apparitions]" and chatted with McDonnell for a few minutes. Some Baysiders interpreted this transaction to mean that John Paul II had officially endorsed the Bayside Prophecies, which would naturally trump any condemnation made by a bishop. When Bishop John R. Quinn of San Francisco published an article in a church bulletin calling the Baysiders "a bogus group," a local devotee wrote an angry letter citing the incident with John Paul II as evidence that the Baysiders were right and that Quinn was in error.[15]

In reality, John Paul II was well known for his Marian piety and probably did have a special fondness for groups like the Baysiders. However, his impromptu remark was clearly not an official endorsement from the Holy See. Someone took a picture of McDonnell handing the package to John Paul II which now appears on the Baysider website, These Last Days Ministries. When I met McDonnell in person at a vigil, he had brought a copy of this photograph with him to the park. His black hair had since turned to gray but he was still very proud of his encounter with John Paul II and claimed he had spoken with him on several occasions, usually for twenty minutes at a time.

A more elaborate example of this kind of creative endorsement concerns a statue of Mary that was "given" to Lueken by Cardinal Cushing of Boston. Published books of the Bayside Prophecies contain notes stating simply that the statue was a "gift" from the Cardinal. But an interview with Lueken reveals that the statue was not really a gift from Cushing at all—at least not in any ordinary sense. Lueken wrote Cushing repeatedly during her early visions and Cushing did sometimes write back. The Cardinal remained neutral on the status of the Bayside apparitions, so Lueken requested that should he die he send a message from beyond the grave as to whether her messages were true or false. After Cushing died, Lueken was visited by a woman who lived on "Cushing" Street in Dorchester, Massachusetts. The woman explained that she felt compelled to give her a statue of Our Lady of Mount Carmel. She then explained that the statue had been given to her years ago by Father Cushing, long before he became a cardinal. For Lueken, this was the sign she had been waiting for: Cushing had "given" her the statue from beyond the grave, thereby endorsing her visions.[16]

Plenty of Church authorities were willing to fully endorse the Bayside Prophecies. All the Baysiders had to do was seek them out. One shrine worker told a reporter, "Finding a bishop or priest to support them is like finding a needle in a haystack."[17] But needles did turn up, often in the developing nations of the Global South. For instance, the website for OLR declares:

> Bayside Messages have the Imprimatur of the Most Reverend Fidel Cortes-Perez, Bishop of Chilapa, Guerrero, Mexico, and the approval of the Most Reverend Alphonse Gallegos, Auxiliary Bishop of Sacramento, California, and Silvio Cardinal Oddi in Rome.[18]

A letter from Kerala, India, complained that a Dominican friar had been endorsing Lueken and her messages.[19] A priest in Guatemala wrote the Baysider shrine workers, expressing his faith in their movement.[20] On Palm Sunday, 1982, Father Robert J. Skurla, a Byzantine Rite priest and Blue Army chaplain, pronounced the following declaration in Saint Peter's Cathedral in Scranton, Pennsylvania, "I want to go on record as personally accepting the messages [of Bayside] until proven otherwise by our good, kind, loving Holy Father.... We have been told that acceptance by the Diocese of Brooklyn will come very soon."[21] These kinds of endorsements are not canonically valid: a bishop in Mexico has no authority over an apparition in Brooklyn. But this hardly matters for Baysiders, who are more interested in proving their legitimacy to other lay Catholics than winning over the Brooklyn Diocese.

In addition to these outspoken advocates, there have always been priests, monks, and nuns who endorsed the Baysiders in an unofficial or quasi-official capacity. During the Battle of Bayside, a letter from the BHCA to Bishop Mugavero reported seeing priests and nuns present during vigils. "Who are they?" demanded the letter, "Have they been asked to identify themselves?"[22] Mugavero likely had no idea who these priests were or even what diocese they had come from. There were almost certainly more priests and nuns who attended vigils in street clothes so as not to be recognized. This sort of unofficial participation from clergy has been noted at other apparition sites.[23]

There is limited data regarding clergy who support apparitions because such clergy are often in defiance of their superiors and not at liberty to share their views. However, from the limited evidence available the motivations of these clergy seem very similar to those of lay Baysiders. They are traditionalists and seem to long for a more direct encounter with the divine. Philip Nobile met a nun of the order of St. Joseph who was attending vigils against the orders of her superiors. She explained, "There's nothing against the faith here, but I can take you to any Catholic church in the United States and show you things against the faith."[24] Anne Cillis interviewed a priest named Clement Shank for *The Canadian Layman*. Shank was a priest of the Oblates of Mary Immaculate from Ottawa, Canada. He had been fascinated by the Garabandal apparitions and had journeyed to Bayside to see Lueken. Not only did Lueken impress him, but he reported seeing her levitate during a vigil. Shank's account of the Bayside vigils is just like those of lay Catholics who were inspired by Lueken's charisma. He describes his elation at receiving a blessed rose from her. Shortly before the interview with Cillis, Shank received permission to leave his order so that he could become a monk.[25]

During my time with SMWA, it was clear that despite their hostile relationship with the Brooklyn diocese, they were supported by a network of priests, both local and abroad. These priests aided them by blessing sacramentals and offering sacraments during vigils. Sacramentals such as the rosary, St. Benedict medal, and the crucifix, are central to the Baysider worldview and are believed to convey supernatural protection. Aside from the rosary, the most important sacramental is the brown scapular. The scapular was originally part of a medieval monk's habit and resembled a broad length of cloth that would be draped around the shoulders and hang as low as the knees. Over time, it evolved into a smaller and less cumbersome form. The scapulars worn by the Baysiders are essentially lengths of string with rectangles of embroidered fabric on either end. The scapular became especially important to modern Marian piety after Lucia Dos Santos, one of the seers of Fatima, explained that Mary wanted her followers to wear it. According to tradition, an apparition of the Virgin Mary gave the first such scapular to St. Simon Stock in the year 1251. She is supposed to have told him, "Anyone who dies clothed in this shall not suffer eternal fire, and if they die wearing it, they shall be saved." It is also said that Pope John XXII issued a bull in 1322 affirming that those who wear the scapular consistently and die with chastity and prayers to Mary shall be freed from Purgatory on the first Saturday following their death. However, many Catholic scholars regard this bull as apocryphal and note that the scapular was not widely worn until the sixteenth century. Regardless, Lueken knew the story of Simon Stock and invoked it in urging her followers to wear the scapular.[26]

At almost every vigil I attended, members of both Our Lady of the Roses Shrine and Saint Michael's World Apostolate asked me if I wore the brown scapular. They made it clear that, given the benefits of wearing this sacramental, to not wear it was not only dangerous but profoundly foolish. I was also given numerous brown scapulars by Baysiders. However, to receive the full benefit of the brown scapular one must be "enrolled" through a special blessing ceremony performed by a priest. The scapulars that were handed out needed to be blessed by a priest also. Finding amenable priests was difficult. In one message, Lueken stated:

> Therefore, because so few priests in My Son's Church are willing to intercede with the Scapular, and enthrone those who wish it, it has become necessary to give a Scapular to every child upon earth; and he or she of reasonable age shall go forth and find a kindhearted and true, holy priest to enroll them.[27]

"Kindhearted and true" priests who would enroll Baysiders and bless their scapulars were rare. One woman who gave me several scapulars explained that she knew a priest from Haiti who would regularly bless large quantities of scapulars and other sacramentals for distribution at vigils.

At least three priests were present at SMWA's vigil for the forty-second anniversary of the apparitions of Bayside. While the congregation said the rosary, two folding chairs were set up behind the statue of Mary so that the priests could take confessions. A small line of penitents formed that wound its away around the bushes that surrounded the vigil site. These sorts of outdoor confessions are common at apparition sites throughout the United States.[28] The following day, these priests presided over Sunday holy hour, standing alongside shrine workers and reciting several prayers into the microphone. That afternoon, the priests were honored by name at a banquet to welcome pilgrims who had attended the anniversary. A shrine worker explained to me that the priests who appear publicly during vigils are usually from outside the Brooklyn diocese. This arrangement causes fewer conflicts with the hierarchy.

The visibility of priests at unapproved apparition sites always emboldens the apparitional movement and undermines the authority of the local bishop.[29] Not surprisingly, Church authorities are often resentful of priests who provide these sorts of endorsements. The conservative Catholic magazine *Fidelity* quoted one priest as saying, "These claims would not get too far if there wasn't always a certain number of credulous priests meddling and muddling to give credit to it all."[30] For religion scholars, the presence of these priests, monks, and nuns also complicates the imagined lines between ecclesiastical and popular religion. The presence of these priests at vigils is controversial precisely because it demonstrates that these definitional boundaries are not static or self-evident but contested.

The Bishop Speaks

By the 1980s, it was clear that the statements put forward by Chancellor King would not be sufficient to quell the Baysider movement. Not only did the movement continue to spread across continents, but it was effectively cobbling together a form of clerical approval by collecting endorsements from priests around the world. In 1986, Baysiders began to claim that the diocese was on the verge of reversing its decision and approving the apparitions at Bayside. The diocese realized that Bishop Mugavero's silence on the matter had been taken as tacit consent. As King's successor Anthony Bevilacqua explained, "Followers of Bayside still feel they are in obedience to the Church because they claim the Bishop has not really taken a stand of condemnation. Of course, the Diocese could not be clearer in its stand on the apparitions but people do not want to hear it."[31] During the Battle of Bayside, Mugavero had delegated the task of dealing with Lueken entirely to his chancellor and vicars. He was far more interested in issues of social justice than adjudicating claims of the supernatural. He is also remembered as thoughtful and slow to act. But on November 4, 1986, he wrote a formal declaration condemning Lueken and her movement.

Although Mugavero never uses the language of heresy or excommunication explicitly, he nevertheless goes after the Baysiders with hammer blows. The declaration is replete with the use of scare-quotes, as if to challenge the legitimacy of every aspect of the Baysider worldview: Their "vigils" are not really vigils, their "movement" is not really a movement, and so on. He begins by directly addressing the legalistic arguments promoted by the Baysiders, namely their claims that the Brooklyn Diocese never produced an "official" position on Lueken. Mugavero also addresses a legal question regarding whether Catholics may publish literature about private revelations. In 1917, an amendment to canon law (canon 1399, 5) forbade Catholics from publishing anything about "new apparitions, revelations, visions, prophecies, miracles" or publishing "new devotions, even private" without the local bishop's authorization and eventual *imprimatur*. [32] This law lasted until Vatican II when, on October 14, 1966, it was declared in the Congregation of Propaganda that Church authority was not required to publish material about apparitions. This change had nothing to do with the Church's stance on private revelation. Rather, it was done in keeping with Vatican II's ideas about modern political life and the need for freedom of expression and piety. However, Baysiders frequently cite this reform to claim that their movement does not violate canon law. Mugavero specifically rejects this interpretation, explaining that the reforms of 1966 did not pertain to publishing religious materials of "authoritative moral value."[33] He adds that he has consulted with the Congregation for the Doctrine of Faith in this matter.

After dismissing the Baysiders' legalistic claims, he invokes his full ecclesiastical authority, declaring, "I, the undersigned Diocesan Bishop of Brooklyn, in my role as the legitimate shepherd of this particular Church, wish to confirm the constant position of the Diocese of Brooklyn that a thorough investigation revealed that the alleged 'visions of Bayside' completely lacked authenticity." This phrasing is far less ambiguous than that of Chancellor King, whose letters during the 1970s explained that the visions "lacked complete authenticity."

The next paragraph frames the messages in terms of spiritual danger and is probably as close as a progressive bishop like Mugavero would come to making an accusation of heresy. He writes, "Moreover, in view of the confusion created by published reports of messages and other literature by this 'Movement,' I consider it my obligation to offer Christ's faithful pastoral guidance, lest their faith be endangered by 'messages' and 'teachings' relayed by 'visionaries,' which are contrary to the Faith of our Catholic Church."

Finally, Mugavero makes a five-point declaration, explaining that: 1) No credibility can be given to the claims of Lueken or her followers. 2) The messages violate Church teachings. Here, Mugavero gives a single example: the imposter pope theory. This is a rare case in which Church authorities actually engaged the Bayside Prophecies sufficiently to articulate *how* they contradict Church teachings. However, it is important to note that Lueken had not yet made this claim about an imposter pope in 1973, when the diocese held their official investigation. 3) Promoting the Baysider movement does, in fact, violate canon law. 4) Loyal Catholics are directed to refrain from attending vigils and from disseminating or reading literature about Bayside. Mugavero adds that this order is given "out of concern of the spiritual welfare" of lay Catholics. 5) Anyone who attends vigils or assists the Baysiders is assisting in spreading confusion throughout the Church.[34]

Mugavero sent this declaration to three hundred bishops in the United States and to one hundred conferences of bishops around the world. It was reprinted in Catholic newspapers and parish bulletins around the country. In cities such as Los Angeles, it was disseminated in Spanish as well as English. An accompanying article in the *New York Post* reported that Cardinal Joseph Ratzinger, Prefect of the Congregation for the Doctrine of Faith, had concluded that the diocese's verdict on the Baysiders was correct.[35] Cardinal Ratzinger, of course, went on to become Pope Benedict XVI.

The declaration came as a heavy blow to the Baysiders but, as during the Battle of Bayside, opposition only caused Lueken's supporters to become more entrenched in their views. Frank Albas, a shrine leader, explained to reporters that Bishop Mugavero failed to investigate "hundreds and hundreds and hundreds of testimonials of cures, conversions, and visions," adding, "The clergy are misleading the flock. They are taking souls to hell with them."[36] The Baysiders are justified in claiming that the diocese did not really conduct "a thorough investigation" as claimed in Mugavero's declaration. In 1973, Chancellor King was under tremendous pressure to produce an official statement from the diocese and his investigation was intended to be quick, not thorough. The investigation represented the position of the diocese but it failed to produce arguments that might persuade someone not already skeptical of Lueken's visions. When Baysiders criticized the investigation, diocesan officials insisted that it had been official, thorough, and conclusive and thereby painted themselves into a corner. To produce a more thorough investigation would be to admit that the first one had been insufficient. Mugavero's claim that there had been a thorough investigation was, in this sense, revisionist history.

Despite the apparent finality of Mugavero's declaration, it had relatively little effect on the Baysider movement. Such a declaration would almost certainly have had more impact in 1970. But by 1986, the movement had reached a kind of critical mass and was now too large for any one bishop to control. In fact, even shrine leaders were beginning to find that they could not control the raw excitement that the Bayside Prophecies inspired.

The Sect-Church Process

Sociologists Roger Finke and Rodney Stark outline a cycle of religious change that they describe as the "sect-church process." The difference between a sect and a church, as Finke and Stark define these terms, is the degree of tension between the religious organization and the culture at large.[37] Religious organizations often begin with prophetic vision that demands strict adherence to ideals and often entails a rejection of institutions and practices valued by mainstream society. Thus new religious groups or sects often exist in tension with society as a whole. Historically, such groups have been mistrusted, mocked, and even killed for their beliefs. Over time, these groups gain acceptance but at the cost of compromising their original otherworldly vision. The group's standards of conduct become more permissive and concessions are made to the dominant culture. Instead of being a persecuted minority, the religious organization becomes a center of community life, a church. But there will always be members of a religious community who find these changes unacceptable and call for a renewal of the original otherworldly vision. These individuals break away from their churches to form new sects, which once again exist in tension with society. As Finke and Stark explain, "The result is an endless cycle of sect formation, transformation, schism, and rebirth."[38]

While the rational choice approach of Finke and Stark is certainly not applicable to the development of every religious group, in many ways the Baysiders and their relationship with the Catholic Church is a classic example of the sect-church process. In the United States, Catholics have historically experienced a level of tension with American culture more consistent with a sect than with a church. From their arrival in the Maryland colony in the seventeenth century through the election of John F. Kennedy in 1960, Catholics in America were religious outsiders. Protestant Americans portrayed Catholic devotional life as superstitious and idolatrous. They also questioned whether practitioners of a religion with a global hierarchal structure could ever really be patriotic or participate in a democratic society. American Catholics proved they were "real Americans" through patriotism and military service. The nationalistic tone of the messages at Necedah and Bayside are a testament to Catholic patriotism. However, Catholics disagreed over how to respond to Protestant accusations of superstition and idolatry. The majority of Catholics adopted a "fortress mentality" and sought to insulate themselves from Protestant society by creating their own parochial schools, hospitals, and social infrastructure. Conversely, so-called Americanist Catholics advocated making concessions to mainstream American culture in order to fit in. This included adopting a vernacular mass and downplaying devotional practices. In the United States, Vatican II came as a victory for the Americanists. The Church made concessions to the modern world and opened the door to ecumenism. It became more permissive with regard to behavioral norms and downplayed discussion of damnation and ritual transgression. The rise of traditionalist Catholics can be read as a classic sectarian response to these changes: They saw Vatican II as a betrayal of the traditional values and duties of the Church. As a subset of the traditionalist movement, the Baysiders represented a more intense form of this sectarian reaction. The Baysiders not only rejected the reforms of Vatican II but they also condemned as sinful many of the institutions of mainstream American culture such as contemporary fashion, popular music, and television.[39] All of this has brought the Baysiders into a high degree of tension with the Catholic Church as well as mainstream American society. However, the Baysiders have interpreted the hostility of outsiders as evidence that their cause is just and that their values remain uncompromised.

But after arriving in Flushing Meadows, the Baysiders became some-what less sectarian and more church-like in their orientation. Although they were still officially condemned by their Church, they were now in considerably less tension with society than they had been in Bayside Hills. Our Lady of the Roses Shrine was receiving enough money in dona-tions to support full-time shrine workers and maintain a modest office and housing. They had a working relationship with the police and parks departments. There was even hope of reconciliation with Church authori-ties. In Bayside Hills, Veronica Lueken and her followers had nothing to lose. In Flushing Meadows, this was no longer true. This became a prob-lem when Baysiders in other states or on other continents began to take actions that cast Our Lady of the Roses Shrine in a negative light. Often such actions were taken by the most zealous Baysiders who were willing to sacrifice anything in the service of what they considered to be a mis-sion from heaven. Almost as soon as the movement achieved a degree of routinization, Our Lady of the Roses Shrine began struggling to control its own sectarian factions.

Dennis John Malvasi

In 1985, a Vietnam veteran named Dennis John Malvasi carried out the first bombing attack on an abortion clinic ever in the state of New York. He also attended vigils in Flushing Meadows Park. Malvasi's actions are in no way characteristic of the Baysider movement. Tens of thousands of people visited Flushing Meadows every year in the 1980s, most of whom had strong conservative beliefs but were not criminals.[40] However, Malvasi's actions demonstrate how some people were inspired by the Baysider mes-sages in ways that could not be predicted or controlled.

Malvasi was raised in a Catholic orphanage in Peekskill, New York. At seventeen, he joined the army by lying about his age and saw heavy combat in Vietnam in the aftermath of the Tet Offensive. After return-ing to New York, he struggled to reenter civilian life. He served several years in prison first for a knife fight and again for carrying an unregistered handgun. By the mid-1980s, Malvasi had become involved in gun run-ning in Florida and a warrant had been issued for his arrest. He received telephone calls by a pager, picked up his mail at local bars, and lived out of a sea-bag. It was during this time that a fellow veteran introduced him to the Baysiders.

His first bomb consisted of a single tube packed with explosive powder left in the men's room of the Manhattan Women's Medical Center. On December 10, 1985, it burst into flames, causing minimal damage but becoming the first such attack in New York history. On October 29, 1986, a bomb with a half-stick of dynamite exploded at the Eastern Women's Center, shattering windows and blowing a hole in the wall. This was a site where Baysiders had protested for years. Two weeks later on November 11, an anonymous caller reported an unexploded bomb hidden inside a sofa at the Queens Women's Medical Center. This time the device contained three sticks of dynamite. Following this attack three hundred federal agents were employed searching for the bomber. Finally, on December 14, 1986, the bomb squad was called into the Manhattan headquarters of Planned Parenthood. A large bomb had been planted and, apparently impatient or lacking confidence about the timing mechanism, Malvasi had set off a smaller incendiary device, which set the carpet on fire. Officers success-fully entered the burning building and disarmed the larger bomb before it was detonated by the heat. Police were alarmed that the bomber seemed to be using increasingly sophisticated weaponry. However, the undetonated bomb left a vital clue. A reporter for *The New York Times* wrote:

> With 15 sticks of dynamite, the bomb was powerful enough to have collapsed the front of the building at 380 Second Avenue and to have shattered windows one-quarter mile away. With a blasting cap, timer and battery, the bomb showed its architect to be someone of sophistication. And one last component, nestled amid the sticks of dynamite, caught the officer's eyes: a medal of St. Benedict.[41]

St. Benedict medals are one of the most important sacramentals for Baysiders. Lueken associated the Benedict medal in particular with spir-itual warfare. A locution from 1977 states, "The sacramentals—your Rosary, My children, the beads of prayer, your Scapulars, were given for reason. And you must keep the sacramental, given for these very days from Saint Benedict, upon you. I, My child, have always called him the fighter of demons."[42] Malvasi's use of the St. Benedict medal suggests that he regarded the abortion clinic as a spiritual target as much as a tactical one. The explosion was intended as a sort of exorcism in addition to being an act of terror.

By tracing the unexploded dynamite to its vendor, federal agents were able to identify Malvasi as the bomber. Despite his extensive police profile,

Malvasi continued to evade arrest for months. He successfully discerned several attempts by police to lure him out using a sting operation. In the end, it was not federal agents but Cardinal O'Connor that effected Malvasi's arrest. On February 23, O'Connor made a televised plea for the bomber to turn himself in. The next day Malvasi surrendered to authorities. "Cardinal O'Connor is a prince of the church," he explained from prison. "If the Cardinal says something and you don't listen, then when you stand before the magistrate in the celestial court, you got problems. And I got enough problems without God being mad at me."[43]

In 1992, Cardinal O'Connor led a prayer vigil at Eastern Women's Center, a site that Malvasi had bombed less than ten years before. The vigil began with a speech and procession from St. Agnes Church. O'Connor did not mention Malvasi by name but referenced "the mad bomber" in calling for non-violent protest. Several Baysiders were in attendance at this vigil and took pictures of the altar, presumably to see if any messages from heaven manifested in the film. In 2001, Malvasi and his wife, Loretta Mara, were arrested for conspiracy to aid and abet James Charles Kopp, a fugitive who had shot and killed Barnett Slepian, a physician who performed abortions.[44] The pair had allegedly been sending him money abroad and arranging for him to return to New York with a new identity.

Malvasi's relationship to the Baysider movement is complicated. On April 11, 1970—approximately one month before the first apparition at Bayside—the state of New York passed one of the most permissive abortion laws in the United States, leading to fears that the state would become an "abortion haven." Soon Lueken was delivering messages such as, "The Eternal Father commands that you stop these murders at once! You will not destroy the lives of the unborn. Human life is sacred in the eyes of your God. No man has the right to destroy a life."[45] When *Roe v. Wade* was decided in 1973, Lueken's followers saw it as the fulfillment of prophecy.[46] In covering Malvasi, *The New York Times* reported that Lueken had declared those who promote abortions "worthy of death."[47] However, this exact phrasing appears nowhere in Bayside Prophecies. Lueken frequently asserted that those who carry out abortions are murderers and will eventually be punished by God for their actions. However, this is quite different from an open call to violence.

Malvasi was not dangerous because he was a mindless drone obeying the rhetoric of conservative religious groups. On the contrary, he was dangerous because he interpreted and acted on the message of conservative Catholics in deviant and radical ways. In one sense, Malvasi was the consummate sectarian because he became almost entirely dedicated to an otherworldly ideal rather than worldly matters. In order to wage his war on abortion, he was willing to live on the lam almost completely outside of societal norms. Yet paradoxically, he turned himself in at the request of Cardinal O'Connor. While Malvasi's connection to the Baysider movement may have been marginal, his conflicted feelings toward authority were shared by many Baysiders. Malvasi longed for both a sense of radical participation in what he considered to be a spiritual battle against evil and to show deference to Catholic authorities. These desires were ultimately irreconcilable.

"The Rosary Ladies"

Malvasi's connections to the Baysider movement received little media attention. However, in 1995 a pair of Baysiders in Greensburg, Pennsylvania, produced a series of headlines that embarrassed Our Lady of the Roses Shrine. On April 13, Holy Thursday, two women were arrested by sheriff's deputies and escorted out of the Blessed Sacrament Cathedral for "praying too loudly" and disrupting the service.[48] Joan Sudwoj, forty-three, and Cynthia Balconi, sixty, were part of a Baysider group in western Pennsylvania, which organized buses to Queens and claimed 1,200 members. The women lived together and were former Carmelite nuns. Sudwoj was the daughter of concentration camp survivors. Fellow Baysiders described her as militant, recalling how she did most of the driving on a bus trip from Pennsylvania to New York. George Sprys, an organizer for the pilgrimage, described her as "high-strung and gung-ho. Like a marine."

The sectarian impulse entails a desire to return to the original values and worldview of a religious community. Significantly, the actions of Sudwoj and Balconi, whom the media eventually dubbed "the rosary ladies," frequently resembled the actions of Lueken herself during the Battle of Bayside. In 1993, the two women, along with one Cecelia Miscovich, attempted to spread the Bayside message in their home parish of Holy Cross Church in Youngwood, Pennsylvania. The trio took to saying the rosary so loudly during mass that it drowned out the priest and the choir. As during the Battle of Bayside, the sound of rosary prayers became a form of protest and a technology of power. According to some accounts, the women would not explain *why* they were praying so loudly.

There was some speculation that the loud praying was in response to parishioners staying in the church after mass to chat—a practice that they claimed would not have occurred before Vatican II. Another theory is that they were fulfilling an order given during one of Lueken's locutions in 1985 that the faithful should say three sets of rosaries twice a day. They also delivered warnings about the coming Chastisement. Bishop Anthony Bosco of the Diocese of Greensburg spoke with the trio for two hours, asking them to sign a statement pledging that they would not disrupt services with loud praying. Only Miscovich signed the pledge. Sudwoj and Balconi refused, claiming that this gesture would seem "unfaithful to Bayside."

When Sudwoj and Balconi refused to yield to the bishop, Our Lady of the Roses Shrine was alerted to the situation. Shrine officials consulted with Lueken and agreed that the rosary ladies should cease their disruptions. Shrine leaders were likely concerned that the pair threatened their already tenuous relationship with the Catholic hierarchy. Officials contacted Sudwoj and Balconi and asked them to obey Church authorities. James Donahue, then deputy director of Our Lady of the Roses Shrine, told reporters, "We told them to obey the pastor. We asked them to be obedient to the clergy." This censure from Our Lady of the Roses Shrine had little effect.

In February, the two moved their campaign to Blessed Sacrament Cathedral in Greensburg. The congregation tolerated their behavior at first, but the last straw came shortly before Holy Week when their shouting interfered with priests who were giving instruction to children preparing for their first communion. This incident was a sort of mimesis of the Battle of Bayside when Lueken's activities prevented priests from performing baptisms at St. Robert Bellarmine's. The rosary ladies were not only re-enacting Lueken's struggles, but the story of Bernadette Soubirous and, indeed, every Marian seer who had ever been persecuted by Church authorities for their piety.

Bishop Bosco obtained a court order barring the two women from entering the cathedral. Two days before the rosary ladies were arrested, Our Lady of the Roses Shrine made an effort to contact them and convince them to call off their campaign. Shrine director Michael Mangan attempted to reach the women by phone. When this failed, he wrote them a letter using the only leverage he had—threatening to take them off the shrine's mailing list. The irony is that Mangan likely felt the same sense of helplessness in trying to rein in the rosary ladies that Chancellor King felt when he attempted to control Lueken and her followers.

On Holy Thursday the women ignored the bishop, Mangan, and the court order and continued to say the rosary aloud during mass, insisting that they were following orders from heaven. The pastor summoned police, who escorted the women out. Undeterred, they knelt on the sidewalk in front of the church and recited the rosary even as passing motorists honked and shouted, "Shut up!"[49] They next day, Good Friday, the women returned to the cathedral. This time they were arrested and charged with criminal trespass and contempt of court. They embraced their role as martyrs and refused a lawyer, saying that Jesus would defend them. They also saw their arrest as the will of heaven and believed it provided important publicity for the Bayside Prophecies. However, in the ensuing weeks, the rosary ladies ceased their disruptive behavior and the charges were dropped. Shrine leaders in New York disavowed their actions, but local Baysider organizer George Sprys supported them, saying, "Joan and Cindy are just trying to lead people to atonement."[50]

The rosary ladies did indeed bring publicity to the Bayside Prophecies. The story made national news and inspired headlines such as "Pair's Prayers Piercing" and "Praying or Braying?" Bishop Bosco commented, "This has become a global story and, with some mixed emotions, I find that Greensburg is bigger than O. J. Simpson right now. They believe that since this is now international, you [the press] have done the work of Bayside for them."[51] Reporters swarmed the house where the two lived, but (again like Lueken) they refused to be interviewed. Sudwoj attempted to drown out the cries of belligerent journalists by turning on her lawnmower—a tactic that the BHCA had once used against Lueken during the Battle of Bayside. On May 24, Balconi left a note announcing that she was quitting her job as a computer operator at a local community college and the two left town. They moved to Youngstown, Ohio, where they were closer to other Baysiders. They also joined the Holy Rosary Chapel where a traditional Tridentine mass was still said.[52] The rosary ladies were never heard from again.

This episode presents an interesting twist on Stark and Finke's model of the sect-church process. Our Lady of the Roses Shrine actually played both roles simultaneously. Compared to the Mother Church, it acted as a sect and existed in a state of greater tension with mainstream culture. But compared to the rosary ladies, it acted as a church as it attempted to rein in more radical segments of its own movement. So instead of a clean break between a church and a sect, the Baysiders represent a segmented or stratified process in which several groups exist in different degrees of tension with society and yet remain chained together, unable to extricate themselves from each other.

One reason why the church-sect model does not neatly fit the Baysiders is that the ideal types of churches and sects were first employed in English-language scholarship to describe the formation of Protestant denominations. Catholics are just as diverse in their orientation to the sacred as Protestants, but unlike Protestants they are extremely reluctant to sever ties with the Mother Church. For Lueken, at least, this was unthinkable. For this reason, Catholics with an extremely fervent otherworldly worldview can never fully separate themselves from Catholic moderates. Malvasi's surrender at the behest of Cardinal O'Connor is perhaps the starkest example of this aspect of Catholicism. Malvasi could evade the FBI but not his sense of deference to the Catholic hierarchy. This inability to break away from the Mother Church gives rise to the paradox that defines Catholic traditionalism and explains the difficult position of the Baysiders, who simultaneously condemn Church authorities and seek reconciliation with them.

Apostate Baysiders

While Baysiders could not break away from Catholicism, they were free to break away from the Baysider movement. Some of these apostates were minimally invested to begin with or found the movement's views too extreme. Michael Cuneo met with a heating contractor named Dan Callegari, who claimed that Baysiders had advised his wife to divorce him. He told Cuneo, "I guess it was pretty obvious I wasn't really buying into their foolishness about Balls of Redemption and zombies and imposter popes and whatever, and so they insisted that my wife divorce me." Some of the movement's greatest critics were ardent Baysiders who became disillusioned with the movement. These individuals demonstrated the same zeal in attacking the Baysider movement that they had once used to promote it. Callegari formed a group of apostates who set out to investigate and debunk Lueken. The other members of this group included Ben Salomone and detective Hank Cinotti, both former bodyguards who had previously expressed their willingness to die for Lueken. The details of Cinotti's apostasy are unknown. Salomone was apparently banished from the movement in the late 1970s. He grew concerned that some aspects of Lueken's lifestyle seemed too worldly. He alleged that Lueken had been seen dining in restaurants, that her household owned three television sets and a subscription to the Playboy Channel, and that when he voiced these concerns he was told his entire family was condemned to hell. This cadre of former Baysiders also accused Lueken of malingering to establish her status as a victim soul. Because of her health problems, Lueken would sometimes arrive at vigils in a wheelchair. But Callegari claimed he had spotted Lueken at her home before a vigil and had seen her load the wheelchair into the trunk of her car unaided. They also accused her of putting on make-up before her vigils to make her look "white as a ghost." I spoke with a Baysider from California who expressed that he too was initially concerned when he heard stories that Lueken attended vigils in heavy makeup. However, he came to believe that her suffering as a victim soul had so ravaged her face that the makeup was necessary.

The charges of these apostates were essentially the same fraud narrative that had been raised by the BHCA decades before. Some apostates, however, insisted that Lueken really was performing miracles but that they were demonic in nature. Salomone came to believe that Lueken had been sent by Satan to exploit the spiritual vacuum that formed in the wake of Vatican II. In an interview, he advised Cuneo that by researching Lueken he was placing himself not only in spiritual danger, but physical danger as well.[53]

More than any other apostate, Anne Cillis became one of Lueken's greatest critics and repeatedly accused her of being a Satanic fraud. Like Salomone and Cinotti, she had once been an avid supporter and confidante. Cillis had long been interested in Marian apparitions. Her uncle, Frederick McGuinn, had been a priest and the first pastor in Canada to acquire a statue of Our Lady of Fatima for his parish. Cillis even named the oldest of her four daughters "Jacinta" after the Fatima seer. In 1971, she founded a magazine called *The Canadian Layman*. She also founded the Padre Pio Institute, a nonprofit organization headquartered in Ottawa and dedicated to studying the twentieth-century Italian stigmatic and saint, Padre Pio. In 1974, the Pilgrims of St. Michael began writing Cillis and urging her to investigate Bayside (in the hope she would confirm its authenticity). She and her family made their first visit to Bayside on a bus pilgrimage in 1975. Cillis was so impressed that she began organizing bus tours herself. In March 1977, she ran a special issue of *The Canadian Layman* about the Bayside apparitions. This happened to coincide almost exactly with the defection of the Pilgrims of Saint Michael in early 1977 over the beret fiasco. At the end of that year, *The Canadian Layman* passed into other hands and Cillis began a new magazine, *Sancta Maria*. Although *Sancta Maria* was created primarily to cover news relevant to the Fatima apparitions, Cillis became inundated with mail requesting more coverage of Bayside. Before long, Cillis's writings had replaced the Pilgrims of Saint Michael publication *Vers Demain* as Bayside's primary media outlet.[54] It was also Cillis who engaged Chancellor King in a surprise interview about his investigation of Lueken, the results of which greatly emboldened the Baysiders' claim that the diocese's position was null and void.

Cillis became a close confidante of Lueken and was given her private telephone number. Lueken would sometimes call Cillis in the middle of the night, talking for hours. Cillis would frequently drive to vigils at Flushing Meadows and stay at the Johnson Motel on the Long Island Expressway before returning to Ottawa. Lueken would often arrive at her hotel room unannounced to visit. However, Cillis became increasingly disillusioned when given the chance to observe Lueken more closely, finding her behavior erratic and obnoxious. Lueken's late night phone calls began to strain their friendship. According to Cillis, when one of her daughters answered one of these calls and refused to wake her mother. Lueken responded, "You don't understand. This is VERONICA! You just go and get your mother."[55]

Like Salomone, Cillis also became disillusioned by Lueken's apparent material prosperity. Lueken had repeatedly warned that televisions were a tool of Satan and that her followers should not have them in their homes. Cillis took this order seriously and did not own a television. The Lueken household, however, had several. Lueken allegedly suggested that Cillis purchase a tiny television and store it in her closet, watching it only when her daughters were not around. Cillis found this suggestion hypocritical and repugnant.[56]

Also like Salomone, Cillis came to reinterpret the miracles associated with Lueken, seeing them as "occultism." She was particularly bothered by Lueken's apparent contact with the dead. Lueken did, of course, sometimes claim to see spirits of the dead during her visions, notably her son Raymond ascending to heaven. But as an apostate, Cillis claimed that Lueken regularly functioned as a medium. She describes one episode she found especially disturbing:

> She called me at 3:00 a.m. and told me Our Lady had told her to do this. She spoke for a few minutes on trivial matters and then her voice abruptly changed altogether and became the voice of a dear

friend of mine who had died some months previously. She did not know my friend—and had never heard her voice—and yet the imitation was so perfect. I was chilled by it. She said it was the "spirit" of my friend, speaking through her. I didn't know enough about Spiritualist mediums then to realize what had happened. I only know that I was frightened and very disturbed by this.[57]

By 1982, Cillis had broken her ties with Bayside but remained heavily involved in the traditionalist Catholic movement. She now became an implacable critic of Lueken and her followers. The articles she had written that spoke favorably of Bayside had been incorporated into *The Blue Book*, then published by The Apostles of Our Lady in Lansing, Michigan. In June, Cillis wrote the publishers declaring that this material was copyrighted and must not be included in any future edition of *The Blue Book*.

Cillis also became an asset for media outlets seeking to do sensational coverage of the Baysiders. In 1985, *The National Enquirer* consulted Cillis for a piece on Tony Bronson, son of action star Charles Bronson, who had taken up residence as a full-time shrine worker.[58] The story featured a picture of a man—presumably Tony—wearing a white beret and sunglasses and holding a rosary. It described how Tony had dropped out of graduate school and was now living in communal housing and mailing out Baysider literature. "Tony is ruining his life," Charles said. "He doesn't do anything but work for that woman for nothing, and talks about her and her visions every minute that he's awake. ... It's as if he's been brainwashed."[59] Lueken's daughter Linda Doherty was interviewed for this piece as well and expressed her annoyance with her mother. "Tony Bronson is just one of thousands who have been sucked in by my mother," she told *The Enquirer*.[60]

In 1986, *Sancta Maria* ran an entire issue entitled "Bayside Backstage," claiming to reveal the hypocrisy of Lueken and her movement. "Bayside Backstage" printed a photograph of Lueken's house in Long Island complete with her address. A caption pointed out that she drove a Chrysler New Yorker and appeared to have a large TV aerial for her numerous television sets. A blurb in the issue asked, "Have YOU or someone you know, had an unfortunate experience concerning Bayside? We want to hear about it. Please write us the details."[61]

The accounts of Callegari, Salomone, and Cillis are indeed lurid, but we should regard this data with caution. Apostates are, by definition, critical of their former religious community. Since the 1970s, apostates have been a key resource through which American media have confirmed a ready-made narrative about marginalized religious groups.[62] Tellingly, the accusations of these apostates only confirmed narratives that were first created about Lueken during the Battle of Bayside, namely that Lueken must be a charlatan, mentally ill, or some combination thereof.

It is significant that the most vocal apostates did not leave because they felt Lueken had become too rigid and zealous. Rather, they felt she had compromised the messages of heaven by owning a television and indulging in other material comforts. The feelings of disillusionment expressed by Salomone and Cillis can be read as another manifestation of the sect-church process. These individuals have experienced a kind of double apostasy finding themselves alienated first from mainstream Catholicism and then from the Baysiders. Catholic traditionalists are sometimes accused of trying to be "more Catholic than the pope." By the same token, apostates like Cillis could be characterized as trying to be "more Baysider than Veronica Lueken."

New Seers

The sect-church process describes a pattern in which religious groups fracture based on different levels of commitment to an otherworldly ideal. This dynamic is at stake in the Baysider movement, but its effects are countered by a Catholic aversion to schism. In the case of apparitional movements there is also a second process at play. Unlike most Christian groups, apparitional movements claim direct access to new revelation. These movements may focus around a single seer, as at Lourdes, Necedah, and Bayside, or a small group of seers, as at Fatima and Garabandal. But these seers do not have a monopoly on revelation. In fact, almost everyone present at an apparition site typically experiences some form of supernatural revelation. Almost all of the Baysiders I spoke with had seen a minor vision, experienced their rosary glow, pulse, or turn to gold, or had at least taken a miraculous Polaroid. Historian Paolo Apolito describes a distinction between "strong" visionaries who define the apparition and "weak" ones whose supernatural experiences seem to follow their lead. He explains, "The physical presence of the strong visionary allows for an epidemiology of weak visionaries, that is, more attenuated forms of contact with heaven, which extends potentially to all worshippers."[63] This "contagious" quality of apparitions provides a powerful form of agency that, for many people, is the appeal of apparitional movements. However, it also creates an inherent instability because there is always the possibility of new and contradictory revelations.

One of Lueken's messages states, "The Eternal Father has a plan, and everyone who comes to the sacred grounds has been called there by the Father."[64] At Flushing Meadows, several people told me that everyone who finds their way to the apparition site was called there by God for a reason. I heard multiple stories from women who said they had first learned about the Baysider movement through a piece of trash they had serendipitously found on the ground. One woman described how she had found only a fragment of a Bayside flyer. The address was missing and she had no clue where the vigil grounds were. She prayed to Mary for weeks before she finally found a complete flyer. Many come to Flushing Meadows because they are desirous of profound mystical experiences similar to the ones Lueken had.[65] For some, this sense of propinquity with the divine is fulfilled through fairly minor supernatural experiences. There have also been several instances of collective visions at Flushing Meadows in which many people claim to have seen supernatural wonders such as the sun spinning. On the night of December 30, 1995, 150 vigil attendees reported seeing nearly a thousand "luminous birds" or doves that circled the grounds several times and appeared to be made out of light.[66]

However, some people have especially profound mystical experiences rivaling those of Lueken herself. One such woman is Antonia Rehrl, a long-time volunteer for SMWA, who experienced a prolonged mystical experience that culminated with a vision in which the sun was transformed into an enormous communion host in the sky over Flushing Meadows. The host then descended upon her rapidly in a manner similar to the miracle at Fatima before returning to its normal position in the sky. Other visitors to the park saw nothing. SMWA has supported Rehrl's vision and she has repeatedly been interviewed about it at the group's annual banquet.[67]

Other visions are less amenable to maintaining the status quo of an established movement. I spoke with a woman from Guatemala who had been coming to Flushing Meadows since the 1980s. She described a dream she had in February of 1995 in which she saw a vision of Jesus. For nearly five minutes she described to me in vivid detail how she had seen the full and gruesome extent of Jesus's wounds. In addition to the traditional five wounds of Christ, nearly all of his skin had been cut and mangled. She could see exposed nerves and ligaments all over his body. From this experience, she came to believe that she had been called to share her vision with the world so that they could know the truth about Christ's suffering. She explained that she had spoken with a seer who had agreed to make a life-size painting of Jesus as he appeared in her dream. She had also procured a large enough piece of canvas and had it blessed by a priest. She believed that the world will see her painting and know the truth before a comet strikes the Earth as described in the Bayside Prophecies. Unlike Rehr's vision, which merely affirms the significance of Flushing Meadows as a holy site, this woman's painting of Christ steers the Bayside Prophecies in a slightly different direction and inserts a new element into the prophetic scheme. Apolito explains that, "The strong seer was able to reshape entirely the real, the usual in its everyday clarity; the weak seer, in contrast, could only work in the shadows."[68] But by networking with other seers and priests to talk about her dream, this woman had begun to transition from a weak seer into a strong one.

This phenomenon is not unique to the Baysiders. Within apparitional culture, individuals who visit one apparition site as pilgrims may go on to create a new apparition site as seers. The apparition site of Medjugorje, located in a tiny mountain village in Bosnia-Herzegovina, epitomizes the state of apparitions in a globalized age. Medjugorje has drawn pilgrims from all over the world who then carry the seed of revelation back to their own countries. Several seers throughout the United States can be traced back to this site. Linda Santo of Worchester, Massachusetts, brought her daughter Audrey to Medjugorje after a pool accident had left her in a coma-like state. After their return to Worchester, numerous supernatural phenomena were attributed to the unconscious girl. Audrey would remain in a vegetative state until her death in 2007, but many Catholics regarded her as a victim soul like Lueken and a community formed around her.[69] In February 1988, three charismatic Catholics returned from Medjugorje to Lubbock, Texas, and began having regular meetings during which they would receive locutions. Pope John Paul II had declared 1988 a Marian year and by August the trio had gathered some fifteen thousand followers outside their Lubbock church. Many in attendance reported seeing the sun spin in the sky. Nancy Fowler of Conyers, Georgia, also began having mystical experiences following a pilgrimage to Medjugorje. She eventually became a seer as famous as Lueken. The remote mountain village has not only spawned daughter sites but granddaughter sites. Fowler's apparition in Conyers inspired Rosa Lopes of Florida and Catalina Rivas of Bolivia to become seers as well.[70] The Medjugorje phenomenon reflects the international web that has come to characterize modern apparitional culture.

The same process happened with the Bayside apparitions. Letters from Baysiders to the Diocese of Brooklyn indicated that people around the country were experiencing visions which they felt were related to Lueken and the Bayside Prophecies.[71] Like the rosary ladies, these seers represented a radical element that neither the Church hierarchy nor Our Lady of the Roses Shrine had any ability to control. Occasionally these seers could become a serious liability to the movement they emerged from. In the 1980s, a former Baysider named William Kamm created his own apparitional movement in Australia and called himself "The Little Pebble." Kamm's activities produced fodder for critics who sought to construct a narrative of phony apparitions promoted by unscrupulous charlatans.

A former bank employee, Kamm made his first trip to Bayside in 1980 and returned again the following year. An article on Kamm in the *Sydney Morning Herald* interviewed Anne Cillis, who was no doubt eager to indict both Kamm and Lueken as false seers. Cillis described visiting the apartments owned by Our Lady of the Roses Shrine where she and her four daughters volunteered to help stuff envelopes. At that time, Kamm was living in the apartment as a shrine worker. Cillis accused Kamm of using this arrangement as an opportunity to sexually harass female volunteers, including her daughters. Lueken herself called Frank Albas, the current shrine director, and asked him to convince Kamm to leave, citing numerous complaints from female shrine workers. Albas was reluctant to confront Kamm and so Lueken asked Cillis to support him. When asked to leave, Kamm allegedly remarked, "Well, I guess it's time Australia got its own seer."[72]

A year later, Kamm had returned to Australia and reinvented himself as "The Little Pebble." He founded an organization called Marian Work of Atonement. Cillis remarked, "See, he'd been at Bayside and watched the money rolling in in bags. He'd learned the ropes of how to operate a bogus seer operation." Kamm's ministry focused on many of the same issues as the Baysiders. He condemned receiving communion in the hand and other liturgical innovations. He encouraged women to wear head coverings, and all men to wear clerical dress. He also offered similar warnings of nuclear war and other disasters and claimed Freemasons had infiltrated the Church hierarchy. He even reproduced the Jacinta 72 image in his organization's literature and explained that this photograph held the key to determining the date of the coming Chastisement.[73]

Kamm's emergence in Australia as The Little Pebble followed the same pattern as Lueken's movement in the early 1970s. In 1982, William

Murray, the Bishop of Wollongong, urged Catholics to avoid his mission, saying that Kamm had no connection whatsoever to the Catholic Church. Despite the ire of local Church authorities, his movement attracted crowds of up to one thousand. In 1984, he began constructing a community near Cambewarra featuring a brick chapel, a school, and a reservoir. Families from Japan and elsewhere gave up their savings and moved to Australia to live in a planned community. By 1991, Kamm claimed to have an international readership of over two million.[74]

Kamm also mimicked the Baysider strategy of traveling abroad to find Church authorities and charismatic leaders who would validate him. He was apparently unique among Marian seers in that he sought out other seers from around the globe. From 1988 to 1989, The Little Pebble travelled throughout the world and finally succeeded in finding Catholic clergy who would recognize his mission. These were primarily priests from such places as Uganda, Kenya, and southern India.[75]

While Lueken had defied her diocese, Baysiders have always distinguished themselves from sedevacantists by professing their loyalty to papal authority. Kamm, however, did not engage in the Baysiders' dance of deference and defiance. In 1987, he prophesied that he would become the next pope. The following year, Kamm convinced an eighty-three-year-old American missionary priest to proclaim him pope. This caused a Japanese bishop to publicly rebuke not only Kamm, but the priest who endorsed him. Kamm was also accused of using his position as a visionary to initiate sexual relationships with his female followers and maintaining simultaneous marriages with a number of women. At the time of this writing, he is serving multiple consecutive prison sentences in Australia for sex crimes.[76]

Our Lady of the Roses Shrine likely kept track of Kamm's activities. In 1985, Lueken gave a prophecy of a "coming tribulation in Australia," explaining, "There will be many deaths, My children. That is why We do hope that the world will recognize two seers in Australia. The one who has presently come forth must be placed aside. There are two legitimate seers which shall come forward in Australia."[77] The "seer who must be placed aside" is presumably Kamm.

If Kamm's activities were an embarrassment to the Baysiders, they were no doubt horrifying to Church authorities. In an age where anyone could claim to see the Virgin Mary and travel the world in a jet seeking followers, what was to stop an army of William Kamms from springing forth and wreaking havoc on the authority of the magisterium? Kamm's activities in the early 1980s may well have influenced Bishop Mugavero in issuing his formal declaration against Lueken in 1986, which was sent throughout the world.

At a vigil held by OLR, the vigil leader complained to me that people in Florida and Michigan had the audacity to create websites promoting Lueken's messages, even though they were located nowhere near Flushing Meadows. At first, I did not understand why this was objectionable if these groups were not altering Lueken's messages.

"So space matters?" I asked.
"Truth matters!" she retorted.

This exchange seemed to encapsulate the problems of authority inherent in a movement like the Baysiders. What was at stake was ultimately neither space, nor truth, but power. Or rather, whoever controlled the movement's sacred site claimed the power to determine what the truth of Bayside is. But while OLR's access to Flushing Meadows does provide them with a form of epistemological authority, it is not an exclusive authority. Anyone with a website may claim to represent the Bayside Prophecies. Much like the Catholic polity as a whole, the boundaries of the Baysider community are both imagined and contested. And the larger the community becomes, the less ability the forces at the center have to determine where these boundaries are drawn. It was perhaps inevitable, then, that Lueken's death in 1995 would result in a schism between rival factions of Baysiders.

6

After Veronica

VERONICA LUEKEN EXPERIENCED chronically poor health throughout her career as a seer. Her followers, in keeping with their understanding of Lueken as a victim soul, tallied the full extent of her pain and suffering. They reported that she suffered from ongoing cancer in her spine as well as spinal arthritis and chronic kidney infections that often left her bedridden or confined to a wheelchair. A massive heart attack in 1978 permanently impaired the function of her heart. Afterward, she would often have to be administered oxygen. This was followed by a gangrenous gallbladder, gall stones, angina pectoris affecting the tissue around her heart, and tinnitus. Near the end of her life, she lost more than fifty pounds and her right kidney was removed.

For Baysiders, Lueken's final months are remembered as a kind of passion narrative. Every affliction was evidence of her holiness and the righteousness of the Baysider mission. A particularly significant story concerns Michael Mangan and James Donahue, two long-time shrine workers who visited Lueken in the hospital on May 29, Memorial Day, 1995. They asked her, "Veronica has Our Lady come to you?" She answered that she had. They asked what Our Lady had said. Veronica, in great pain, responded, "You will be ... " But her visitors could not make out the final word. "You will be studied?," asked Mangan. Lueken repeated herself but the final word was still indistinguishable. Mangan tried again, "You will be saved?" Finally, Lueken lifted her head and stated, "You WILL BE SCOURGED."[1] The visitors interpreted this to mean that Lueken's final months on Earth were to involve heavy suffering for the sins of the world and especially for the benefit of priests.

On August 3, 1995, Lueken died of congestive heart failure. Dates are always significant within the Baysider theology of history and correspondences were soon discovered between the timing of Lueken's death and that of other significant figures. Some claimed that Lueken had died—down to the minute—on the anniversary of Robert Kennedy's death. Others found significance in the fact that she lived to be seventy-two. Thomas Aquinas speculated that this was the approximate age when Mary herself quit her mortal life and was assumed into heaven.

Father Robert Skurla, who had risked his career to advocate the Bayside messages, presided over her wake. Over four hundred Baysiders attended the funeral service. The Lay Order of Saint Michael in their white berets served as pallbearers. In keeping with the movement's media culture, the funeral was videotaped. Lueken was buried in Mount St. Mary's cemetery in Flushing, Queens, and her grave is a common pilgrimage site for Baysiders. Once a year, SMWA brings a statue of Mary to her gravesite to say rosaries and sing hymns. Shrine workers began preparing her for beatification by dubbing her "Veronica of the Cross," a title that Lueken had first mentioned in a locution given in 1980.[2]

In Flushing Meadows, I was able to purchase a photograph called "Veronica in Repose." It portrays the seer of Bayside in her coffin, her hair covered by a veil. A large rosary rests on her chest and a folded American flag supports her head. Her face appears peaceful but also very wan. The image is the total opposite of pictures taken during vigils, where she appears heavyset and in a state of religious ecstasy. On the back of the photograph is the message "Veronica of the Cross, pray for us."

When I travelled to Lueken's gravesite, I entered the cemetery office and asked for help finding a grave. A woman with a distinct Queens accent asked me, "What is the last name of the deceased." When I said "Lueken," she answered, "Oh, Veronica?"

"You've probably had other people visiting this grave," I said.
She pursed her lips and answered sarcastically, "Oh, one or two."

A rose granite tombstone carved with the Virgin Mary marks the final resting place of Veronica, Arthur, and their son Raymond. Although the grave was unremarkable, an inordinate amount of flowers and wreaths were heaped upon it.

Lueken had been the heart and soul of the Baysider movement. Four months after her death, shrine donations dropped by fifty percent and attendance at the vigils began to decline. One Baysider explained, "It's just not the same without Veronica. Veronica's the reason we've all been coming. I can't tell you how much I miss her."[3] Without a living seer, the movement's sacred space took on even greater significance. So too did the body of Lueken's messages, which was now a closed canon.

The authority derived from Lueken's charisma now passed on to those who had been close to her. In Weberian terms, this was the formation of the charisma of office.[4] The death of a prophet often leads to a crisis of succession. Muhammad's death set the stage for the eventual split between Sunni and Shia Islam, and the murder of Joseph Smith led to a crisis of succession for the Latter-Day Saint movement. Among the Baysiders, many of Lueken's companionable spirits were now in a position to lay claim to the movement's leadership and assets. The candidates included Ann Ferguson, Lueken's longtime friend and secretary; Arthur Lueken, her widower and the nominal president of Our Lady of the Roses Shrine; and Michael Mangan, the shrine director who had taken over much of the daily operations of the movement. Within three years of Lueken's death, rivalries between these individuals split Our Lady of the Roses Shrine into rival factions who vied for material assets as well as symbolic capital.

After Lueken's death, Michael Mangan quickly emerged as the movement's new leader. While Arthur Lueken was the organization's president, it was Mangan who made most of the decisions. In his bid for authority, Mangan had several advantages over his rivals. Ronald Brown, who observed the Baysiders in New York both before and after Lueken's death, has suggested that Mangan's access to the shrine's mailing list was his greatest asset. This allowed him to communicate with Baysiders around the world, a distinct advantage.[5] Mangan was also a generation younger than Arthur Lueken, who was seventy-one when his wife died. Mr. Lueken did not have the energy to appear at vigils or to run a vigorous campaign against his rival. Another advantage was that Mangan had been drawn to the shrine as a teenager and worked for almost two decades as a full-time shrine worker. He had no career or obligations outside of the movement and knew its inner workings intimately. Finally, other than Arthur Lueken, all of Mangan's rivals were women. Despite the fact that the Baysider movement is centered on a female seer and receives the majority of its donations from women, it remains patriarchal in its view of authority. Many of Lueken's messages affirm that women may never be priests, must remain silent in church, and must be submissive to their husbands. In 1972, her messages condemned the proposed Equal Rights Amendment, claiming that equal rights for women was a rebellion against the divine order.[6] This notion of gender roles has been an obstacle for Ann Ferguson and other female Baysiders who have made bids for leadership.

Mangan came from a large Catholic family in Boston. Despite a strict Catholic upbringing, he underwent a period of worldliness in his mid-teens that he later described as "leading a very sinful life." In December 1976, at the age of seventeen, he learned about Veronica Lueken through a relative who had been attending vigils. Simply hearing about Lueken and her visions effected a change in Mangan's life. He began saying the rosary and receiving the sacraments again and reading through the Bayside Prophecies. After high school, he enrolled in the Culinary Institute of New York in Hyde Park. From there he was able to a take a train into New York to attend vigils in Flushing Meadows. He soon felt the call of a religious vocation and in the summer of 1978, he visited the Society of St. Pius X seminary in Armada, Michigan.

The Society of St. Pius X (SSPX) was founded by traditionalist bishop Marcel Lefebvre, who believed that Vatican II had been infiltrated by Freemasons. Lefebvre was placed under a series of suspensions and eventually excommunicated for ordaining bishops without proper authorization. Mangan's brief involvement with SSPX is another manifestation of the divided loyalties that many traditional Catholics experience. On the one hand, the seminary faculty loved Catholic tradition and rejected the reforms of Vatican II. On the other hand, they expressed contempt for Pope Paul VI. That proved to be intolerable for Mangan. In an interview with Michael Cuneo he recalled:

> The rector was also ridiculing Pope Paul VI, and I knew from Bayside that Pope Paul wasn't to blame for all the problems that had befallen the Church. ... I also knew from the Bayside messages that the new Mass was valid and that we were supposed to stay in our parish churches, not separate and start our own little churches. Needless to say, I didn't stick around for long.[7]

Baysiders pride themselves on being "traditional but not traditionalist." The shrine workers at SMWA were particularly eager to distinguish themselves from schismatic groups like SSPX. When I met with Mangan, he seemed embarrassed when I brought up his summer in Armada.

In October 1978, Mangan was invited to join the Lay Order of Saint Michael and became a full-time worker for Our Lady of the Roses Shrine. He was only nineteen. Mangan showed promise and by 1979 he was travelling across the country to organize groups of Baysiders in places like Spokane, Washington. In the 1980s, Lueken dismissed Frank Albas, the rector of the Lay Order of Saint Michael. Albas relocated to Miami, Florida, claiming that he had been ousted in a coup led by Arthur Lueken and Mangan.[8] In 1989 Mangan replaced Albas as rector.

Mangan became very close to Lueken in a relationship that lasted nearly two decades. Lueken would reportedly call Mangan whenever she received new revelations, which was often late at night. This is entirely plausible considering her relationship with her previous confidante, Anne Cillis. It is even possible that Mangan, who joined the shrine as a teenager, reminded Lueken of her son Raymond. Today, SMWA's website hosts the text of the Bayside Prophecies as well as a smaller set of messages called "locutions/home visitations." These are mostly short messages described by Lueken to Mangan over the telephone between 1990 and 1994. Having this kind of access gave Mangan a strong claim to become Lueken's successor. As conflicts developed over control of shrine resources, these "home visitations" became the focus of a power struggle.

The Great Schism of 1997

In the months following Lueken's death, Arthur Lueken and Ann Ferguson became worried that Mangan was usurping Arthur's authority as shrine president. The most obvious source of tension was the question of who would have control over the shrine's substantial assets. However, a failed prophecy became the issue that catalyzed a schism. In late 1996, Mangan sent out an issue of the Shrine's newsletter *Rose Notes* relating a prophecy that a supernatural event called "The Warning" would occur in 1997. The idea of a "world-wide warning" that would shock mankind away from its sins before the Chastisement first entered Marian discourse through the apparitions at Garabandal, which occurred from 1961 to 1965. Many Baysiders believe that the two great chastisements predicted in the Bayside Prophecies—World War III and a comet—will be preceded by a supernatural warning. The claim that The Warning would occur in 1997 was based on a message given privately to Mangan by Lueken before her death on February 5, 1994.[9] By disseminating the message, Mangan was signaling that he had special access to Lueken and her prophecies that others did not.

After the issue of *Rose Notes* went out, Arthur Lueken and Ann Ferguson quickly began raising concerns that Mangan had tied the Bayside Prophecies to a specific date, thus setting the shrine up for embarrassment if this time-line went unfulfilled. Ferguson claimed that Veronica had always shared private revelations with her and was suspicious that she would have been left out of the loop. On January 8, 1997, Ferguson disseminated a letter cit-ing four passages from the Bayside Prophecies emphasizing that no dates would be given as to when the divine plan will occur. The letter, however, makes no specific mention of Mangan or the prediction of a warning in 1997.[10] Frank Albas's website features a letter, allegedly written by Arthur Lueken on February 10 to Gary Wohlsheid, an influential Baysider in Lowell, Michigan, who founded the independent group These Last Days Ministries in 1996. Lueken wrote, "Gary, between you and me and the light post; someone, not me, is full of 'monkey dust', and also I might be a 'doubting Thomas', [but] I just don't believe that there will be a Warning this year. What will happen to the Shrine then? – Lord help us!"[11]

By October, Arthur decided there was little enough chance of a world-changing supernatural event occurring in 1997 and decided to make his move. The attorney for Our Lady of the Roses Shrine asked Mangan to step down as shrine director. Mangan was accused of taking the shrine's vans and computers as well as $130,000 of the shrine's money, which was allegedly spent to secure the support of the police and parks departments. Further, he was accused of usurping Arthur's authority by referring to himself as president of the shrine organization in a general mailing. But the accusation that was likely most important to Baysiders was that Mangan had altered or invented some of Lueken's messages. The most damning evidence of this was that the Warning seemed unlikely to occur in 1997 as predicted.[12]

On November 29, 1997, Arthur's supporters distributed a letter to Baysiders that specifically attacked Mangan on the issue of the Warning of 1997. This letter alleged that any "private" locutions discussed by Mangan were null and void and that Mangan had published this locution in *Rose Notes* without authorization from the shrine's board of directors. It then claimed there were no fewer than seventy-five passages in the Bayside Prophecies asserting that no dates were to be given. Meanwhile, Frank Albas, whom Mangan had replaced as shrine director, gleefully weighed in through a newsletter he published from Miami. Albas accused Mangan of having a "fertile imagination"—the two most stinging words that can ever be applied to a Baysider.[13]

When I visited Flushing Meadows, Mangan said that he doubted Arthur Lueken had ever believed in his wife's visions. Arthur's grandson,

Jeremy, expressed similar suspicions during an interview. Shrine workers alleged that he had been spotted receiving communion in the hand—one of the gravest transgressions possible for Baysiders.[14] As both sides lobbied for supporters, Arthur and Mangan went to court. On December 24, 1997, a judge ruled in favor of Arthur Lueken, awarding him all of the organization's assets and facilities as well as the name "Our Lady of the Roses Shrine." The news was immediately announced to some three hundred Baysiders attending a Christmas Eve vigil at Flushing Meadows Park where it elicited "weeping and lamentations" from Mangan's followers.[15]

Mangan may have lost his date in court but he still had more knowledge of the organization's inner workings as well as strong relationships with many of the movement's followers. With the help of James Donahue and some of the other full-time shrine workers, he quickly started his own group, St. Michael's World Apostolate (SMWA). One of their first orders of business was to fend off attacks over the failed prophecy of 1997. In April of 1998, SMWA produced a document explaining that all of the Bayside Prophecies are conditional and can be delayed or even averted through prayer. The issue of *Rose Notes* describing The Warning of 1997 had been sent all over the world and they claimed that the prayers it had inspired were so powerful that Heaven had chosen to set back its apocalyptic clock.

This conditional view of prophecy had previously been established by Lueken herself and is common among Marian prophecies. Scholars have noted that where Protestant dispensationalism is often fatalistic, popular Catholic apocalyptic discourse emphasizes an ongoing and personal relationship between heavenly personages and the faithful on Earth.[16] On several occasions, Lueken delivered messages that the Earth had been granted "a reprieve" because of the piety demonstrated during vigils. Chancellor Anthony Bevilacqua also noticed the conditional nature of Lueken's prophecies and remarked, "She is constantly talking about this horror that is going to happen—this ball of fire. It has never happened. Then she keeps postponing it and postponing it. Then she claims, well, 'we prayed.' And it is so frightening to people."[17]

Just as Arthur Lueken and Ann Ferguson had cited passages stating that no dates would be given, SMWA's letter cited passages that *did* give specific dates and time tables. SMWA even found passages where Heaven appeared to have completely reversed its decision. For instance, in 1988 it was declared that no cure would ever be found for AIDS. But in 1990, it was declared that a cure would be found.[18] By the time of her death, Lueken had produced over three hundred messages from heaven. Complete printed copies of the Bayside Prophecies filled six volumes. There was no shortage of ammunition for either side of the argument.

In many ways the debate over the Warning of 1997 resembled the "beret fiasco" of 1977 that had split Lueken's movement from the Canadian group, The Pilgrims of Saint Michael. A dispute over the color of the berets was the official reason for the split but the underlying issues had to do with power and authority. Similarly, the Baysiders were accustomed to having prophecies of imminent warnings and chastisements and most were not likely to leave the movement over one missed deadline. I spoke with a Baysider from the state of Washington who acknowledged that some of Lueken's prophecies had never been fulfilled. A locution delivered in 1983 announced that there would be "a devastating plague within six months." The Baysider conceded that this had simply never happened but that this did not deter his faith in Bayside or the mission to restore the Church.[19]

The Warning of 1997 became the public arena in which a power struggle between Mangan and his critics played out. Most Baysiders were spread throughout the world and likely unconcerned with the politics of the shrine organization in New York. Prophecy, however, was important. To discredit Mangan, Lueken and Ferguson sought to challenge his unique access to Lueken and portray him as a poor steward of Lueken's messages.

In December 1998, SMWA published the first issue of their own newsletter, *Golden Warrior*. This shored up Mangan's bid as Lueken's successor with an article entitled "Jesus and Mary Chose Michael Mangan." The article emphasized Mangan's close relationship with Lueken, describing how the two would speak daily on the telephone, often for hours at a time. It also cited a series of incidents that confirmed that Mangan had been chosen not only by Lueken but by heaven as well. On January 10, 1994, Lueken allegedly asked Mangan to promise three times that he would continue the work after she died. On February 7, 1994, Lueken stated in a taped interview that Mangan would be "the head of the Order of St. Michael." Finally, the article describes an event on June 19, 1995, in which Mangan and Regina Fox, a pilgrimage coordinator, visited Lueken at her home. By this time Lueken was quite ill and announced that she was going to die. She extended her hands and asked Mangan to hold on to her fingertips. Mangan did this several times after which Lueken placed her hands on his face, kissed his forehead, and told him to "pray for Artie." While the meaning of this encounter is ambiguous, the article stated, "With Heaven nothing is by accident, but by design. Through this profound gesture witnessed by Regina and Arthur, the scepter was 'handed' over to Michael by Veronica shortly before her death, fulfilling God's Will."[20] In the end, Mangan succeeded in winning over the majority of remaining Baysiders to his cause. His success was as much a result of his management and organizational skills as his claim to Lueken's charisma. At one of SMWA's vigils, I asked a long-time Baysider why he chose to follow Mangan after the schism. He answered, "Lueken named Mangan. It's on tape. That's all I need to hear."[21]

With both sides entrenched, a battle quickly formed over the move-ment's resources. These included the physical and financial assets of the Shrine. But even more important were sources of symbolic capital. The greatest of these was access to the vigil grounds at Flushing Meadows. The sacred site remained the ultimate technology of power. Here, Mangan had the upper hand. As shrine director, he had experience working closely with police and park officials to obtain the necessary permits to hold vig-ils in the park. Frank Albas, commenting on the situation from Florida, remarked that winning a court case was nothing compared to controlling the vigil site. He wrote, "Arthur Lueken continues to fiddle while Michael remains in control of the Vigil Grounds—a disastrous position to take, as Michael maintains a power base to continue his control over the Bayside believers."[22]

On June 10, 1998, Arthur Lueken's group began holding their first vigils since the schism. The group still displays banners during vigils that read, "Welcome to the official and original shrine of Our Lady of the Roses, Mary Help of Mothers." Because Mangan already had the permits to be present at the Vatican Pavilion monument, Arthur's group was ini-tially displaced to other parts of the park. As Lueken and Ferguson were both aging, they asked the younger Vivian Hanratty to lead their vigils. With her twin sister, Yvonne, Hanratty had done video editing for a cable access show about Bayside prior to the schism.[23]

On June 18, 1998, the twenty-eighth anniversary of the first apparition at Bayside, both factions attempted to hold vigils at the same time. Police were out in force to keep the peace just as they had been in Bayside Hills. According to some accounts, Mangan asked police to remove the other faction, but they remained neutral.[24] A New York Times reporter described accusations and insults, but no physical violence. Arthur Lueken's faction produced another important source of symbolic capital: They had the ori-ginal fiberglass statue that Lueken had purchased in 1974 to bring to vigils at St. Robert Bellarmine's. A journalist described the statue as "the secret weapon" of Arthur Lueken's faction. It was kept in a van and guarded by "beefy young men." A guard explained, "We are afraid St. Michael's will steal her."[25] Perhaps to make up for this "statue gap," SMWA's statue is adorned with an oversized rosary, which they explain was blessed by Mary and Jesus during one of Lueken's locutions. Adoring this rosary has become part of their vigil liturgy. At the end of each vigil, pilgrims are invited to kiss the crucifix on this rosary. A shrine guard attends with a cloth to clean the rosary after each kiss.

The apparition's twenty-eighth anniversary also marked a shift of physical resources. Lueken's group decided they could no longer maintain the shrine's workshops and printing apparatus. On June 18th the printing equipment was sold at auction. One of Mangan's shrine workers noticed the ad and arranged to buy the equipment for $25,000. A couple was willing to grant SMWA a cash loan to facilitate the purchase. SMWA boasted of this transaction in *Golden Warrior*, "God works in mysterious ways!"[26]

Not long after this, SMWA acquired a complex in College Point that became their new workshop. It was a five-thousand-square-foot plot with a large three-story, ten-room, brick and wood-framed stucco house built in 1927. Attached was a 2,200-square-foot factory where the mission could store their printing equipment. The site had been a bakery with an attached stable until World War II when it used to manufacture aviation parts. What particularly delighted SMWA was the date in which the city approved the attached factory—June 18, 1930. The correspondence of this date with the date of the first apparition at Bayside was taken as a sign that heaven intended this location as their new home.[27]

By the end of 1998, the parks department brokered a deal in which the two groups would have alternate access to the Vatican Pavilion monument for every vigil and Sunday holy hour.[28] The arrangement was not unlike a divorced couple scheduling child custody with a judge. Each week the displaced group would hold vigils on a traffic island adjacent to the monument where they would set up their own statue of Mary. This tactic clearly has its precedent in the Battle of Bayside when "the lawns" became a refuge for pilgrims who had been displaced from their sacred site. This situation in which each group alternates from occupying the monument and the traffic island has continued every week for over a decade.

While Baysiders disagreed over whom Lueken's rightful successor was, everyone agreed that having two Marys present at Flushing Meadows was undesirable. Most Baysiders interpreted the schism as a plan of Satan. One Baysider pointed across the street to the other faction and told me,

"You think they're there because two shrines are better than one? No, it's divide and conquer!"[29] The conquerer, in this case, was Satan and the schism was his most successful attack on the Baysider mission.

In Miami, Frank Albas took aim at both Arthur Lueken and Michael Mangan, claiming the schism proved that he was the rightful successor. Albas's claim to succession is based entirely on the fact that Lueken apparently mentioned him by name in one of her locutions. On June 18, 1988, shortly before Albas was dismissed, Lueken explained that Jesus was showing her a vision of a schoolhouse:

> I see what looks to be a school of some kind; and it's a boy's school, and it has them all sitting at desks. But who is the teacher? Oh! I can see that. Oh, it's Frank! Yes! Now Jesus is touching His lips:
>
> JESUS: "My child, there are lessons to be learned from that picture. I am going to ask you to seek the wisdom that is necessary for the present crisis. Now I want you to know, My child, that this has not been solved yet. We will depend on you to do what is necessary."[30]

This message is deliberately vague as Jesus explains that Lueken is not allowed to reveal the whole truth of this image. Albas's claim was that Lueken did not understand her own vision. By identifying him as "the teacher," Albas was named as Lueken's successor. He explains, "In order to understand the present Crisis, I will explain it the way I see it. Just as Satan has entered the Church, so he entered the Bayside office and pitted workers against the Teacher."[31] He goes on to describe how Arthur Lueken served as Satan's agent turning Michael Mangan and James Donahue against him, resulting in his dismissal.

Finally, Albas offered a new interpretation of the story in which Lueken delivered the message "You WILL BE SCOURGED." SMWA assumes that in this message Lueken was repeating Mary's words verbatim and that they were addressed to her. Albas claims that Lueken was actually addressing Mangan on behalf of Mary, telling him that he was going to be scourged—presumably for leading to a coup to displace the rightful head of the shrine organization. Despite these arguments, Albas drew few Baysiders to his cause. The most likely reason for this is that he was in Florida and had no way to access the vigil site and had only his newsletter to establish his claims. While it is obvious why this would be a disadvantage, it demonstrates that religious "truth" is best established through embodied practices and ritual repetition and not through intellectual propositions. This is a fact that historians of religion often forget. On January 17, 2013, I received an e-mail from Albas to his followers. It explained that he had decrypted a hidden message in the Jacinta 1972 Polaroid, which had revealed that an "Earth-shaking event" was going to occur on January 18 that would destabilize the government and possibly result in war on American soil. Albas never publicly explained what he believed was going to happen or why the 18th passed without incident.

Arthur Lueken died on August 28, 2002, and was buried beside Veronica in Flushing. Jeremy Lueken recalls Baysiders ransacking his grandfather's belongings and begging for an article of Arthur's clothing. Some even asked him if he had inherited his grandmother's gift of prophecy.[32] Workers from SMWA attended the funeral and arranged for thirty consecutive Gregorian masses to be said for the repose of his soul.[33] However, Arthur's death was not the end of the schism. Vivian Hanratty took over as the new leader of OLR and has continued to lead vigils at Flushing Meadows to this day. The conflict between Hanratty and Mangan appears to be intractable. Under Hanratty, OLR registered all URL addresses that might be useful to SMWA such as smwa.us, veronicaofthecross.org, and orderofstmichael.org. In 2005, after many pleas from Baysiders to end the schism, Mangan wrote to Hanratty seeking a sort of truce. His letter read in part:

> Although this may be a very difficult task—some would say impossible—we have great trust and confidence in Jesus and Mary that if we both act in good faith and in good will only good fruit can result. As the saying goes, let's give it the old college try.
>
> If you are interested in meeting, please contact me and we can arrange a mutually suitable time and location.

According to SMWA, this was met with a three-page "cease and desist" letter drafted by OLR's lawyers.[34] During my fieldwork, Mangan said of Hanratty, "She's like ivy. She's got her roots in and she's not going anywhere."[35]

Hanratty's continued leadership is somewhat remarkable considering that it is unusual for women to hold positions of institutional authority in any American church, but particularly in traditionalist Catholic movements.[36] Unlike Veronica Lueken, Hanratty does not claim to be the recipient of private revelation. Instead, she earned her position by demonstrating leadership abilities under Arthur Lueken and Ann Ferguson. Some Baysiders are certainly resentful of this. A woman who attends SMWA vigils complained to me, "I think she's [Hanratty] like a female priest!" Within Baysider culture, this is a serious charge. However, the female organizers I spoke with from OLR seemed to regard their role as caretakers rather than permanent authority figures. They explained that OLR would one day be accepted by the Church at which point it would be taken over by Church authorities and lay leadership would no longer be required. They saw their job as preserving the truth of the Bayside Prophecies until this transition occurred.

Although the two groups honor the same seer, read the same canon of prophecies, and hold vigils at the same site, they have different orientations toward the world. To return to Stark and Finke's types, SMWA has become more church-like whereas OLR has become more sectarian. SMWA is led by shrine workers who are celibate and have no career outside of their mission. They are ambitious and have rebuilt the infrastructure that was lost during the schism. Mangan continues to travel around the country and to organize events such as the annual banquet. In 2007, SMWA rented twenty billboards throughout Queens declaring "Your Mother Is Looking For You." Most of all, Mangan has shown a desire to work with Church authorities in the hope that Lueken's visions will one day be re-examined and approved.

Some longtime Baysiders expressed concern that all of SMWA's work toward developing infrastructure had become a distraction from the urgent millennial message of the Bayside Prophecies. On the anniversary weekend, there was a Sunday morning holy hour followed by a banquet at the LaGuardia Marriott. After the holy hour, I spoke with Vincent McDonnell who wished me a good time at the banquet but said that he would not be going. He felt that time was short and that the afternoon would be better spent evangelizing or saying the rosary than attending a banquet.[37]

In contrast to SMWA, OLR has no office and does not go to great lengths to evangelize or attract new members. They do not seem the least bit discouraged that SMWA draws two to three times as many visitors at weekly vigils. Instead, they seem to take this as evidence that they themselves have not compromised the Bayside Prophecies. The differences between Mangan and Hanratty are best summed up by an interview given to a *New York Times* reporter in 2003. Regarding the schism, Mangan stated,

"I have 99 percent of the following. She [Hanratty] has nobody." Hanratty countered, "How many people were at the cross when Jesus died?"[38] Both groups believe that Catholic authorities will one day approve the Bayside apparitions and that the movement will return to its original sacred site at St. Robert Bellarmine's Church. However, where Mangan and others are actively striving for this goal, OLR appears to be waiting patiently, certain in their faith that Lueken's prophecies will come to pass.

The Mission Goes On

Despite their apocalyptic worldview, the Baysiders have not retreated from the world but remain engaged in a number of social issues, notably the right-to-life movement. Attendance at pro-life demonstrations has often brought Baysiders into coalitions with more mainstream conservative Christian groups. If other conservative groups found the Baysiders' beliefs unusual, no one complained when they came to swell the ranks of a protest. Lueken frequently spoke about the dangers of mass media and once claimed that televisions "vomit filth" and described them as "boxes created by satan to invade your homes." Baysiders scrutinize media closely and are particularly likely to mobilize against movies that they feel disparage Catholicism. In 1985, Catholics from New York to Italy protested a film by director Jean-Luc Godard entitled *Hail Mary* about a modern woman who miraculously becomes pregnant. Baysiders offered themselves as shock troops in these protests. When a theater in Boston screened the film, Baysiders were bused in from New York to picket it.[39]

These kinds of protests continued even during the height of the schism. In October 1998, SMWA was part of a coalition of conservative Christian protestors who picketed a performance of the play *Corpus Christi*, a reimagining of the gospel narrative with Jesus as a gay youth living in modern-day Corpus Christi, Texas. SMWA was very pleased to get their name in the paper alongside commentary by William Donohue of the Catholic League. In 2006, a musical entitled *Mary, Like a Virgin* debuted in New York City, inspiring a protest led by SSPX. SMWA came out in full support, and participated by saying rosaries and litanies outside the venue for two and a half hours. That same year, SMWA also sponsored a campaign to protest the film *The DaVinci Code*, which they described as a "hate crime" against Christians.[40]

SMWA has also looked for opportunities to evangelize. In 1998 Baysider websites encouraged visitors to see the summer disaster movies *Deep Impact* and *Armageddon*, explaining that the Ball of Redemption would closely resemble the planet-destroying asteroids portrayed in these films. In 2011, SMWA used the Occupy Wall Street protests as an opportunity to evangelize encamped protestors.[41] They have continued to apply their Marian theology of history to many current events from the controversy over the 2000 presidential election, to the Catholic priest sexual abuse scandal, to ongoing tensions with Iran, to the objections of conservative Catholics to the HHS mandate. Each of these events has been interpreted as the fulfillment of one of Lueken's prophecies.

The most significant event for the Baysider worldview since the schism is likely the terrorist attacks of September 11, 2001. This event was, of course, significant to all Americans. Many conservative Christians, including Jerry Falwell and Pat Robertson, claimed that the attack was a form of divine chastisement for the country's sins. Dispensationalist groups saw it as a sign of the end times. The Baysiders naturally saw it as a fulfillment of Lueken's prophecies. Gary Wohlscheid, an independent promoter of the Bayside Prophecies, runs a website which sells sacramentals including "home protection kits" consisting of small crucifixes and superglue to adhere them to doors. After September 11, his business struggled to keep up with orders for the protection kits.

Wohlscheid told the press that Lueken had predicted a terrorist attack on New York City on September 11, 1990.[42] This was yet another example of using corresponding dates to construct a prophetic interpretation. Significantly, this locution was not given during a vigil but was one of the "private locutions" given by telephone to Michael Mangan. In *Golden Warrior*, SMWA framed the terrorist attack as a consequence of ignoring the messages of heaven. One article declared, "Ultimately, our biggest enemy is not Osama bin Laden but legalized abortion, homosexuality, pornography and blasphemy. Worse than bin Laden—the world is sin-laden." Another article declared, "Sadly, there wouldn't be a 9/11 if the prophetic words of Our Lady were taken seriously–if only by just some of the clergy."[43]

Being based near New York City, Baysiders were also personally affected by the attacks. One of the victims had been a member of OLR.[44] Another individual who volunteered at Ground Zero for nine months called OLR and requested blessed rose petals to distribute to his fellow volunteers. He described seeing numerous "crosses" among the debris and, much like the miraculous Polaroids, interpreted this as a sign that those who died in the attack were now with God.[45] Baysiders also volunteered as relief work-ers. Mangan and Bill Dykes, another founding member of SMWA, were allowed to enter Ground Zero where they helped with relief efforts and also used the opportunity to evangelize.

In many ways, September 11 filled a vacuum in American culture and political discourse that had been created by the end of the Cold War. Islamic terrorism replaced communism as an "oppositional other" and the war on terror provided a new national threat that seemed able to strike from any direction. Baysiders took part in this shift as well. Ever since Lucia Dos Santos published her memoirs about Fatima and Mary's request for the consecration of Russia, Marian culture in America has been closely linked to the fight against communism. American seers including Mary Ann Van Hoof, Veronica Lueken, and Nancy Fowler all warned about the dangers of communism. While their true enemy was Satan, the Soviet Union provided a tangible and worldly threat that Marian groups could direct their energy against. On December 18, 1991, as Lueken sat reading a newspaper article about the collapse of the Soviet Union, she heard the voice of Mary tell her, "Do not be deceived. Their father is the father of all liars: satan. Their master plan is in motion. Pray for the light. Minds are clouded. I repeat: it is a ruse. Wake up America or you will suffer much."[46] For conservative Catholics, it was difficult to imagine a world without a rival superpower and Lueken simply did not accept that the Cold War had ended.

Since September 11, a number of Marian groups have begun to cast Islam as the new rival civilization ranged against America and Christianity. By December 2011, Ann Ferguson's son, Gene, was distributing flyers with an American flag and the words, "To End Terrorism & War Say the Rosary Daily." On the reverse of the flyer is the story of the Battle of Lepanto.[47] This was a naval confrontation in 1571 in which a coalition of Catholic states defeated the main fleet of the Ottoman Empire. The victory was attributed to Mary's intercession. Reviving the story of Lepanto suggests the beginning of a new theology of history in which Islam, rather than communism, becomes the ancient menace destined to be put down by Mary and her followers in the last days.

Do the Baysiders Have a Future?

The Baysiders have endured for nearly half a century despite condem-nation from Church authorities and ridicule in the media. They have never stopped meeting at their sacred site in Flushing Meadows. Lueken's messages and the prayers of her followers can still be heard in the park, at protests and demonstrations, and on the Internet. Throughout this process Baysiders have insisted that they are loyal Catholics who are simply taking a stand to preserve tradition. There are a finite number of ways in which the story of the Baysiders can end. One possibility is extinction: The movement will simply die out. Another is that it will languish indefinitely in a limbo of traditionalism, neither a separatist group nor recognized by the Church. Finally, there is the possibility of some sort of reconciliation with Church authorities.

Extinction

One possibility is that the Baysider movement will die out as the leadership of SMWA and OLR ages. This is by no means a forgone conclusion. In Flushing Meadows I saw young people and children among both groups of Baysiders. The youngest of SMWA's full-time shrine workers was only thirty-two. I also met Michael Mangan's nephew, who had recently completed college with a degree in engineering and was helping to organize the anniversary festivities. However, future Baysiders will have to somehow update their message in order to appeal to a generation that never experienced Vatican II or the Cold War.

Younger Baysiders I spoke with were attracted to the devotional culture of the vigils. But the significance of these rituals is different for Catholics born in the later part of the twentieth century. In the 1970s, Baysiders saw the vigils as a restoration of the Catholicism they remembered from their childhood. But for Catholics who grew up after Vatican II, the devotional culture of the vigils is something new. It may appeal as an alternative to the practices of their parish church rather than a restoration of older practices. Younger Catholics may also have a very different understanding of Baysider notions of ritual transgression. For instance, many older Baysiders embraced Lueken's message that communion in the hand is an abomination because this confirmed the religious training they received before Vatican II. For younger Baysiders, especially those from progressive parishes, receiving communion on the tongue is experienced not as a ritual restoration but a ritual innovation.

A similar problem is that the Bayside Prophecies are a reflection of the anxieties of the Cold War. Of course, many of these anxieties are remarkably resilient. Nearly two decades after the collapse of the Soviet Union, conservative pundits and politicians still stigmatize their opponents with the label of "socialism." However, some elements of the Bayside Prophecies such as references to Moscow or the fear of encroaching submarines armed with nuclear missiles are alien to a younger generation. This cultural gap will likely yield new ways of approaching and interpreting the text.

If the Baysider movement persists, it will likely continue to reorient the Bayside Prophecies toward contemporary threats such as Islamic terrorism. The Cold War worldview, which focused on nation-states and geopolitics, will likely be replaced with a new globalist mindset. Instead of Soviet armies or nuclear threats, current Baysider literature has begun to emphasize plots to take over America through economic schemes or false flag terrorist attacks used as precedents to declare martial law. The alleged conspirators are usually not the Freemasons and Soviets described in the Bayside Prophecies but global cabals that operate within the federal government through such organizations as the Bilderberg group, the Trilateral Commission, and the Council on Foreign Relations. The octopus of evil sprouts new tentacles every day.

Baysider ideas about spiritual warfare, conspiracy theory, and theology of history have evolved to be highly adaptable. This resiliency may allow the movement to continue well into the twenty-first century. However, with each passing decade it may become more difficult to root contemporary anxieties in the Bayside Prophecies. The process of bricolage may require more and more outside material to buttress the closed canon of the messages. This means that the Baysider worldview could lose its distinctness as it fades into the larger milieu of conspiracy theory and millennial expectation.

Reconciliation

The greatest obstacle to the movement's reconciliation with Church authorities will be the legacy of the fallout between Lueken and her diocese. With time, the rancor generated by the Battle of Bayside has subsided and may be largely forgotten. However, the Bayside Prophecies are still replete with damning indictments of Church authorities. Lueken repeatedly describes the images of "mitres in hell." In some messages she calls for Church authorities to be excommunicated.[48] Finally, there is the imposter pope theory, which Church authorities have repeatedly cited as evidence that the entire Bayside movement is founded on error.

In the end, the content of the Bayside Prophecies may make approval of the Bayside apparitions impossible, regardless of any actions taken by modern Baysiders. However, indictments of Church authority are not entirely unprecedented among approved Marian apparitions. In fact, many elements of the papal conspiracy outlined in the Bayside Prophecies can be found in the writings of Melanie Mathiew, a Marian seer whose visions were approved in 1851.

On September 19, 1846, an apparition reportedly appeared to two children in the French village of La Salette. Melanie Mathiew, fifteen, and Maximin Giraud, eleven, had each been hired to herd cattle and had agreed to work together. The two took a nap and woke to find their cattle gone. While searching for them, they encountered a bright light that appeared to hover above a boulder. Within the light, they discerned the image of a crying woman. She spoke to the children and warned them that the French had fallen into wickedness. Because of this they would be punished with disaster including famine and disease. Five years later, the bishop of Grenoble declared their vision worthy of belief.

In addition to this message for French Catholics to increase their piety, each child described being given a secret message not issued to the other. After considerable pressure from the local clergy, the two wrote down their secrets on the condition that they were for the pope's eyes alone. Although Pope Pius IX reportedly read them, the Vatican has never revealed their contents. Maximin fell out of the spotlight as an adult, but Melanie continued to play the role of a seer, drifting from one religious order to another. Maximin died insisting that only the pope had ever read his secret. Melanie, however, allowed her secret to be published in a pamphlet in 1870. Critics pointed out that Melanie's "Secret of La Salette" was far too long to have been the original document sent to the Holy See, which was reported to have been only three pages long. The text outlines an apocalyptic scenario in which the corrupt Catholic clergy will become a "cesspool of iniquity" and the seat of the Antichrist. It will be replaced by an "Order of the Mother of God," whose members would be the apostles of the last days.[49]

The primary difference between Melanie Mathiew's message and Lueken's is that Mathiew declared the Church will become a cesspool of iniquity in the future whereas Lueken claimed this had already happened. Mathiew's prediction that the priesthood would be replaced with a Marian order could even be construed as a more direct challenge to Church authority than Lueken's imposter pope theory. Of course, Mathiew made these pronouncements decades after her apparition had already been approved. But the Church never revoked its approval of La Salette. In 1996, Pope John

Paul II wrote a letter to the bishop of Grenoble to honor the 150th anniversary of the apparition. This suggests that the heavy indictment of Church authorities and conspiracy theories found in the Bayside Prophecies may not, in itself, be an insurmountable obstacle to receiving Church approval.

Changing Attitudes of Church Authorities

Finally, the most important factor for the future of the Baysiders is the Church's changing attitude toward claims of the supernatural and private revelation. Only a tiny handful of the hundreds of Marian apparitions reported all over the world have ever been declared worthy of belief. The primary reason for the Church's caution is the possibility of ridicule. For five hundred years, Marian piety has represented an "Achilles's heel" for Catholic apologists. The Church's critics have constantly attacked Marian piety seeking to portray Catholics as either idolatrous or irrational. During the Reformation, Protestant critics accused Catholics of elevating Mary to the equivalent of a pagan deity. Erasmus of Rotterdam, who in his early years had composed prayers in Mary's honor, became a reformer seeking to "purify" the faith. In his satirical colloquy, "A Pilgrimage for Religion's Sake," he attacked Marian devotionalism as an institution established by the venal to take money from the credulous. Regarding Marian relics, he commented that there was so much of "the heavenly milk of the Blessed Virgin" that, "it's scarcely credible a woman with only one child could have so much, even if the child had drunk none of it."[50] Erasmus did not so much disparage Mary as mock material religion. However, it is notable that his critiques of sixteenth-century Marian pilgrimage as fraudulent were essentially the same as those leveled against Lueken by her opponents.

Martin Luther was also originally drawn toward Marian piety. In 1521 he wrote a fifty-seven-page exegesis on "Mary's Magnificat," a devotional hymn found in the gospel of Luke. However, he increasingly came to feel that Marian piety detracted from proper devotion to Jesus. He finally declared, "The text says that he is the Savior. And if this is true, then let everything else go." John Calvin and Huldrych Zwingli shared similar views. In Geneva all of the festivals of Mary were eventually suppressed in the name of "purifying" the Church. In England, almost all Marian shrines were destroyed during the Reformation. In 1645, the House of Commons nearly ordered that all images of the Virgin Mary must be burned.

Marian piety became a liability again during the Enlightenment when rationalist critics attacked the Catholic Church as an institution that used religion to exploit the ignorant. Stories of miracles and Marian apparitions were particularly vulnerable to this sort of ridicule. Enlightenment critiques of Marian devotionalism are still voiced today. In his book on miracles, Richard Dawkins invokes Scottish Enlightenment philosopher David Hume to dismiss the sun miracle of Fatima as impossible. Dawkins also emphasizes that Fatima was approved by the Vatican, apparently to suggest that the Catholic hierarchy is as irrational as the Portuguese "villagers" who reported the miracle. (Dawkins's critique demonstrates a firm knowledge of the solar system but relatively little understanding about what people actually reported experiencing at Fatima or the nuances of the Church's position on this event.)[51]

In the face of such attacks, Church authorities have been extremely reluctant to endorse reports of Marian apparitions. The Church has periodically made attempts to rein in and consolidate popular practices that might present targets to critics. Particularly in the decades after Vatican II, some of the aspects of devotional culture that were most dear to lay Catholics were downplayed out of the fear that they would cause the Church to appear superstitious or alienate a younger generation of Catholics. A memorandum by Chancellor King about the vigils at St. Robert Bellarmine's expressed his fear that, "Many young people hold these people in scorn because of some of their odd devotions."[52]

However, by the 1970s some American priests began to argue that embarrassment about the supernatural was not only unwarranted but a tactical error. In the 1970s, Andrew Greeley blamed Vatican authorities for turning their backs on mysticism and inadvertently driving Catholics into America's spiritual marketplace. Greeley saw this turn as regrettable, and argued that the yearning for direct encounters with the supernatural leaves individuals feeling isolated and spiritually unfulfilled.[53] Chancellor Otto Garcia of the Diocese of Brooklyn concurred with Greeley and blamed Church authorities for creating a spiritual vacuum that the Bayside apparitions ultimately filled. In an interview with *Fidelity*, he stated, "We have taken, unfortunately, the transcendental out of the picture and the mystery out of the Church and that is what has happened ... The moment you take [the transcendent] out, people are going to cling to anything."[54] Church authorities are now finding that many young people are drawn to Catholicism because of, and not in spite of, its overt supernaturalism.

The religious landscape has changed dramatically since the days of Vatican II. The secularization narrative, in which scientific rationalism would inevitably destroy religion, was widely believed in the 1970s. Most sociologists have now rejected this theory.[55] Pentecostalism and charismatic forms of Christianity, with their heavy emphasis on supernaturalism, are currently exploding across the globe. At the same time, the New Atheists led by the likes of Richard Dawkins, do not make a distinction between superstition and "rational religion" as did the Protestant reformers. Instead they take aim at all expressions of religion, giving Church authorities little incentive to restrain the religious practices of their followers. In this new cultural climate, many of the traditions that were considered a liability before Vatican II—such as devotional practices, Marian piety, and material religion—have become assets.

Commentators on American Catholic culture have noted that many churches have begun to reintroduce elements of pre-Vatican II liturgy. One explanation is that these changes are intended to appeal to an American Catholic population that is becoming predominately Latino. Even the practice of indulgences, arguably the Church's single greatest liability during the Reformation, has been revived. In 2000, Pope John Paul II began a campaign to reintroduce indulgences, which was continued by his successor, Benedict XVI.[56]

Church authorities have also shown signs of becoming more amenable to Marian apparitions. On December 8, 2010, a bishop gave official approval to a Marian apparition within the United States: Our Lady of Good Help in Champion, Wisconsin, was deemed worthy of belief. It joins a short list of approved apparitions alongside Guadalupe, Lourdes, and Fatima. The approved apparition has little in common with the most popular American apparitions of the twentieth century in Necedah, Wisconsin, Bayside, New York, and Conyers, Georgia. It is, in fact, a nineteenth-century apparition that dates back to the Age of Mary. In 1859, one year after the famous apparition at Lourdes, Mary reportedly appeared to a young girl named Adele Brise whose family had recently moved to the Green Bay peninsula from Belgium. The apparition ordered Brise to pray for the conversion of sinners and to spread the Catholic catechism to the frontier. A shrine erected near the site of the apparition is said to have healing powers and was adorned with crutches supposedly left behind by pilgrims who had been cured. During the great Peshtigo fire of 1871 in which 1.2 million acres burned and over 1,200 people died, the shrine remained unscathed, sheltering the pilgrims within.

More importantly, the Diocese of Champion was not under any pressure to give a verdict on this apparition. No one can accuse Church authorities of caving to the demands of an apparitional movement. Instead, some journalists suggested that the diocese approved the apparition as a distraction from a recent abuse-related lawsuit, in which diocesan officials were charged with destroying incriminating files on former priests.[57] But even if the abuse scandal were a factor in the diocese's decision, this would only further indicate that the Church hierarchy and lay devotees have begun to move toward a position of harmony rather than discord.

Another important index of the hierarchy's changing attitude toward Marian apparitions is a document devised and recently released by the Congregation for the Doctrine of Faith (CDF) known as "Norms and Process for Judging Private Revelations." This document presents guidelines for assessing and evaluating reported visions including Marian apparitions. Previously, there was very little resembling an official or universal standard. The Norms were drafted in November 1974, at the same time that Lueken's church was erecting a three-hundred-foot fence to keep unwanted devotees off its property. The document received papal approval from Paul VI on February 24, 1978.[58]

While the Norms were mentioned in scholarly texts, the actual text was not promulgated by the Church. The Norms were not listed in the *Acta Apostolicae Sedis*, the official publication of Vatican documents and decrees. The Internet, however, quickly filled with Marian websites purporting to offer either the exact text of the Norms or a summary of their standards for evaluating apparitions. According to Landislas Orsy, a Jesuit at the Georgetown University Law Center, this meant that the Norms were not Church law in the technical sense. Their function was as an internal document for the CDF and a resource for bishops.[59]

Why would the CDF create such a document and not promulgate it? One of the most obvious reasons for creating the Norms is the increasing reports of Marian apparitions. Over fifty new Marian seers and apparition sites emerged between the close of Vatican II and the affirmation of the Norms.[60] Furthermore, it seems that the ability of modern Catholics to circumvent the local authority of bishops necessitated a global response. The first paragraph of the Norms describes the challenge of addressing apparitions in an increasingly interconnected world: "Today more than formerly, the news of these apparitions is spread more quickly among the faithful thanks to the media (mass media) in addition, the ease of travel supports more frequent pilgrimages."[61]

The reason for trying to keep the Norms secret was probably to curtail the sort of legalistic arguments frequently used by apparitional movements. It was likely feared that if the Church's standards were known, lay Catholics could use them to argue that Church authorities had erred in not approving one or another apparition. In theory, would-be seers could even use the Norms as a template for describing their visions. However, keeping the Norms secret proved impossible. Translations began to appear in multiple languages, always in books on Marian apparitions. Marian websites frequently cited the summaries of the Norms to argue that their apparitions had not been properly investigated and that the Church is in error.

In May 2012, the CDF finally relented and posted the official text of the Norms on their website. Cardinal William Levada, Prefect of the CDF, explained this decision by acknowledging that anyone who wanted to read the Norms could already do so. He conceded, "Today, it must be recognized that the contents of these important norms are already in the public domain."[62] That the hierarchy would freely disseminate this once secret material on the Internet suggests two things: First, that the movements inspired by private revelations are not regarded with the same suspicion that they once were; second, that the global networks of lay Catholics can exert leverage over Rome, particularly when they are persistent over decades.

It now seems that Veronica Lueken's mystical experiences suffered from poor timing. Had they occurred in nineteenth-century Europe, Church authorities might have found her charisma an asset rather than a liability. Instead, Lueken began speaking to the Virgin Mary just after Vatican II, in an urban diocese led by a progressive bishop. Rejection by local church authorities drove her into the arms of the emerging global Marian network, replete with conspiracy theories and apocalyptic lore. Once the Bayside Prophecies became entangled in conspiracy theories the odds of ever receiving Church approval dropped considerably.

However, it is possible that the persistence of the Baysiders will someday pay off. At the very least they may one day succeed in getting a truly "complete and thorough" investigation of the apparitions at Bayside. In contrast to Chancellor King's investigation, which consisted of only one meeting, the Diocese of Champion investigated Our Lady of Good Help for two years before proclaiming it worthy of belief. Even if a lengthy investigation concluded that Lueken's apparition was not authentic, it might still go a long way toward repairing the rift between the Baysiders and their hierarchy. A careful pronouncement on Bayside that cited canon law, investigation of alleged healings, and the wisdom of Catholic theologians might finally make some Baysiders feel that their traditions and values, their concerns and anxieties, were taken seriously by the clergy.

Ultimately, the Baysiders do not have to receive formal recognition from the Church or even survive as a movement in order to effect a shift in the definitional boundaries of Catholic culture. Simply by existing, they have asserted what many traditional Catholics consider to be the core values of their tradition and pushed back against the reforms associated with the spirit of Vatican II. This in itself is an impressive demonstration of power.

7

Religious History as a Dance of Deference and Defiance

THE IMAGINED BOUNDARIES of Catholicism are continually being challenged by new innovations, and the story that was played out in Bayside Hills continues to repeat itself across the globe. Conflicts involving twenty-first century apparitions usually present the same elements that culminated in the Battle of Bayside: A seer, a network of traditionalist and millennialist Catholics, angry bystanders, and embarrassed Church authorities. Those who experience revelation frequently attract the same forces that transformed Lueken and Van Hoof from housewives into seers. There is both "pull" from an international network of Marian devotees and "push" from Church and civil authorities.

A case in Windsor, Ontario, in 2010 bore a remarkable resemblance to the events at Bayside. Fadia Ibrahim, also a mother, began receiving messages from the Virgin Mary. Marks such as the letter "M" would spontaneously appear on her body in blood. Ibrahim was an Orthodox Christian, but a Catholic group in nearby Detroit learned of her story and sent her a miraculous statue of the Virgin Mary. The statue—which may have first acquired its miraculous reputation in Los Angeles—appeared to weep tears of holy oil. A small shrine was erected for the statue on Ibrahim's front lawn where it immediately began to draw hundreds of pilgrims to her suburban neighborhood. As at Bayside Hills, the crowds angered neighbors and drew media attention. City officials declared that the shrine did not meet building codes and gave Fadia a deadline to remove it. Fadia vowed that she would not. Her followers began a petition and fund-raising campaign to prepare for a legal battle.

Father John Ayoub of St. Ignatius of Antioch Orthodox Church appeared to find himself in exactly the same position as Chancellor King had been, seeking to strike a delicate balance between uncritical acceptance of Fadia and her statue on the one hand, and stark condemnation on the other. Father Ayoub reported that he had investigated Ibrahim's weeping statue and that it was not miraculous. However, he still considered Ibrahim a beloved member of his parish. He even added, "If you want to believe [Ibrahim], you are free to believe her." Some pilgrims found this diplomatic response unacceptable. At least one woman managed to get his unlisted number and called to scream at him and demand that he confirm the miracle. The conflict ended in a manner reminiscent of the Battle of Bayside, with the seer receiving a divine command to relocate. Shortly before the city's deadline to remove the shrine, Fadia announced that Mary had asked for the statue to be moved to the local church.[1] Once it was inside the church, the statue received far less attention. Perhaps the community simply lost interest. However, for a time the neighborhood shrine demonstrated how the creation of sacred space serves to empower apparitional movements.

Other apparitional movements are not disbanded so easily. In 2008, the CDF wrote a letter to Church authorities in Korea, regarding Julia Youn, a Marian seer who has been active in Naju, South Korea, for two decades. Youn's experiences began when her statue of Mary started to weep. The Archdiocese of Kwangju, where Youn's movement is based, ruled that Youn's visions and miracles were not genuine. As at Bayside, the archdiocese had sought the aid of the Vatican only after the failure of such measures as ordering local Catholics not to attend Youn's vigils. Despite this opposition, Youn's messages emphasize that Catholics must pray for priests and be obedient to the Pope.[2]

In the summer of 2012, Catholic authorities in Mexico spoke out against Our Lady of the Rosary, a Marianist group that burned down two public school buildings rather than submit their children to secular education. Like the Baysiders, Our Lady of the Rosary began as a community of prophecy in the wake of Vatican II. The movement was formed in 1973 by Nabor Cardenas, a traditionalist priest, and Gabina Sanchez, a seer. They founded the town of Nueva Jerusalén, which is now home to over four thousand people. The town is surrounded by stone walls and is semi-autonomous from the Mexican government. The movement teaches that this town will be spared from a coming chastisement. Secular music, modern dress, alcohol, and tobacco are all forbidden in Nueva Jerusalén. Rules are enforced by a group of armed men known as "The Guard of Mary and Jesus." When Cardenas and Sanchez died, they were replaced by a new male cleric and a new female seer. This combination of male organizer and female seer is also common in contemporary North American Marian movements. Mary Ann Van Hoof worked closely with Henry Swan while Veronica Lueken worked with a series of male leaders who organized her movement and promoted her messages. Nueva Jerusalén existed in isolation and relative peace until more progressive members of the community expressed support for public education and violence ensued.[3]

Mexico is also home to a much broader challenge to the boundaries of Catholicism in the cult of Santa Muerte. Santa Muerte or "Saint Death" is a folk saint depicted as a skeleton clad in female attire such as a wedding dress or a queenly robe. Santa Muerte has become the saint most frequently prayed to in Mexico, rivaled only by Saint Jude. Her devotees pray for jobs, the health of their loved ones, success in romance, protection from Mexico's deadly drug wars, and revenge on enemies. In R. Andrew Chestnut's ethnography of Santa Muerte, he visited Enriqueta Romero, "the godmother of Saint Death," who leads rosary ceremonies to Santa Muerte from her home in Tepito, a notoriously dangerous barrio of Mexico City. Like Van Hoof and Lueken, Romero is a working-class woman with little formal education. Catholic clergy in Mexico and the United States have urged their parishioners not to own statues of Santa Muerte, dismissing the practice as idolatrous and Satanic. However, the fact that Catholic authorities feel the need to comment on the issue at all demonstrates that the boundaries of Catholicism must be policed. Tellingly, Cardinal Gianfranco Ravasi of the Vatican's Pontifical Council of Culture described Santa Muerte as a "degeneration of religion," implying that it is not alien to Catholic tradition but rather a sort of corruption that emerged out of it.[4]

This opposition from the Church has led at least some followers of Santa Muerte to form an autonomous religious institution. David Romo comes from a family of traditionalist Catholics who left the Church following Vatican II. He became involved with Catholic separatist movements and eventually formed his own church: Traditional Holy Catholic Apostolic Church, Mex-USA. Romo's church offered all of the services of the Roman Catholic Church but centered on the two figures of Our Lady of Guadalupe and Santa Muerte. Romo's followers were an unexpected mix of traditionalist Catholics and Santa Muerte devotees. His Church was legally recognized in 2003 but its legal status was revoked in 2005. Romo blamed the influence of the Catholic Church, eventually declaring political "holy war" on the Catholic Church in 2009.[5]

Like the Baysiders, these movements problematize the way we think about religious traditions. Their practices and beliefs do not seem normative and yet they are rooted in Catholic tradition. They also represent a complex set of relationships between Church authorities and lay practitioners. The laywomen and men who become leaders of these movements generally do not set out to form new religions. Instead, they either formed new movements in protest of the reforms of Vatican II or gradually took on greater leadership roles in the face of opposition from Church authorities. They are simultaneously more conservative and more eclectic than their clerical counterparts. Furthermore, the response of Church authorities is almost never uniformly negative. There are always some priests, nuns, or monks who are sympathetic to these movements. Sociologists, historians, and anthropologists have offered a number of models by which to think about the relationship of such movements to Catholic tradition as a whole.

One approach favored by sociologists is to categorize Marian apparitional groups as new religious movements (NRMs). This approach generally assumes that Marian movements are either independent of the Catholic Church or on their way to becoming so. An article on the "Global Network of Divergent Marian Devotion" appears in a reference guide to new religions alongside such Christian movements as the Branch Davidians and the Children of God.[6] The strength of this approach, when it is done well, is that it attends to the ongoing tensions between Church authorities, seers, and their followers. David Bromley and Rachel Bobbitt note that Marian movements never develop on their own but only through "interactive exchange between allies and opponents."[7] Pressure from Church authorities, they argue, is likely the greatest factor in a movement's trajectory.

A potential risk of this approach is that an intricate web of religious meaning is reduced to a naked power struggle. When Church authorities endorse an apparition, Bromley and Bobbitt do not describe this as a reconciliation but a "co-opting" or "domestication" of a popular movement.[8] This approach can become almost teleological, as if forming a schismatic sect is the goal of all such movements and compromise with Church authority represents failure. While the toolkit used to study NRMs can be usefully applied to Marian movements, it must be remembered that apparitional movements think of themselves as Catholic and generally do not aspire to become sectarian movements. Like Veronica Lueken and her followers, what they want is for their understanding of the core values of their tradition to be taken seriously. Success as a sectarian movement is at best a consolation prize after this battle for legitimacy has been lost. Apparitional groups that have broken away from the Church, such as Van Hoof's movement, have done so only when they feel Church authorities have left them no further options.

An alternative approach, favored by historians, is the move toward "lived religion." Robert Orsi has called lived religion "an awkward neologism," and what this approach signifies is sometimes vague.[9] David Hall has explained that lived religion is concerned with circumventing the divisions into "high" and "low" that often come with the study of popular religion. Most discussions of the lived religion approach emphasize the experiences of lay practitioners over those of clergy and theologians and the experience of "the everyday" and the actual over the ideal and the prescribed.[10] This shift is accomplished by focusing on vernacular religion or "local worlds." Orsi explains, "Religious cultures are local and to study religion is to study local worlds."[11]

Lived religion provides another useful tool for understanding groups like the Baysiders. However, the emphasis on agency over structure has potential drawbacks. A historiographic emphasis on the personal, the vernacular, and the local tends to lose sight of how movements spread and evolve at the national and global level. The Baysiders are often characterized as a localized phenomenon, particular to Queens. This is to ignore the movement's global missionary efforts as well as the complex relationships between independent cells of Baysiders around the country. Additionally, the emphasis on the everyday and the local may suggest that the practitioners of vernacular religion are not invested in the prescribed and the ideal or not communicating with religious authorities. However, the Baysiders are preoccupied with what Catholics *ought* to be doing. In some cases, they have chided priests for administering communion in ways they feel are improper.

The lived religion approach is at its best when local worlds are regarded as the products of interplay rather than lonely islands of personal meaning. Thomas Tweed, a historian associated with the lived religion approach, defines religions in terms of "confluences" of "cultural flows."[12] This model, which Tweed compares to hydrodynamics, emphasizes that religions are both "dynamic and relational." Orsi has also emphasized the significance of interplay, especially "the necessary and mutually transforming exchanges between religious authorities and the broader communities of practitioners."[13] It is only with attention to such relationships that groups like the Baysiders can be understood. As Orsi points out, these relationships usually involve individuals in positions of authority and therefore entail dynamics of power as well as culture.

Finally, an underutilized model of how religious cultures evolve is the anthropologist Anthony Wallace's theory of "revitalization movements."[14] Wallace outlined a complicated ten-point model in which a culture undergoes stress, stress leads to the emergence of charismatic individuals, charisma leads to social movements and cultural change, and cultural change leads to routinization until finally a new "steady state" is achieved. The advantage of Wallace's model is that it leaves room to examine both the individual project of creating a meaningful world to inhabit and the collective project of constructing a "steady state," which entails defining an imagined community and setting new definitional boundaries. Wallace also describes some of the strategies employed by these movements to revitalize their religious traditions. These include nativism and the move to "purify" the culture of alien elements, the move to import alien elements into the tradition, and the move to messianism and millennialism. The Baysiders used all three of these strategies. In fact, although Wallace was writing in the 1950s, his model applies to the history of the Baysider movement surprisingly well. Lueken's transformation into a seer can be interpreted as a product of the "stress" following the reforms of Vatican II. However, while the Baysiders did form a social movement and undergo a process of routinization, the end result has been much messier than in Wallace's model. Lueken's charisma did not produce a new "steady state" for Catholics but rather several new variations on what it means to be Catholic and what it means to be a Baysider.

Clifford Geertz characterized religious studies as suffering from "the pigeonhole disease." He wrote, "All the social sciences suffer from the notion that to have named something is to have understood it, but nowhere is this more true than in the comparative study of religion."[15] The danger of labels such as "NRM," "vernacular religion," and "revitalization movement" is that these terms may become pigeonholes that distort the data rather than explaining it. The definitional boundaries that separate movements like the Baysiders from their larger traditions are not static but contested and evolving. As Meredith McGuire observes in her work on lived religion, they must be historicized in order to be understood.[16] Traditionalist Catholic groups do not strike out to become independent from Catholic authority nor are they uninterested in what Catholic author-ities think of them. Rather they are asserting what they feel to be the core values of their tradition. Their protest is a reaction to actions of Church authorities as well as broader social and political changes. And while their beliefs and practices often involve a struggle with Church authorities, it is a struggle tempered by respect for a shared religious tradition. It is not through a contest of raw power but through a dance of deference and defiance that the daily project of personal meaning-making is weighed against the views and concerns of ecclesiastical authorities and defini-tional boundaries are renegotiated. "Mainstream" forms of religion, schis-matic movements, NRMs, and folk pieties are not the dance itself but its byproducts.

The future of religious historiography does not lie in devising new taxonomies of religious traditions but in becoming more attentive to how and why the boundaries of imagined communities are challenged, policed, and negotiated. Church authorities tend to exert power over these boundaries through encyclicals, letters, and proclamations. Historians are fond of texts and this may explain why one half of the dance has received a disproportionate amount of analysis. Lay practitio-ners are more likely to exert their influence through material culture, performance, and embodied practices. While prayers, ritual, songs, and images have just as much power to define a religious culture, they do not leave the same kind of archival record. To understand how defi-nitional boundaries are challenged, it will be necessary to focus more attention on the technologies of power employed by lay practitioners such as the use of sacred space and sound. What is at stake when reli-gious groups use vigils and processions to assert their presence and claim sacred space? How do these groups inscribe their own mean-ings and utilize the "symbolic surpluses" of religious sites? If repetition "articulates absolute reality," as J. Z. Smith has argued, then what reali-ties are new religious practices seeking to affirm? If we are sensitive to these questions, the religious landscape ceases to be a static collection of institutions and types and can be understood as truly "lived"—that is, dynamic, responsive, and adaptable. On my first visit to Flushing Meadows, the confused cyclist asked me which group was Roman Catholic. At the time, I did not know how to respond. I now believe the answer is that the boundaries of Catholic culture are being negotiated every day in Flushing Meadows Park, just as they are in the suburbs of Windsor, Ontario, Naju, South Korea, and the barrios of Mexico City.

Notes

PREFACE

1. Chaim M. Rosenberg, *America at the Fair: Chicago's 1893 World's Columbian Exhibition* (Chicago: Arcadia Publishing, 2008).
2. Jonathan Z. Smith, *Relating Religion: Essays in the Study of Religion* (Chicago: University of Chicago Press, 2004), 253.
3. Robert Orsi, *Between Heaven and Earth: The Religious Worlds People Make and the Scholars Who Study Them* (Princeton, NJ: Princeton University Press, 2005), 188. More recently, Orsi has emphasized that this hidden moral framework has multiple threads and is not solely the product of Western Protestant hegemony. See "The 'So-Called' History of the Study of Religion," *Method and Theory in the Study of Religion* 20, no. 2 (2008): 134–38.

CHAPTER 1

1. John Whelan, "From the Archbishops Desk: Stay Away From Bayside," *Hartford Connecticut Catholic Transcript Weekly*, September 5, 1986. Archives of the Diocese of Brooklyn.
2. Benedict Anderson, *Imagined Communities: Reflections on the Origin and Spread of Nationalism*, rev. and extended ed. (London: Verso, 1991); Leonard Norman Primiano, "Vernacular Religion and the Search for Method in Religious Folklife," *Western Folklore* 54 (January 1995): 45.
3. Clifford Geertz, *Islam Observed: Religious Development in Morocco and Indonesia* (Chicago: University of Chicago Press, 2004), 56; John Ireland, *The Church and Modern Society: Lectures and Addresses* (New York: D.H. McBride & Co., 1896), 390.
4. Charles Savitskas, "The Church and 'Apparitions,'" *Visitor*, August 8, 1982, 4.
5. Field notes (June 14, 2012).

6. Veronica Lueken, *Virgin Mary's Bayside Prophecies: A Gift of Love* (Lowell, MI: These Last Days Ministries, 1998), 2:373.

7. "2010 New York Code RCO—Religious Corporations Article 5—(90 - 92) ROMAN CATHOLIC CHURCHES 90—Incorporation of Roman Catholic Churches," accessed February 3, 2011, Justia.com.

8. William A Varvaro, a canon lawyer for the Brooklyn Diocese, wrote Judge Arthur Lonshein to specifically reiterate that Lueken did not have the approval of the Catholic Church. His letter cites canon law 1327, which states that a diocese is under the authority of a bishop, and 1329, which specifies that pastors require catechetical instruction. See William A. Varvaro to Arthur W. Lonshein (October 6, 1978). Archives of the Diocese of Brooklyn.

9. Supreme Court of New York, "In the Matter of Veronica Lueken (Our Lady of the Roses, a Proposed Corporation)," November 29, 1978, accessed February 3, 2011. Lexis Nexus archive.

10. Philip Nobile, "Our Lady of Bayside," *New York Magazine*, December 11, 1978, 57–60; Charles Montgomery, "Charles Bronson's Secret Heartache: His Son Drops Out of Graduate School to Join Religious Cult," *The National Enquirer*, August 23, 1985, 3.

11. An analysis of Veronica Lueken from a new religion studies perspective appears in David Bromley and Rachel S. Bobbitt, "Visions of the Virgin Mary: The Organizational Development of Marian Apparitional Movements," *Nova Religio* 14, no. 3 (February 2011): 5–41. For a discussion of the Baysiders in the context of re-enchantment, see Christopher Partridge, *The Re-Enchantment of the West* (London: T & T Clark International, 2004), 1:43. For a discussion of the Baysiders as folk religion, see Daniel Wojcik, "Polaroids from Heaven: Photography, Folk Religion, and the Miraculous Image Tradition at a Marian Apparition Site," *Journal of American Folklore* 109, no. 432 (Spring 1996): 129–48.

12. Meredith B. McGuire, *Lived Religion: Faith and Practice in Everyday Life* (New York: Oxford University Press, 2008), 43.

13. Robert Orsi, "Everyday Miracles: The Study of Lived Religion," in *Lived Religion in America: Toward a History of Practice*, ed. David D. Hall (Princeton, NJ: Princeton University Press, 1997), 9.

14. In the 1990s, Nancy Fowler, another Marian seer, began drawing thousands of pilgrims to Conyers, Georgia. As at Bayside, the physical apparition site was important to the success of the movement. However, Fowler operated on a farm where the crowds caused relatively few problems for the surrounding community. While the local diocese expressed concern about Fowler's movement, church authorities neither approved the apparition nor formally condemned Fowler. See Deborah Halter, "Field Note: Charisma in Conyers: A Journey from Visionary to Apparition Site to Church," *Nova Religio* 14, no. 3 (February 2011): 108–14.

15. *Catechism of the Catholic Church* (New York: Continuum International Publishing Group, 2002), 511.

16. Victor W. Turner and Edith L. B. Turner, *Image and Pilgrimage in Christian Culture: Anthropological Perspectives* (New York: Columbia University Press, 1978), 212.

17. Caroline Walker Bynum, *Jesus as Mother: Studies in Spirituality of the High Middle Ages* (Berkley: University of California Press, 1982); Mary Jo Weaver, *New Catholic Women: A Contemporary Challenge to Traditional Religious Authority* (Bloomington: Indiana University Press, 1986), 53.

18. Robert Orsi, *Thank You, St. Jude: Women's Devotion to the Patron Saint of Hopeless Causes* (New Haven, CT: Yale University Press, 1999), 210.

19. Christian Williams Jr. records two cases in the 1930s in which seers were forcibly committed to a mental institutions. See Christian Williams Jr., "Religious Apparitions and the Cold War in Southern Europe," in *Religion, Power and Protest in Local Communities: The Northern Shore of the Mediterranean*, ed. Eric Wolf (New York: Walter de Gruyter, 1984), 255. Similarly, Angie Heo describes the controversy surrounding Samia Youssef Basilious, a seer from Port Said, Egypt. In 1990, shortly after Basilous reported seeing the Virgin Mary and miraculously exuding oil from her hand, Egyptian state security officers requested that she visit the Ministry of Interior, who ordered that she be removed to a convent and kept out of the public eye. Basilious's visions were deemed a threat to the authority of the state. See Angie Heo, "The Bodily Threat of Miracles: Security, Sacramentality, and the Egyptian politics of Public Order," *American Ethnologist* 40, no. 1 (2013): 149–64.

20. Roger Friedland and Richard Hecht, "The Bodies of Nations: A Comparative Study of Religious Violence in Jerusalem and Ayodhya," *History of Religions* 38, no. 2 (November 1998): 101–49.

21. Jonathan Z. Smith, *Map Is Not Territory: Studies in the History of Religion* (Chicago: University of Chicago Press, 1993), 291.

22. Malachi Martin, *Hostage to the Devil* (New York: Reader's Digest Press, 1976), 14. One Baysider told me that Martin, who lived in New York, regularly dined with a Baysider family. He believed that Martin was initially skeptical but that before his death in 1999 he had come to believe in the movement. Field notes (June 16, 2012).

23. Mircea Eliade, *The Sacred and the Profane*, trans. Willard R. Trask (New York: Harcourt Brace, 1961), 20–65.

24. Smith, *Map Is Not Territory*, 92.

25. Michel Foucault, "Space, Knowledge, and Power," in *The Foucault Reader*, ed. Paul Rabinow (New York: Pantheon, 1984), 252.

26. David Chidester and Edward T. Linenthal, eds., *American Sacred Space* (Bloomington: Indiana University Press, 1995), 15.

27. Isaac Weiner, *Religion Out Loud: Religious Sound, Public Space, and American Pluralism* (New York: New York University Press, 2013).

28. Jonathan Z. Smith, *Imagining Religion: From Babylon to Jonestown* (Chicago: University of Chicago Press, 1982), 54.

29. Robert Orsi, *Between Heaven and Earth: The Religious Worlds People Make and the Scholars Who Study Them* (Princeton, NJ: Princeton University Press, 2005), 160–66.

30. Field notes (June 16, 2012).

31. Field notes (June 9, 2012).

32. J. Z. Smith popularized this line of analysis as a tool for religious studies. He attributes it to literary critic Viktor Shklovsky. See Smith, *Imagining Religion*, xiii.

33. Field notes (June 16, 2012).

34. Field notes (June 13, 2012).

35. See Anthony Wallace, "Revitalization Movements," *American Anthropologist* 58, no. 2 (April 1956): 265–81; I. M. Lewis, *Ecstatic Religion: An Anthropological Study of Spirit Possession and Shamanism* (Harmondsworth, UK: Penguin, 1978); Len Oakes, *Prophetic Charisma: The Psychology of Revolutionary Religious Personalities* (Syracuse, NY: Syracuse University Press, 1997); and Rodney Stark, "A Theory of Revelation," *Journal for the Scientific Study of Religion* 38, no. 2 (1999): 287–308.

CHAPTER 2

1. Sandra L. Zimdars-Swartz, "Religious Experience and Public Cult: The Case of Mary Ann Van Hoof," *Journal of Religion and Health* 28, no. 1 (Spring 1989): 36.

2. Michael Carroll, *The Cult of the Virgin Mary: Psychological Origins* (Princeton, NJ: Princeton University Press, 1986), 139–40.

3. The only support for the claim that Van Hoof and Lueken ever met in person is that Lueken's husband Arthur was born in Indiana and the Luekens may have lived in Indianapolis during the 1950s—still 400 miles from Necedah, Wisconsin. Michael Cuneo spent six days in Necedah and was unable to find any evidence of correspondence with Lueken. Arthur and Veronica's grandson Jeremy confirms that his grandparents always lived in New York. See Michael Cuneo, *The Smoke of Satan: Conservative and Traditionalist Dissent in Contemporary American Catholicism* (New York: Oxford University Press, 1997), 155; James Donovan, "Bayside Unveiled: The Blessed Mother Takes a Beating from Her 'Friends'," *Fidelity* (March 1988): 40; Jeremy Lueken, phone interview (May 21, 2013).

4. Ann Ferguson, "My Memories of Veronica Lueken by Mrs. Ann Ferguson," accessed June 30, 2012, http://www.tldm.org/news4/MemoriesOfVeronica.htm.

5. On this model of religious communities, see Danièle Hervieu-Léger, *Religion as a Chain of Memory* (New Brunswick, NJ: Rutgers University Press, 2000).

6. David Yamane, "Narrative and Religious Experience," *Sociology of Religion* 61, no. 2 (2000): 184.

7. Courtney Bender, "Touching the Transcendent: Rethinking Religious Experience in the Sociological Study of Religion," in *Everyday Religion: Observing Modern Religious Lives*, ed. Nancy T. Ammerman (New York: Oxford University Press, 2007), 201–18.

8. Robert Wuthnow, *After Heaven: Spirituality in America since the 1950s* (Berkeley: University of California Press, 1998), 134.

9. Zimdars-Swartz, "Religious Experience and Public Cult," 52

10. Mark Garvey, *Waiting for Mary: America in Search of a Miracle* (Cincinnati, OH: Emis Books, 2003), 216–18. Visions of people dying from radiation or germ warfare were common among Marian seers during the Cold War. Van Hoof's visions were preceded by those of the Dutch seer Ida Peerdeman, who likewise had visions of people dying from toxins carried by long-range missiles.

11. "Urge Bishop Impose Sanction on Vigils," *The Bayside Times* 34, no. 40 (May 8, 1975): 1, 3.

12. Zimdars-Swartz, "Religious Experience and Public Cult," 40.

13. Zimdars-Swartz, *Encountering Mary: From La Salette to Medjugorje* (Princeton, NJ: Princeton University Press, 1991), 251–70; Michael Barkun uses the term "super conspiracy" to refer to conspiracy theories in which "multiple conspiracies are believed to be linked together hierarchically." This category applies to the worldview of Van Hoof as well as Lueken. See Michael Barkun, *A Culture of Conspiracy* (Berkeley: University of California Press, 2003), 6.

14. Garvey, *Waiting for Mary*, 229.

15. Zimdars-Swartz, "Religious Experience and Public Cult," 53. For an additional account of Van Hoof's deteriorating relationship with Church authorities, see Thomas A. Kselman and Steven Avella, "Marian Piety and the Cold War in the United States," *Catholic Historical Review* 72 (July 1986): 403–24.

16. The Archives of the Diocese of Brooklyn contained one of Lueken's checkbooks. It is a joint checking account with one Roy J. McDonald, possibly her stepfather.

17. Donovan, "Bayside Unveiled," 40.

18. Lueken's detractors claim that she made a cassette of herself singing background to a recording to MacDonald and Eddy. She remarked that St. Therese had asked her to sing. According to Ann Cillis, an apostate Baysider and one of Lueken's most vocal critics, Lueken's exertions in recording this tape resulted in a hiatal hernia. Cillis also points out that June 18th, the anniversary of the apparitions at Bayside, is MacDonald's birthday. See Donovan, "Bayside Unveiled," 40; Paul Hamilton, "The Reality behind the Roses" *Sancta Maria* (December 8, 1986): 8.

19. Phone interview with Jeremy Lueken (May 21, 2013).

20. Kevin Farrelly reports that Lueken's apartment was about a mile from St. Robert Bellarmine's. Interview with Kevin Farrelly (June 14, 2012).

21. Ann Ferguson, "My Memories of Veronica Lueken."

22. Roberta Grant, "War of the Roses," *Rolling Stone*, February 21, 1980, 44–45. Some claimed that to supplement the family income, Veronica began telling

fortunes using tarot cards. The source of Lueken's career as a fortune-teller is Ann Cillis, an apostate Baysider, who claimed to have heard it from Lueken's son, Butch. See Donovan, "Bayside Unveiled," 40; Cuneo, *Smoke of Satan*, 155. Jeremy Lueken reported that his grandmother never demonstrated any interest in the New Age milieu.

23. Baysider literature uses the spellings Therese and Theresa interchangeably.

24. These Last Days Ministries, *Our Lady of the Roses, Mary Help of Mothers* (Lowell, MI: These Last Days Ministries, n.d.), 14.

25. These Last Days Ministries, *Our Lady of the Roses*, 14.

26. Veronica Lueken, *Virgin Mary's Bayside Prophecies* (Lowell, MI: These Last Days Ministries, 2003), 2:xiii.

27. Significantly, Lueken was not the only Catholic to have mystical experiences related to this event. Jeffrey Kripal gives an account of his friend "Adam," a former Benedictine monk, who spontaneously awoke at 3:00 a.m. on June 5, 1968, in his home in Toronto, Canada. Not knowing why he was suddenly wide awake, he turned on a transistor radio near his bed. By some strange coincidence the AM band was receiving a station from California. In this way, Adam was able to hear the immediate aftermath of the shooting, which occurred as Kennedy was being interviewed for a Los Angeles radio station. Adam attributed this coincidence to a kind of paranormal "link" that he had formed with Robert Kennedy after shaking hands with him during his campaign in the fall of 1968. Kripal goes on to mention the work of Alan Vaughan, a writer who helped to coauthor a book entitled *Dream Telepathy* (1973). Vaughan had recorded two precognitive dreams on May 25, 1968, which he subsequently recorded as predicting Robert Kennedy's death. See Jeffrey J. Kripal, *Authors of the Impossible: The Paranormal and the Sacred* (Chicago: University of Chicago Press, 2010), 3–4. What is significant is not the plausibility of these explanations, but that multiple people have incorporated this event into the narratives about their relationship to the supernatural and the sacred. The assassination of Robert Kennedy created a vacuum of meaning and for some the supernatural rushed in to fill the space.

28. These Last Days Ministries, *Our Lady of the Roses*, 28.

29. This is most likely a paraphrase of Job 27:11 as found in the Douay-Rheims Bible. In his ethnography of contemporary Fundamentalist culture, Robert Glenn Howard heard similar stories of Bible text glowing so as to highlight one verse while rendering the rest of the page invisible. See Robert Glenn Howard, *Digital Jesus: The Making of a New Christian Fundamentalist Community on the Internet* (New York: New York University Press, 2011).

30. These Last Days Ministries, *Our Lady of the Roses*, 15.

31. Since Lueken's death, SMWA president Michael Mangan has sometimes signed his correspondences JMJTV. The added "V" naturally stands for Veronica.

32. An eagle also gives this message in Revelation 8:13; however, Baysider literature makes no mention of this connection.

33. Lueken, *Virgin Mary's Bayside Prophecies*, 1:xxiii–xxiv.

34. Lueken, *Virgin Mary's Bayside Prophecies*, 1:xxxv–xxxvi.

35. St. Robert Bellarmine's Roman Catholic Church, "The Parish of St. Robert Bellarmine at Bayside," accessed April 21, 2011, http://www.stroberts.org/.

36. Lueken, *Virgin Mary's Bayside Prophecies*, 1:xl.

37. Lueken, *Virgin Mary's Bayside Prophecies*, 1:li.

38. Lueken, *Virgin Mary's Bayside Prophecies*, 1:xlvi.

39. Lueken, *Virgin Mary's Bayside Prophecies*, 1:lxii.

40. Lueken, *Virgin Mary's Bayside Prophecies*, 1:lxx.

41. Lueken, *Virgin Mary's Bayside Prophecies*, 1:lii–liii.

42. Lueken, *Virgin Mary's Bayside Prophecies*, 1:2.

43. Field notes (June 17, 2012); "Miracle Lady Packs Them In," *The Bayside Times* 30, no. 4 (August 30, 1973): 2.

44. Teresa of Avila describes these experiences in her autobiography and is a major influence on the Catholic understanding of locutions. She writes, "Though perfectly formed, the words are not heard with the bodily ear; yet they are understood much more clearly than if they were so heard, and, however determined one's resistance, it is impossible to fail to hear them." See E. Alison Peers, *The Life of Teresa of Jesus: The Autobiography of Teresa of Avila* (New York: Doubleday, 1991), 196.

45. This image of roaming bands of homosexuals occurs three times in the Bayside Prophecies. This is a window into conservative fears regarding increasing tolerance for different sexual orientations.

46. Lueken, *Virgin Mary's Bayside Prophecies*, 6:281–82.

47. Daniel Wojcik, *The End of the World as We Know It: Faith, Fatalism, and Apocalypse in America* (New York: New York University Press, 1996), 80.

48. David Morgan, *Visual Piety: A History and Theory of Popular Religious Images* (Berkeley: University of California Press, 1998).

49. In 1921, Abbe Paulin Giloteaux published his book, *Victim Souls: A Doctrinal Essay*, which located victim souls within a teleological view of history. He writes, "For in the darkest hours of this world's history, when godlessness is rife or immorality parades itself before men's eyes, it pleases God to summon certain souls to sacrifice themselves, freely in imitation of the Crucified, for the advantage of the Church and the salvation of the world." Paula M. Kane, "'She Offered Herself Up': The Victim Soul and Victim Spirituality in Catholicism," *Church History* 71, no. 1 (March 2002): 88–92.

50. Lueken, *Virgin Mary's Bayside Prophecies*, 6:102.

51. St. Michael's World Apostolate, "Gethsemani to Calvary: Sufferings of Veronica of the Cross," accessed May 15, 2011, http://www.smwa.org/Veronica_of_the_Cross/Document_Gethsemani_to_Calvary_Sufferings_of_Veronica.htm.

52. Field notes (June 10, 2012).

53. Lueken, *Virgin Mary's Bayside Prophecies*, 1:72.

54. Lueken, *Virgin Mary's Bayside Prophecies*, 2:lxxxviii.

55. Garvey, *Waiting for Mary*, 152–53. The lore that seers do not blink when in ecstasy appears to have originated with the apparitions at Garabandal. This was the first apparition in which film and photographs of the seers were widely disseminated. One Baysider told me when he first saw Lueken she never blinked, despite numerous flash bulbs going off in front of her. This convinced him her visions were authentic. Field notes (June 14, 2012).

56. Lueken, *Virgin Mary's Bayside Prophecies*, 2:222. It was while discussing the need for women to be submissive to their husbands that her voice became higher.

57. Lueken, *Virgin Mary's Bayside Prophecies*, 1:lxxi.

58. Roberta Grant, "War of the Roses," *Rolling Stone*, February 21, 1980, 45.

59. Analogous arguments are made in other prophetic traditions. Muslim apologists sometimes argue that Muhammad was illiterate and therefore could only have produced the Qur'an through revelation. Similarly, Mormon apologists note that Joseph Smith had little formal education to argue that he could not have invented the *Book of Mormon*.

60. Veronica Lueken, to Chancellor James P. King (October 15, 1974). Archives of the Diocese of Brooklyn. This "double voice" recalls the female mediums of the nineteenth century, who used mediumship to orate at a time when women were discouraged from public speaking. Ann Braude, *Radical Spirits: Spiritualism and Women's Rights in Nineteenth-Century America* (Bloomington: Indiana University Press, 2002), 91–92.

61. The first "instant" camera was invented by Edwin Land in 1948. However, the average consumer could not afford an instant camera until the Polaroid SX-70. See Daniel Wojcik, "Polaroids from Heaven: Photography, Folk Religion, and the Miraculous Image Tradition at a Marian Apparition Site," *Journal of American Folklore* 109, no. 432 (Spring 1996): 137.

62. Evelyn Murphy, Polaroid Company customer service to anonymous (December 11, 1968). Archives of the Diocese of Brooklyn.

63. Daniel Wojcik, "Polaroids from Heaven: Photography, Folk Religion, and the Miraculous Image Tradition at a Marian Apparition Site," *Journal of American Folklore* 109, no. 432 (Spring 1996): 157.

64. These Last Days Ministries, *Our Lady of the Roses*, 23.

65. Suzann Weekly Chute and Ellen Simpson visited the Baysiders in 1976 and were among the earliest researchers to do field work on the movement. They describe one of Lueken's early messages in which the Virgin Mary designated the SX-70 as her preferred camera. No such message appears in any of the publicly available versions of the Bayside Prophecies. See Suzann Weekly Chute and Ellen Simpson, "Pilgrimage to Bayside: 'Our Lady of the Roses' Comes to Flushing Meadow," Paper presented at the American Folklore Society Annual Meeting, Philadelphia, PA (November 11, 1976), 4.

66. Rene Laurentin, *The Apparitions of the Blessed Virgin Mary Today*, trans. Luke Griffin (Dublin: Veritas Publications, 1991), 72; Zimdars-Swartz, "Religious Experience and Public Cult," 48.

67. Daniel Wojcik, "Spirits, Apparitions, and Traditions of Supernatural Photography," *Visual Resources: An International Journal of Documentation* 25, nos. 1–2 (March–June 2009): 109; Tom Gunning, "Phantom Images and Modern Manifestations: Spirit Photography, Magic Theater, Trick Films, and Photography's Uncanny," in *Fugitive Images: From Photography to Video*, ed. Patrice Petro (Bloomington: Indiana University Press, 1995), 64.

68. Wojcik, "Polaroids from Heaven," 136. Jessy Paglioroli cites an image of an iceberg resembling the Virgin Mary taken in 1905 off the shore of Newfoundland. This photograph, shot by an amateur with a Kodak camera, was significant in Canadian Catholic culture. Michael Francis Howley, the archbishop of St. John's Newfoundland composed a sonnet about the photograph entitled, "Our Lady of the Fjords." While this story does show an early connection between popular photography and Catholic piety, strictly speaking, "Our Lady of the Fjords" is a simulacrum rather than miraculous photography. See Jessy C Pagliaroli, "Kodak Catholicism: Miraculous Photography and Its Significance at a Post-Conciliar Marian Apparition Site in Canada," *Historical Studies* 70 (2004), 77.

69. Pagliaroli, "Kodak Catholicism," 71; E. Ann. Matter, "Apparitions of the Virgin Mary in the Late Twentieth Century: Apocalyptic, Representation, Politics," *Religion* 31, no. 2 (2001): 135.

70. Jean Baudrillard, *America*, trans. Chris Turner (New York: Verso, 1989), 37; Edward Berryman, "Taking Pictures of Jesus: Producing the Material Presence of a Divine Other," *Human Studies* 28, no. 4 (2005): 432.

71. Brian Britt, "Snapshots of Tradition: Apparitions of the Virgin Mary in Georgia," *Nova Religio* 2, no. 1 (1998): 115; Paolo Apolito, *The Internet and the Madonna: Religious Visionary Experience on the Web* (Chicago: University of Chicago Press, 2005), 11–12.

72. Norman D. Caron to Charles Savitaskas, Associated Editor, *Our Sunday Visitor*, August 14, 1982, 2. Archives of the Diocese of Greater Brooklyn.

73. Ewa Kurluk, *Veronica and Her Cloth: History, Symbolism, and Structure of a "True" Image* (Cambridge, MA: Basil Blackwell, 1991).

74. A version of this story, including the name "Robert Franzenburg" and his home address, appear in a letter by Veronica to Chancellor King. (Veronica Lueken to Chancellor King, January 27, 1974. Archives of the Diocese of Brooklyn.) Another version of this story appears in the document *Conversations with Jesus*, based on tapes of Lueken's memories recorded in 1980. "Conversations with Jesus" is reprinted in Lueken, *Virgin Mary's Bayside Prophecies*, vol.2.

75. Mike Gershowitz, "Lourdes and Fatima. Why Not Bayside?," *Long Island Press*, August 30, 1973, 19.

76. Cuneo, *Smoke of Satan*, 165. To duplicate the Jacinta 1972 photograph, Bill Wuest employed a complicated procedure in which he used a time exposure in a dark studio to write his name on the wall using a flashlight. He then did a double exposure to impose this image onto an ordinary Polaroid. If such a technique was used to create the Jacinta 1972 photo, it seems unlikely that Franzenburg could have taken the Polaroid in the manner described by Lueken. See Gerowitz, "Lourdes and Fatima," 19.

77. Hamilton, "The Reality behind the Roses," 6.

78. Lueken, *Virgin Mary's Bayside Prophecies*, 2:lx. "Satan" is never capitalized in Baysider literature.

79. Lueken, *Virgin Mary's Bayside Prophecies*, 2:lxv.

80. Mike Gershowitz, "Lourdes and Fatima. Why Not Bayside?," *Long Island Press*, August 30, 1973, 19.

81. The chronology in "Conversations with Jesus" is confusing. The incident with Father McL. occurred in January and is described as taking place after the Jacinta 1972 Polaroid. But the Polaroid was taken in September 1971 while the mass with Father McL allegedly occurred in January 1971.

82. Interview with Kevin Farrelly (June 14, 2012).

83. Ferguson, "My Memories of Veronica Lueken."

84. Frank Albas, "Pinocchio Introducing His New Soul Mate," accessed June 30, 2011, http://www.rosesfromheaven.com/michael.html. Other Baysiders have used similar warnings as a kind of supernatural copyright. At a vigil a Baysider sold me a joke book he had written from a Baysider perspective. It begins with a warning that unauthorized reproduction of the book will be detected by angels. Although this warning is delivered in a whimsical style, the threat of observant angels appears to be serious. See John T. Watkins, *Charles Chickens & the Chicken Joke Yolk Book* (Print on Demand: Just Between Us Publishers, 2010).

85. Field notes (June 16, 2012).

86. Lueken, *Virgin Mary's Bayside Prophecies*, 2:263.

87. Antonio Maria Martins, *Novos Documentos de Fátima* (São Paulo: Edições Loyola, 1984), 62–63.

88. Field notes (June 16, 2012).

89. Lueken, *Virgin Mary's Bayside Prophecies*, 1:94.

90. Lueken, *Virgin Mary's Bayside Prophecies*, 1:98.

91. Lueken, *Virgin Mary's Bayside Prophecies*, 1:278.

92. Lueken, *Virgin Mary's Bayside Prophecies*, 1:380.

93. Jim Greene, "Bayside Church Statue Removed to Curb Spurious Marian Rites," *The Tablet* 66, no. 45 (December 6, 1973): 1. In 1973, a number of emerging religious groups made prophecies about the comet Kohoutek. David Berg, founder of the Children of God, also warned that Kohoutek would bring about dire calamity. J. Gordon Melton believes that fear of Kohoutek convinced numerous

members of the Children of God to emigrate to other countries. See J. Gordon Melton, *Encyclopedic Handbook of Cults in America* (New York: Garland, 1992), 226. Conversely, Timothy Leary, then incarcerated in Folsom Prison, explained that he had been receiving mental transmissions from Kohoutek, which he renamed "Starseed." Starseed had come to help humanity achieve its destiny of reaching beyond the womb of Earth and finding immortality among the stars. See Joanne Harcourt-Smith, "Word from Folsom Prison," *The New Yorker*, December 3, 1973, 44–45.

94. James P. King to Sister M. Christine (March 22, 1974). Archives of the Diocese of Brooklyn.

95. Norman D. Caron to Charles Savitaskas, Associated Editor, *Our Sunday Visitor*, August 14, 1982, 2. There are literally thousands of miraculous Polaroids taken by Baysiders. I have not seen the one described in the letter.

96. Lueken, *Virgin Mary's Bayside Prophecies*, 6:498.

97. Gershowitz, "Lourdes and Fatima. Why Not Bayside?," 19.

98. Diocese of Brooklyn, "Chronology of Bayside" (September 8, 1977). Archives of the Diocese of Brooklyn.

99. Gershowitz, "Lourdes and Fatima. Why Not Bayside?," 19. The discarded crutch is a trope common to Marian shrines, which are sometimes decorated with the canes and crutches of formerly disabled people. See Robert Orsi, *The Madonna of 115th Street* (New Haven, CT: Yale University Press, 1985), 12.

100. Gershowitz, "Lourdes and Fatima. Why Not Bayside?," 19.

101. Chancellor King to Bishop Mugavero (May 4, 1973). Archives of the Diocese of Brooklyn.

102. "Miracle Lady Packs Them In," *The Bayside Times* 30, no. 4 (August 30, 1973): 2.

103. Chancellor King to Bishop Mugavero (September 17, 1973). Archives of the Diocese of Brooklyn.

104. James P. King, Memorandum (October 9, 1973). Archives of the Diocese of Brooklyn.

105. Lueken recalls at least 200 people present on December 7, 1973. Ann Ferguson recalls 450. See Lueken, *Virgin Mary's Bayside Prophecies*, 2:lxviii; Ferguson, "My Memories of Veronica Lueken."

106. Ferguson, "My Memories of Veronica Lueken." Here, they draw on the writings of the seventeenth-century French missionary Louis-Marie Grignion de Montfort. De Montfort's book, *Treatise on the True Devotion to the Blessed Virgin*, describes an apocalyptic battle between Mary and Satan, in which Mary will be aided by a group of spiritual elite.

107. Ferguson, "My Memories of Veronica Lueken."

108. Cuneo, *Smoke of Satan*, 156. Here, Cuneo is drawing on telephone interviews with members of the Pilgrims of Saint Michael.

109. Lueken, *Virgin Mary's Bayside Prophecies*, 2:562.

110. Kevin J. Farrelly, "Vigil Chronology" (May 1995).

111. Lueken, *Virgin Mary's Bayside Prophecies*, 3:231.

112. In their analysis of data from the Baylor Religion Survey, Christopher Bader et al. found that while women reported a higher rate of belief in subjugated discourses such as fortune-telling and mediumship, men were more likely to believe in conspiracy theories. The combination of a female seer and a male conspiracy theorist appears to be a potent formula behind a number of apocalyptic Marian worldviews. See Christopher Bader, David, Frederick Carson Mencken, and Joe Baker, *Paranormal America: Ghost Encounters, UFO Sightings, Bigfoot Hunts, and Other Curiosities in Religion and Culture* (New York: New York University Press, 2010), 107–8.

113. Chancellor James P. King to Veronica Lueken (October 23, 1974). Archives of the Diocese of Brooklyn.

114. I. M. Lewis, *Ecstatic Religion* (New York: Routledge, 2003).

115. Interview between Monsignor Anthony J. Bevilacqua and Monsignor James P. King (February 20, 1979). Archives of the Diocese of Brooklyn.

116. Returning to Lewis's example of the distressed women who become shamans, he adds that acknowledging women when they are possessed also functions to keep them in subservient positions by allowing them to vent their frustrations and staving off more radical social changes. Church authorities did not grant Lueken such an outlet; perhaps because of this she became a powerful charismatic leader. Lewis, *Ecstatic Religion*, 7.

117. These Last Days Ministries, "The Truth about the So-Called Investigation," accessed May 15, 2011, http://www.tldm.org/no-invest/veronica.htm.

118. David Bromley and Rachel S. Bobbitt, "Visions of the Virgin Mary: The Organizational Development of Marian Apparitional Movements," *Nova Religio* 14, no. 3 (February 2011): 9.

119. Lueken, *Virgin Mary's Bayside Prophecies*, 6:49.

120. Field notes (June 3, 2012).

121. James M. O'Toole, *The Faithful: A History of Catholics in America* (Cambridge, MA: Belknap Press of Harvard University Press, 2008), 243.

122. Norman D. Caron, to Charles Savitaskas, Associated Editor, *Our Sunday Visitor*, August 14, 1982, 3.

123. Donovan, "Bayside Unveiled," 34.

124. Michael Mangan (May 6, 2012), accessed June 30, 2012, http://www.smwa.org/Vigil_Information/Audio_streaming/2012_Holy_Hours/05-06-12-HH/05-06-12-HH.htm.

125. Brown, Interview (September 24, 2012).

126. Cuneo, *The Smoke of Satan*, 165.

127. Letter to the Diocese of Brooklyn. Archives of the Diocese of Brooklyn.

128. Daniel Martin, *Vatican II: A Historic Turning Point* (Bloomington, IN: AuthorHouse, 2011), 126.

CHAPTER 3

1. Chancellor King to Monsignor McDonald (April 6, 1971). Archives of the Diocese of Brooklyn.
2. Susan Cheever Cowley, "Our Lady of Bayside Hills," *Newsweek*, June 2, 1975, 46.
3. Mrs. Irene Cash to Chancellor King (October 18, 1973). Archives of the Diocese of Brooklyn.
4. Benedict Groeschel, *A Still, Small Voice* (San Francisco: Ignatius Press, 1993), 122.
5. Personal communication with Joseph Coen, archivist for the Diocese of Brooklyn (March 18, 2011).
6. Ari L. Goldman, "Francis J. Mugavero, 77, Is Dead; Was Bishop of Brooklyn 22 Years," *The New York Times*, July 13, 1991, http://query.nytimes.com/gst/full-page.html?res=9D0CE2DF153CF930A25754C0A967958260.
7. "Church Schedules Easter Services," *The Bayside Times* 37, no. 37 (April 8, 1971): 1.
8. Chronology of Bayside (September 8, 1977). Archives of the Diocese of Brooklyn.
9. Chancellor King to Veronica Lueken (March 23, 1973). Archives of the Diocese of Brooklyn.
10. Chancellor King to Bishop Mugavero, Memorandum (May 4, 1973). Archives of the Diocese of Brooklyn.
11. James T. Fisher, *The Catholic Counterculture in America, 1933-1962* (Chapel Hill: University of North Carolina Press, 1989), 158.
12. Mark Garvey, *Waiting for Mary: America in Search of a Miracle* (Cincinnati, OH: Emis Books, 2003), 91.
13. James Donovan, "Bayside Unveiled: The Blessed Mother Takes a Beating from Her 'Friends,'" *Fidelity* (March 1988): 38–39. In addition to apparitions, there are numerous accounts of American Catholics from this period constructing and visiting springs and grottos replicating the one at Lourdes. See Robert Orsi, "Everyday Miracles: The Study of Lived Religion," in *Lived Religion in America: Toward a History of Practice*, ed. David D. Hall (Princeton, NJ: Princeton University Press, 1997), 3–21, and also Thomas A. Kselman and Steven Avella, "Marian Piety and the Cold War in the United States," *Catholic Historical Review* 72 (July 1986): 403.
14. Paolo Apolito, *The Internet and the Madonna: Religious Visionary Experience on the Web* (Chicago: University of Chicago Press, 2005), 89–90.
15. Apolito, *The Internet and the Madonna*, 90.
16. Groeschel, *A Still, Small Voice*, 20–21.
17. This institution was founded by Pope Paul III in 1542. At that time, it was known as "The Sacred Congregation of the Universal Inquisition" and was charged with protecting the Church from heresy. The designation "Universal" is significant as this organization was charged with policing local expressions of Catholicism to ensure uniformity. The word "Inquisition" was dropped from

the group's title in 1908. It received its current title from Pope Paul VI in 1965. "Congregation for the Doctrine of Faith," http://www.vatican.va/roman_curia/congregations/cfaith/documents/rc_con_cfaith_pro_14071997_en.html.

18. "Interview between Monsignor Anthony J. Bevilacqua and Monsignor James P. King" (February 20, 1979), 6. Archives of the Diocese of Brooklyn.

19. In 1971, the Diocese of Brooklyn was divided into five vicariates, each overseen by a vicar subordinate to the bishop. These were Vincent J. Powell, William J. Cullen, Peter L. Altmain, Martin P. Bannan, and George T. Deas. "Five Vicars Installed in Ceremony," *The Bayside Times* 38, no. 14 (October 28, 1971): 12.

20. In one of Lueken's letters, she mentions approaching these priests about her experiences. Lueken to Bishop Mugavero (October 14, 1974). Archives of the Diocese of Brooklyn.

21. Chancellor King to Bishop Mugavero, "Memorandum" (June 29, 1973). Archives of the Diocese of Brooklyn.

22. Chancellor King to James S. Rausch (June 19, 1974). Archives of the Diocese of Brooklyn. The investigation of June 29, 1973, only considered the content of Lueken's visions, not alleged miracles. King's reference to "our investigation" in this letter may indicate ongoing assessment of the situation rather than the formal investigation of the committee.

23. Anne McGinn Cillis, "Investigation of Veronica by Church officials, a Sham," *Sancta Maria*, 2, n.d. Archives of the Diocese of Brooklyn.

24. Interview with Adrian K. Cornell (July 5, 2012).

25. Lueken to Bishop Mugavero (October 14, 1974). Archives of the Diocese of Brooklyn.

26. Cillis, "Investigation of Veronica," 2.

27. Anthony Bevilacqua, "Critique of News Article by Anne McGinn Cillis." Archives of the Diocese of Brooklyn.

28. Michael Mangan, Speech given in honor of the passing of Veronica Lueken (August 5, 2007). Available in Saint Michael's World Apostolate, "Special Report: Is Bayside Condemned," Audio CD.

29. Rene Laurentin, *The Apparitions of the Blessed Virgin Mary Today*, trans. Luke Griffin (Dublin: Veritas Publications, 1991), 141.

30. Charles Savitskas, "The Church and 'Apparitions,'" *Visitor* (August 8, 1982): 4.

31. Bernadette Ives to Francis J. Mugavero (January 18, 1981). Archives of the Diocese of Brooklyn.

32. Chancellor Anthony Bevilacqua, "Critique of New Article by Ann McGinn Cillis," 6. Archives of the Diocese of Brooklyn.

33. Archives of the Diocese of Brooklyn.

34. Savitskas, "The Church and 'Apparitions,'" 5.

35. Quoted in Donovan, "Bayside Unveiled," 38. James LeBar was the chief exorcist of the Archdiocese of New York. He was also a leader in the Catholic counter-cult movement and described the Baysiders pejoratively as a "cult."

36. Savitskas, "The Church and 'Apparitions,'" 5.

37. Paul Hamilton, "The Reality behind the Roses," *Sancta Maria* (December 8, 1986): 7. Archives of the Diocese of Brooklyn.

38. Parish Council of St. Robert Bellarmine to Monsignor J. Emmet McDonald (September 13, 1973). Archives of the Diocese of Brooklyn.

39. Mary Jeffers to Bishop Francis J. Mugavero (June 15, 1981). Archives of the Diocese of Brooklyn.

40. Bryan Robert Eyman to Bishop Francis J. Mugavero (1981). Archives of the Diocese of Brooklyn.

41. Alison McKay, *Bayside* (Portsmouth, NH: Arcadia Publishing, 2008), 51.

42. Adrian K. Cornell, *What?? Who?? King Cornell?!?! Who's He????* (Self-published memoir), 152; Associated Press, "Veronica Disrupts Baptisms," *The Morning Record*, April 14, 1975, 12.

43. Kevin Farrelly, Interview (June 14, 2012).

44. William Caulfield, "The Vigils," *Bayside Hills Beacon*, September 1974, 3. Both Bayside residents I interviewed mentioned the problem of public urination. As Farrelly explained it, the area around St. Robert Bellarmine's was a residential neighborhood with no public facilities whatsoever. The pilgrims truly did have no alternative.

45. *Bayside Hills Beacon*, October 1974, 8. Isaac Weiner describes the case of *Harrison v. St Marks*, which occurred in Philadelphia in 1877 and concerned whether an Episcopal church could ring bells in a residential neighborhood. Plaintiffs in that case also invoked what the bells would do to their property values. See Isaac Weiner, *Religion Out Loud: Religious Sound, Public Space, and American Pluralism* (New York: New York University Press, 2013), 47.

46. Cornell, *King Cornell?*, 152.

47. Bayside Hills Civic Association, "Memorandum" (April 30, 1975). Archives of the Diocese of Brooklyn.

48. Chancellor James P. King to Luis J Montinola (November 29, 1973). Archives of the Diocese of Brooklyn.

49. Veronica Lueken to Chancellor James P. King (June 12, 1974). Archives of the Diocese of Brooklyn.

50. Anonymous to Chancellor James P. King (1976). Archives of the Diocese of Brooklyn. Kevin J. Farrelly suggests that accounts of heckling teenagers at the vigils may have been something of a myth. By his own recollection, it was not teenagers but adults who were responsible for most of the heckling.

51. Anonymous to Chancellor King. Archives of the Diocese of Brooklyn.

52. Kevin Farrelly, Interview (June 14, 2012).

53. David Chidester and Edward T. Linenthal, eds., *American Sacred Space* (Bloomington: Indiana University Press, 1995), 18.

54. In her study of apparitions in al-Warraq, Egypt, in 2009, Angie Heo notes that churches are significant not only to Christians but also have significance within

secular polities. Marian apparitions at church sites effect political shifts and expansions that involve multiple polities. See Angie Heo, "The Virgin Made Visible: Intercessory Images of Church Territory in Egypt," *Comparative Studies in Society and History* 54, no. 2 (2012): 361–91.

55. Adrian K. Cornell, Interview (July 5, 2012).

56. Chancellor James P. King to Bishop Francis J. Mugavero (June 29, 1973). Archives of the Diocese of Brooklyn.

57. Form letter to Chancellor King (September 28, 1973). Archives of the Diocese of Brooklyn. Joseph Coen, the archivist who prepared a copy of this letter for me, was somewhat flabbergasted by the claim that St. Robert Bellarmine's was "unused."

58. Peter Freiburg, "Queens Simmers After 'Vigil,'" *New York Post*, April 7, 1975.

59. Joseph E. Geoghan to Monsignor McDonald (September 13, 1973). Archives of the Diocese of Brooklyn.

60. Monsignor McDonald to Bishop Mugavero (September 14, 1973).

61. Lawrence G. Norris, Sr. Corporate Attorney, Polaroid to Lawrence Finnegan, J., Esquire (September 12, 1973). Archives of the Diocese of Brooklyn.

62. Chancellor King to Monsignor Powell (October 30, 1973). Archives of the Diocese of Brooklyn.

63. Chancellor James P. King to Veronica Lueken (September 20, 1973). Archives of the Diocese of Brooklyn.

64. Jim Greene, "Bayside Church Statue Removed to Curb Spurious Marian Rites," *The Tablet* 66, no. 45 (December 6, 1973): 1.

65. Greene, "Bayside Church Statue Removed to Curb Spurious Marian Rites," 1.

66. Jo-Anne Price, "Church Removes Statue in Dispute Over Visions," *The New York Times*, December 2, 1973, 158.

67. Price, "Church Removes Statue in Dispute Over Visions," 158.

68. Jay Itkowitz, "Removal of Statue Fails to Dissuade Vigil Keepers," *Long Island Press*, December 3, 1973, 1.

69. Farrelly, Interview (June 14, 2012).

70. Our Lady of the Roses Shrine, "20 Years 5 of 7" (online video), accessed September 10, 2012, http://www.youtube.com/watch?v=WKwQDSa0BoY&feature=plcp.

71. These Last Days Ministries, *Our Lady of the Roses: Mary Help of Mothers* (Lowell, MI: These Last Days Ministries, n.d.), 29

72. Philip Nobile, "Our Lady of Bayside," *New York Magazine*, December 11, 1978, 55.

73. These Last Days Ministries, *Our Lady of the Roses*, 29.

74. Ann Ferguson, "My Memories of Veronica Lueken," accessed September 10, 2012, http://www.tldm.org/news4/MemoriesOfVeronica.htm.

75. Veronica Lueken to Chancellor James P. King (July 7, 1974). Archives of the Diocese of Brooklyn.

76. Donovan, "Bayside Unveiled," 39.

77. Lueken, *Virgin Mary's Bayside Prophecies*, 2:128.

78. Bayside Hills Civic Association to Bishop Francis J. Mugavero, (June 19, 1974). Archives of the Diocese of Brooklyn.

79. "Homeowners Seek Court Ban on Vigils," *The Bayside Times* 30, no. 46 (June 20, 1974): 1; Chancellor James P. King to Bishop James S. Rausch (June 19, 1974). Archives of the Diocese of Brooklyn.

80. Farrelly, "Chronology of Bayside."

81. King to Mugavero (August 11, 1974). Archives of the Diocese of Brooklyn.

82. Farrelly, Interview (June 16, 2012).

83. Veronica Lueken, " 'The Truth about the So-Called Investigation' in Veronica Lueken's Own Words," accessed September 10, 2012, http://www.tldm.org/no-invest/Veronica.htm.

84. Chancellor James P. King, "Memorandum" (September 8, 1974). Archives of the Diocese of Brooklyn.

85. Lueken, "The Truth about the So-Called Investigation."

86. Veronica Lueken to Chancellor King and Bishop Mugavero (October 15, 1974). Archives of the Diocese of Brooklyn.

87. Lueken, "The Truth about the So-Called Investigation." In an interview with *Rolling Stone*, Veronica and Arthur later claimed that a resident of Bayside Hills had attempted to throw acid on her. See Roberta Grant, "War of the Roses," *Rolling Stone*, February 21, 1980, 46.

88. Chancellor James P. King, "Memorandum" (September 17, 1974). Archives of the Diocese of Brooklyn.

89. Marlene Maloney, "Necedah Revisited: Anatomy of a Phony Apparition," *Fidelity* (February 1989): 23.

90. Archives of the Diocese of Brooklyn.

91. Chancellor King to Bishop Mugavero (November 22, 1974). Archives of the Diocese of Brooklyn.

92. Cornell, Interview (July 5, 2012).

93. Lueken, *Veronica Lueken's Bayside Prophecies*, Vol. 2, 549.

94. Peter Freiburg, "Queens Simmers After 'Vigils,'" *New York Post*, April 7, 1975.

95. William Caulfield, "Editorial: The 'Vigils.'" Archives of the Diocese of Greater Brooklyn.

96. Isaac Weiner, *Religion Out Loud*, 6. For an analysis of the history of this assumption in American law and politics, see Stephen L. Carter, *The Culture of Disbelief: How American Law and Politics Trivialize Religious Devotion* (New York: BasicBooks, 1993).

97. "Vigils: Tensions Continue to Mount," *Bayside Times* 34, no. 34 (March 27, 1975): 1.

98. Cornell, Interview (July 5, 2012).

99. Ann Ferguson, "My Memories of Veronica Lueken by Mrs. Ann Ferguson," accessed June 30, 2012, http://www.tldm.org/news4/MemoriesOfVeronica.htm.

100. "Vigils: Tensions Continue to Mount," 10.

101. Chancellor King to Commissioner Codd (December 11, 1974). Archives of the Diocese of Brooklyn.

102. Susan Cheever Cowley, "Our Lady of Bayside Hills," *Newsweek*, June 2, 1975, 46; Farrelly, Interview (June 16, 2012).

103. Robert Kalfus, *Long Island Press*, April 14, 1975.

104. "Vigils: Tensions Continue to Mount," 10.

105. A document entitled "Vigil Chronology" describes the number of residents who visited the precinct as over 500. However, Kevin Farrelly currently believes this number is exaggerated. See Farrelly, "Vigil Chronology" (May 1995).

106. "Uneasy Truce over Vigils Faces Its Toughest Test," *Bayside Times* 34, no. 35 (April 3, 1975): 14.

107. Farrelly, Interview (June 16, 2012).

108. "Arrests cap demonstration at Vigil Site, College Gate" *Bayside Times* 34, no. 36 (April 10, 1975): 1–2; Farrelly, Interview (June 16, 2012).

109. Lueken, *Virgin Mary's Bayside Prophecies*, 3:80.

110. Ann Ferguson to King (April 1975). Archives of the Diocese of Brooklyn; Farrelly, Interview (June 14, 2012); Lueken to Chancellor King (May 19, 1975). Archives of the Diocese of Brooklyn; Roberta Grant, "War of the Roses," *Rolling Stone*, February 21, 1980, 45; These Last Days Ministries, "The Truth about the So-Called Investigation in Veronica Lueken's Own Words" (February 13, 1977), accessed July 12, 2012, http://www.tldm.org/no-invest/veronica.htm.

111. "5 years of Vigils Rile Some in Bayside," *The New York Times*, April 14, 1975, 35.

112. "'Vigils' Averting Major Confrontation," *Bayside Times* 34, no. 37 (April 17, 1975): 1.

113. Monsignor James P. King to Commissioner Michael J. Codd (April 15, 1975). Archives of the Diocese of Brooklyn; Lueken, "The Truth about the So-Called Investigation."

114. Cornell, *King Cornell?*, 156; Interview (July 5, 2012).

115. Petition (April 30, 1975). Archives of the Diocese of Brooklyn.

116. "Urge Bishop, Impose Sanction on Vigils," *Bayside Times* 34, no. 39 (May 8, 1975): 1–3.

117. "Padavan Bids Lefkowitz Probe Vigils," *Bayside Times* 34, no. 38 (April 24, 1975): 1.

118. Farrelly, "Bayside Chronology" (May 1995).

119. Ann Ferguson, "My Memories of Veronica Lueken."

120. Lueken, "The Truth about the So-Called Investigation." Lueken claims that no one from the diocese ever attempted to contact her before 1975. However, the archives of the Diocese of Brooklyn contain copies of letters addressed to Lueken from Chancellor King.

121. Memorandum (April 29, 1975). Archives of the Diocese of Brooklyn.

122. King, "Interview with Monsignor James P. King," 1.

123. Lueken, "The Truth about the So-Called Investigation."

124. Ferguson, "My Memories of Veronica Lueken." These sorts of improvised and spontaneous rituals that sacralize everyday objects are common in vernacular religion and especially in apparitional movements. In the 1940s and 1950s, Spanish visionaries would identify "sacred trees." Believers then took branches from these trees for use as cures or talismans. See William Christian Jr., "Religious Apparitions and the Cold War in Southern Europe," in *Religion, Power and Protest in Local Communities: The Northern Shore of the Mediterranean*, ed. Eric Wolf (New York: Walter de Gruyter, 1984), 252.

125. Chancellor King claims that during one round of negotiations, she was nearly persuaded to move the vigils to nearby Cunningham Park. She expressed that she would prefer Alley Pond Park because it was located in the precinct of a police captain sympathetic to her cause. See King, "Interview with Monsignor James P. King," 1.

126. Robert Thomas Jr., "Woman Agrees to Change Site of Virgin Mary Vigils," *The New York Times*, May 23, 1975, 41; Susan Cheever Cowley, "Our Lady of Bayside Hills," *Newsweek*, June 2, 1975, 46.

127. Lueken, *Virgin Mary's Bayside Prophecies*, 3:106–7. This language of "passing a test of faith" is a common strategy by which prophetic movements rationalize disappointment. See Lorne L. Dawson, "When Prophecy Fails and Faith Persists: A Theoretical Overview," *Nova Religio* 3, no. 1 (1999): 67.

128. Ferguson, "My Memories of Veronica Lueken by Mrs. Ann Ferguson."

129. Arthur Everett, "Religious Street Vigils in N.Y. Ended," *St. Petersburg Times*, May 24, 1975, 4-A.

130. "Peace Returns to Bayside Hills," *Bayside Times* 34, no. 43 (May 29, 1975): 1–12.

131. "Peace Returns to Bayside Hills," *Bayside Times* 34, no. 43 (May 29, 1975): 1–12.

132. Jubilation Day Program, 1975. Archives of the Diocese of Brooklyn.

133. Chidester and Linenthal, *American Sacred Space*, 8; For a discussion of the Battle of Bayside in terms of civil religion, see Jane Yager, *The Rosary and the Lawnmower: The Making of Public Religion in the Contemporary American City* (Honors paper, Macalester College, 2001).

134. Farrelly Interview (June 14, 2012); Jane H. Lii, "Neighborhood Report: Bayside Hills; A Cherished Memory: Banishing Veronica," *The New York Times*, June 4, 1995, 9.

135. Cuneo, *Smoke from Satan*, 173.

136. Lueken, *Virgin Mary's Bayside Prophecies*, 4:20.

137. Ann Ferguson, "My Memories of Veronica Lueken."

138. Mike Gershowitz, "Lourdes and Fatima. Why Not Bayside?," *Long Island Press* August 30, 1973, 19.

139. Veronica Lueken to Chancellor James P. King (October 15, 1974). Archives of the Diocese of Brooklyn.

140. Lueken, *Virgin Mary's Bayside Prophecies*, 5:477.

141. Lueken, *Virgin Mary's Bayside Prophecies*, 6:421–33.

142. Mangan, Speech given in honor of the passing of Veronica Lueken.

CHAPTER 4

1. "Bill Adds 'Corona' to Fair Site's Name," *The New York Times*, February 5, 1964, 32.

2. These Last Days Ministries, "Audio Recording of Veronica Lueken, June 18, 1994," accessed September 11, 2012, http://ia700200.us.archive.org/6/items/BaysideMessageOfJune181994/940618.mp3; Veronica Lueken, *Virgin Mary's Bayside Prophecies: A Gift of Love* (Lowell, MI: These Last Days Ministries, 1998), 6:498.

3. Lueken, *Virgin Mary's Bayside Prophecies*, 6:334.

4. See Jonathan Z. Smith, *Imagining Religion: From Babylon to Jonestown* (Chicago: University of Chicago Press, 1982), 89. On the function of sacred space, see Smith's essay "The Wobbling Pivot," in *Map Is Not Territory: Studies in the History of Religion* (Chicago: University of Chicago Press, 1993).

5. Lueken, *Virgin Mary's Bayside Prophecies*, 1:436–37. Michael Barkun has noted that there is a rich mythology involving malevolent aliens living under the earth that has appeared in a number of modern conspiracy theories and apocalyptic movements. For a genealogy of this mythology, see Michael Barkun, "Myths of the Underworld in Contemporary American Millenialism," in *Experiences of Place*, ed. Mary N. MacDonald (Cambridge, MA: Harvard University Press, 2003), 147–62.

6. I use the term "subjugated discourses" to refer to those ideas and beliefs that are stigmatized or otherwise repressed by mainstream society. In their analysis of the Baylor Religion Survey, Christopher D. Bader et al. found that nearly two-thirds of Americans reported belief in a least one "paranormal" idea such as UFOs, hauntings, or astrology. However, Bader et al. also found evidence that Americans who discuss these ideas too much are mocked or stigmatized. Sociologists have put forward a number of terms to describe how a pool of such repressed knowledge is a permanent feature of modern society. Colin Campbell coined the term "cultic milieu" in 1976. Christopher Partridge has used the term "occulture" in a similar fashion. Michael Barkun has used the term "stigmatized knowledge" to describe the pool of ideas employed in conspiracy theories and apocalyptic expectations. In using the term "subjugated," I draw on Michel Foucault's notion of "subjugated knowledge" or knowledge that has been dismissed as naive or unscientific. Foucault noted that subjugated knowledge was often employed as a critique of dominant regimes of knowledge. See Christopher D. Bader et al., *Paranormal America* (New York: New York University Press, 2010), 71–72; Colin Campbell, "The Cult, the Cultic Milieu, and Secularization,"

in *The Cultic Milieu: Oppositional Subcultures in an Age of Globalization*, ed. Jeffrey Kaplan and Heléne Lööw (Walnut Creek: AltaMira Press, 2002), 12–25; Christopher Partridge, *The Re-Enchantment of the West: Alternative Spiritualities, Sacralization, Popular Culture, and Occulture* (London: T & T Clark International, 2004), vol. 1; Michael Barkun, "Conspiracy Theories as Stigmatized Knowledge: The Basis for a New Age Racism?," in *Nation and Race: The Developing Euro-American Racist Subculture* ed. Jeffrey Kaplan and Tore Bjorgo (Boston: Northeastern University Press, 1998), 58–72; Michel Foucault, *Society Must Be Defended: Lectures at the College de France, 1975-76* (New York: Picador, 2007).

7. Meredith B. McGuire, *Lived Religion: Faith and Practice in Everyday Life* (New York: Oxford University Press, 2008), 4.

8. On combinativeness, see Catherine Albanese, *A Republic of Mind and Spirit: A Cultural History of American Metaphysical Religion* (New Haven: Yale University Press, 2007).

9. Paolo Apolito, *The Internet and the Madonna: Religious Visionary Experience on the Web* (Chicago: University of Chicago Press, 2005), 179.

10. E. Ann Matter, "Apparitions of the Virgin Mary in the Late Twentieth Century: Apocalyptic, Representation, Politics," *Religion* 31, no. 2 (2001): 127.

11. Claude Lévi-Strauss, *The Savage Mind* (Chicago: University of Chicago Press, 1966), 17–19. Michael Barkun notes that millennial speculation is frequently a process of putting the pieces together. He identifies the "apocalyptic bricoleur" as an emerging style of millennialism that combines traditional Protestant dispensationalism with secular apocalyptic scenarios and New Age discourses. See Michael Barkun, "Politics and Apocalypticism," in *The Encyclopedia of Apocalypticism*, ed. Stephen J. Stein (New York: Continuum, 1998), 3:442–60.

12. Christian Williams Jr., "Religious Apparitions and the Cold War in Southern Europe," in *Religion, Power and Protest in Local Communities: The Northern Shore of the Mediterranean*, ed. Eric Wolf (New York: Walter de Gruyter, 1984), 258.

13. Thomas E. Bullard, "UFOs: Lost in the Myths," in *UFOs and Abductions: Challenging the Borders of Knowledge*, ed. David M Jacobs (Lawrence: University of Kansas, 2000), 141.

14. Veronica Lueken (October 21, 1973). Quoted in Saint Michael's World Apostolate, *Heaven Speaks Today*, no. 7, accessed September 12, 2012, http://www.smwa.org/HST/HST_007/HST_7_UFOs.htm.

15. Daniel Wojcik argues that UFOs tend to map naturally onto millennial expectations. In 1974, Protestant dispensationalist Hal Lindsey published his book, *Planet Earth—2000 A.D*, in which he explained that UFOs exist and are demonic in origin. This is the same position presented in the Bayside Prophecies. Lindsey still maintains this position and in 2010 he appeared on CNN to argue that UFOs are real. See Wojcik, *The End of the World as We Know It*, 274; Mark

Hulsether, "Aliens are Fattening Us Up for the Rapture," *Religion Dispatches* (October 18, 2010), accessed July 4, 2011, http://www.religiondispatches.org/dispatches/guest_bloggers/3566/aliens_are_fattening_us_up_for_the_rapture/.

16. Billy Graham, *Angels: God's Secret Agents* (Garden City, NY: Doubleday, 1975).

17. Ann Ferguson, "My Memories of Veronica Lueken," accessed September 10, 2012, http://www.tldm.org/news4/MemoriesOfVeronica.htm.

18. Philip Nobile, "Our Lady of Bayside," *New York Magazine*, December 11, 1978, 59–60.

19. Lueken (October 21, 1973). Quoted in Saint Michael's World Apostolate, *Heaven Speaks Today*, no. 7.

20. Veronica Lueken (October 28, 1973). Quoted in Saint Michael's World Apostolate, *Heaven Speaks Today*, no. 8, accessed September 12, 2012, http://www.smwa.org/HST/HST_008/HST_8_Unholy_Ray.htm.

21. Veronica Lueken (December 31, 1974). Quoted in Saint Michael's World Apostolate, *Heaven Speaks Today*, no. 8.

22. Lueken, *Virgin Mary's Bayside Prophecies*, 2:506.

23. Lueken, *Virgin Mary's Bayside Prophecies*, 4:458

24. Rapture theology relies heavily on two passages from Paul: 1 Corinthians 15:51–52, "We will not all sleep, but we will all be changed in a flash, in the twinkling of an eye, at the last trumpet," and 1 Thessalonians 4:16, "We who are still alive and left will be caught up together with them in the clouds to meet the Lord in the air." The Catholic Church does not regard these passages as a cogent scriptural basis for the Rapture. According to the 2006 Baylor Religion Survey, 32 percent of Americans believe in the rapture. Bader et al., *Paranormal America*, 163.

25. Field notes (June 16, 2012).

26. Theologians on the retreat were inspired by the Acts of the Apostles as well as the book *The Cross and Switchblade* (1936) by David Wilkerson. From Duquesne, the movement soon spread to the campus of Notre Dame. See Randall Balmer, *The Encyclopedia of Evangelicalism* (Louisville, KY: Westminster John Knox Press, 2002), 182.

27. Catherine L. Albanese, *America, Religions, and Religion* (Belmont, CA: Wadsworth, 1999), 95.

28. Philip Jenkins. *The Next Christendom: The Coming of Global Christianity* (New York: Oxford University Press, 2002), 68.

29. Lueken, *Virgin Mary's Bayside Prophecies*, 2:288.

30. James Donovan, "Bayside Unveiled: The Blessed Mother Takes a Beating from Her 'Friends,'" *Fidelity* (March 1988): 39.

31. Roberta Grant, "War of the Roses," *Rolling Stone*, February 21, 1980, 43.

32. Philip Nobile, "Our Lady of Bayside," *New York Magazine*, December 11, 1978, 57.

33. Lueken, *Virgin Mary's Bayside Prophecies*, 3:114–15.

34. Lueken, *Virgin Mary's Bayside Prophecies*, 3:241.

35. Portavoz, "Mensajes dados a la Portavoz Mexicana," accessed September 20, 2012, http://www.portavozmexicana.info/html/12avo_mensaje.html; Michael Cuneo, *The Smoke of Satan: Conservative and Traditionalist Dissent in Contemporary American Catholicism* (New York: Oxford University Press, 1997), 99; Millie and Mary LaCava to Anthony Bevilacqua (June 18, 1976). Archives of the Diocese of Brooklyn.

36. Lori Pieper, "Was Pope John Paul I Murdered?," *On Pilgrimage* (August 22, 2008), accessed May 15, 2011, http://subcreators.com/blog/2008/08/22/was-pope-john-paul-i-murdered-part-i/; Lueken, *Virgin Mary's Bayside Prophecies*, 3:358.

37. David Frankfurter, in his work on demonic conspiracy theories, describes how demonic evil can be mimetically "performed" either directly or indirectly. Lueken's description of the Satanic rites she sees in her visions is an indirect performance of evil. A possessed woman describing a conspiracy on behalf of demons is a direct performance of evil. See David Frankfurter, *Evil Incarnate: Rumors of Demonic Conspiracy and Satanic Abuse in History* (Princeton, NJ: Princeton University Press, 2006), 168–203.

38. Jean Marty, *Warnings from Beyond: Warnings from the Other World to the Contemporary Church (Confessions of Hell)*, trans. Nancy Knowles-Smith (Fort Lauderdale, FL: Catholic Books and Tapes, n.d.).

39. Elizabeth Isichei found conservative Catholics in New Zealand who were also influenced by this text. See Elizabeth Isichei, "Visions and Visionaries: The Search for Alternative Forms of Authority among Catholic Conservatives," *Archives de Sciences Socials des Religions* 36, no. 75 (July–September 1991): 122.

40. Isichei, "Visions and Visionaries," 122; Cuneo, *Smoke of Satan*, 99–133; Peter Gilmour, "Pius to the 13th Degree?," *U.S. Catholic*, August 1, 2005, 6.

41. Anne Cillis, "Investigation of Veronica by Church Officials, a Sham," *Sancta Maria*, 2–3. Archives of the Diocese of Brooklyn.

42. E. Michael Jones, "The Cult, the Statue, and the Fall of the Canadian Layman," *Fidelity* (May 1989): 37.

43. Lueken, *Virgin Mary's Bayside Prophecies*, 5:127.

44. Field notes (June 10, 2012).

45. Daniel Martin, *Vatican II: A Historic Turning Point* (Bloomington, IN: AuthorHouse, 2011), 39.

46. Field notes (June 17, 2012); Martin, *Vatican II*, 44–45. Traditionalist Catholics have repeatedly accused Bugnini of being a Freemason; however, there is no evidence to support this claim.

47. Lueken, *Virgin Mary's Bayside Prophecies*, 3:230.

48. Bill Ellis, *Raising the Devil: Satanism, New Religions, and the Media* (Lexington: University Press of Kentucky, 2000), 138. In 2000, SMWA explained that this locution actually refers to Nelson Rockefeller's younger brother, David. An article in SMWA's newsletter described comments attributed to Rockefeller

at a meeting of the Bilderberg group that appeared to outline a secret globalist agenda. See Michael Mangan, "Election Debacle Paves the Way," *Golden Warrior* 4 (December 2000): 2.

49. Pilgrims of Saint Michael, "Pawns in the Game: A Satanic Conspiracy to Control the World," *Michael Journal*, accessed June 11, 2011, http://www.michaeljournal.org/pawns.asp.

50. James J. Hennesey, *American Catholics: A History of the Roman Catholic Community in the United States* (Oxford: Oxford University Press, 1981), 317.

51. Scott Bonn, "Serial Killer David Berkowitz, aka Son of Sam, Tells Professor, 'I was once an evil person,' in prison conversation," *CBS News* (March 18, 2013), accessed March 11, 2014, http://www.cbsnews.com/news/serial-killer-david-berkowitz-aka-son-of-sam-tells-professor-i-was-once-an-evil-person-in-prison-conversation/.

52. See Donovan, "Bayside Unveiled," 38.

53. Grant, "War of the Roses," 46.

54. Leonard Buder, "Officer Who Pursued Clues on 'Son of Sam' Facing Police Charges, *The New York Times*, January 3, 1980, B3. For a discussion of law enforcement endorsing Satanic conspiracies during the 1980s, see Robert D. Hicks, "The Police Model of Satanic Crime" and "Law Enforcement and the Satanic Crime Connection: A Survey of 'Cult' Cops," both in *The Satanism Scare*, ed. James T. Richardson, Joel Best, and David G. Bromley (Hawthorne, NY: Aldine de Gruyter, 1991).

55. Lueken, *Virgin Mary's Bayside Prophecies*, 6:510.

56. Lueken, *Virgin Mary's Bayside Prophecies*, 1:18.

57. Lueken, *Virgin Mary's Bayside Prophecies*, 6:284. This locution also describes how Lueken has been kept awake at night by "weird chantings" coming from Satanists. Significantly, it was given the day after Halloween.

58. Ellis, *Raising the Devil*, 199.

59. These Last Days Ministries, *Our Lady of the Roses, Mary Help of Mothers* (Lowell, MI: These Last Days Ministries, n.d.), 59.

60. Lueken, *Virgin Mary's Bayside Prophecies*, 2:507 and 4:501; Martin, *Vatican II*, 132; Miri Rubin, *Gentile Tales: The Narrative Assault on Late Medieval Jews* (New Haven, CT: Yale University Press, 1999).

61. Terry's account is corroborated by documents found in the Diocese of Brooklyn archives. An untitled page of notebook paper appeared to be an attempt to keep addresses and phone numbers for Lueken, her family, and close associates. Along with other addresses where Lueken had lived or owned property, the document stated, "Lived 3 1/2 years with Emma Wagner at 577 Van Duzer Ave, Staten Island."

62. See Maury Terry, *The Ultimate Evil* (New York: Bantam Books, 1989), 191–92.

63. See Terry, *The Ultimate Evil*, 192–93.

64. Terry, *The Ultimate Evil*, 241–43.

65. Grant, "War of the Roses," 46.

66. Cuneo, *Smoke of Satan*, 173.

67. Field notes (June 16, 2012).

68. Don Sharkey, *The Woman Shall Conquer: The Story of the Blessed Virgin in the Modern World* (Milwaukee, WI: Bruce Pub. Co, 1952), 34. A memorandum from Chancellor James King to Bishop Mugavero indicates that King wrote the Montfort Fathers in May 1973 in an effort to reign in Lueken's movement. The letter apparently met with no response. See James P. King to Francis J. Mugavero, "Memorandum" (May 4, 1973). Archives of the Diocese of Brooklyn.

69. Lueken, *Virgin Mary's Bayside Prophecies*, Vol. 2, 20.

70. Baysiders explained to me that only the Douay-Rheims Bible was valid. The key passage was Genesis 3:15, in which God tells the serpent, "I will put enmities between thee and the woman, and thy seed and her seed: She shall crush thy head, and thou shalt lie in wait for her heel." More modern translations use the male pronoun "He will crush your head and you will strike his heel." For Baysiders, this translation denies Mary's victory over the serpent. Field notes (June 9, 2012).

71. Sharkey, *The Woman Shall Conquer*, 3.

72. Zimdars-Swartz, *Encountering Mary*, 262.

73. Michael Barkun, *Disaster and the Millennium* (New Haven, CT: Yale University Press, 1974), 127–28.

74. The Blackout: Night of Terror," *Time Magazine*, July 25, 1977, accessed March 26, 2011, http://www.time.com/time/magazine/article/0,9171,919089-1,00.html.

75. Lueken, *Virgin Mary's Bayside Prophecies*, 4:357.

76. Frances Duke to Bishop Francis J. Mugavero (August 28, 1979). Archives of the Diocese of Brooklyn.

77. Lueken, *Virgin Mary's Bayside Prophecies*, 4:349.

78. Lueken, *Virgin Mary's Bayside Prophecies*, 5:203.

79. Nobile, "Our Lady of Bayside," 57.

80. Mark Garvey, *Waiting for Mary: America in Search of a Miracle* (Cincinnati, OH: Emis Books, 2003), 157.

81. David M. Lindsey, *The Woman and the Dragon: Apparitions of Mary* (Gretna, LA: Pelican Pub, 2000), 161.

82. Lueken, *Virgin Mary's Bayside Prophecies*, 5:406.

83. Our Lady of the Roses Shrine, *Roses*. Copy provided by David Frankfurter.

84. See Grant, "War of the Roses," 43–46.

85. Field notes (June 14, 2012).

86. Field notes (June 16, 2012).

87. Lueken, *Virgin Mary's Bayside Prophecies*, 2:222. Similar dress codes were developed in Mary Ann Van Hoof's movement. Female followers were eventually encouraged to wear blue wrap-around skirts, serving much the same function

as the blue berets. Marlene Maloney, "Necedah Revisited: Anatomy of a Phony Apparition," *Fidelity* (February 1989): 20.

88. Cuneo, *Smoke of Satan*, 158; Grant, "The War of the Roses," 45; Nobile, "Our Lady of Bayside," 60.

89. Lueken, *Virgin Mary's Bayside Prophecies*, 2:222.

90. Lueken, *Virgin Mary's Bayside Prophecies*, 3:507.

91. Lueken, *Virgin Mary's Bayside Prophecies*, 3:508.

92. Nobile, "Our Lady of Bayside," 60.

93. Lueken, *Virgin Mary's Bayside Prophecies*, 6:378.

94. Sandra Gurvis, *Way Stations to Heaven: 50 Major Visionary Shrines in the United States* (New York: Macmillan, 1996), 138.

95. Robert Di Veroli, "Apparitions of Mary Ingrained in Catholicism; Rome Accepts Fatima as Fact; U.S. Appearance a Matter of Faith," *The San Diego Union-Tribune*, February 18, 1984, A6; Cuneo, *Smoke of Satan*, 163–73.

96. Cuneo, *Smoke of Satan*, 164.

97. Field notes (June 3, 2012).

98. Our Lady of the Roses, "Shrine Books, Publications, and Recommended Reading," accessed September 20, 2012, http://www.roses.org/pubs/publicat. htm.

99. St. Joseph's Catholic Church, "The Vision of Pope Leo XIII," accessed September 27, 2012, http://www.stjosephschurch.net/leoxiii.htm.

100. Robert Orsi, *Between Heaven and Earth: The Religious Worlds People Make and the Scholars Who Study Them* (Princeton, NJ: Princeton University Press, 2005), 12.

101. These Last Days Ministries, *Our Lady of the Roses, Mary Help of Mothers* (Lowell, MI: These Last Days Ministries, n.d.), 18.

102. In 1979, Pope John Paul II visited Boston and Lueken led a hundred of her followers down from New York to sell blessed rose petals. Megan Rosenfield and Patrick Tyler, "The Souvenir Business: Preparing for the Pope," *The Washington Times*, October 5, 1979, C1.

103. D. Gonzalez, "La Virgen busca casa propia en Queens," *El Diario La Prensa*, December 25, 2007, retrieved January 11, 2011, via Ethnic NewsWatch (ENW), ProQuestWeb. A Latina named Judith Reyes described saving her husband from the brink of heart failure simply by placing a blessed rose petal on his chest. Reyes seemed unperturbed by the unrecognized status of the shrine, pointing out that it took years for the church to approve Our Lady of Guadalupe as well. For Latino-American Catholics, religion has traditionally been focused on the home rather than mass attendance or regular participation in the sacraments. The Baysider's heavy emphasis on healing and the use of material religion such as rose petals likely appealed to Latino Catholics, whose devotional culture incorporates traditions of folk healing such as *curanderismo*. See Gonzalez, "La Virgen busca casa propia en Queens"; Jay P. Dolan, *In Search of an American Catholicism: A History of Religion and Culture in Tension* (Oxford: Oxford University

Press, 2002), 245; Timothy M. Matovina, *Latino Catholicism: Transformation in America's Largest Church* (Princeton, NJ: Princeton University Press, 2012), 164.
104. Field notes (June 10, 2012).
105. Orsi, *Between Heaven and Earth*, 162.

CHAPTER 5

1. Michael Cuneo, *The Smoke of Satan: Conservative and Traditionalist Dissent in Contemporary American Catholicism* (New York: Oxford University Press, 1997), 192; Our Lady of the Roses, "Jesus and His Mother Speak to the World," *Boston Globe*, April 12, 1979, 37; Daniel Wojcik, *The End of the World as We Know It: Faith, Fatalism, and Apocalypse in America* (New York: New York University Press, 1996), 61–70; Susan Paynter, "Coming Soon: The Mother of All Messages," *Seattle Post-Intelligencer*, April 3, 1995, D1; Mark Garvey, *Waiting for Mary: America in Search of a Miracle* (Cincinnati, OH: Emis Books, 2003), 178–79.
2. Adon Taft, "Shrine Ad Not Sanctioned, But Women Are Believers," *The Miami Herald*, February 1, 1985, 5; J. Gordon Melton, "Our Lady of Roses Shrine," *The Encyclopedia of American Religions*, 5th ed. (Detroit, MI: Gale Research Inc., 1996), 229; Paynter, "Coming Soon: The Mother of All Messages," D1.
3. State of Connecticut v. Curtiss Heinz, 3382, App Conn, 1984.
4. David Haldane, "Kneeling in Sin," *Concord Monitor*, July 8, 2006, accessed September 20, 2012, http://www.concordmonitor.com/article/kneeling-in-sin; Saint Michael's World Apostolate, *Golden Warrior Notes* 10 (July 2006), accessed September 20, 2012, http://www.smwa.org/Golden_Warrior/GW_10GW_Notes_July_06.html.
5. Robert Orsi, "Everyday Miracles: The Study of Lived Religion," in *Lived Religion in America: Toward a History of Practice*, ed. David D. Hall (Princeton, NJ: Princeton University Press, 1997), 13.
6. Roger Finke and Rodney Stark, *The Churching of America, 1776-2005: Winners and Losers in Our Religious Economy* (New Brunswick, NJ: Rutgers University Press, 2005).
7. The exceptions were Alabama, Arkansas, Georgia, Hawaii, Idaho, Mississippi, New Hampshire, South Carolina, South Dakota, and West Virginia. However, the absence of evidence should not be considered evidence of absence. The Archive's policy is that researchers may only see material that is at least thirty years old. The archives contained many letters concerning the Baysiders from after 1981, which have never been seen by researchers.
8. Mother Mary Teresa O.C.D. to Bishop Francis J. Mugavero (March 21, 1976). Archives of Diocese of Brooklyn.
9. Steven C. Moore to Chancellor Anthony Bevilacqua (October 3, 1976). Archives of Diocese of Brooklyn.

10. Mrs. Palma Lionetti to Bishop Francis J. Mugavero (September 19, 1980). Archives of Diocese of Brooklyn.

11. Archbishop Jaime Cardinal Sin to Bishop Francis J. Mugavero (May 15, 1979); Lolesio Fuahea to Chancellor Anthony Bevilacqua (December 1, 1977); Bishop William J. McNaighton to Bishop Francis J. Mugavero (January 14, 1981). Archives of Diocese of Brooklyn.

12. James Donovan, "Bayside Unveiled: The Blessed Mother Takes a Beating from Her 'Friends,'" *Fidelity* (March 1988): 38.

13. A. Windbacher to Bishop Bishop Francis J. Mugavero (February 27, 1976). Archives of Diocese of Brooklyn.

14. In the mid-eighteenth century, Pope Benedict XIV endorsed the limited use of apparitions and related phenomena for religious instruction in his treatise *De servorum Dei beatificatione*. Benedict had urged caution regarding visions since long before he became pope. Another of his treatises, *De revelatione*, introduced the distinction between *fides humana* and *fides Catholica*. He specified that, even with approval, there is no guarantee that an apparition has truly taken place. In other words, the hierarchy's endorsement of supernatural phenomena did not render these revelations part of Catholic doctrine, but only "worthy of belief." See Sandra Zimdars-Swartz, *Encountering Mary: From La Salette to Medjugorje* (Princeton, NJ: Princeton University Press, 1991), 9; George H. Tavard, *The Thousand Faces of the Virgin Mary* (Collegeville, MN: Liturgical Press, 1996), 177.

15. Angela from San Francisco to Bishop John R. Quinn, accessed June 6, 2011, http://www.tldm.org/news6/mugaverofiles.htm.

16. Lueken, *Virgin Mary's Bayside Prophecies*, 1:38; Lueken, *Virgin Mary's Bayside Prophecies*, 2:xiii–xiv.

17. Susan Paynter, "Coming Soon: The Mother of All Messages," *Seattle Post-Intelligencer*, April 3, 1995, D1.

18. Our Lady of the Roses; Mary Help of Mothers, accessed June 6, 2011, http://ladyofroses.org/cont18.htm.

19. John S. Hild, CM to Diocese of Brooklyn (March 15, 1980). Archives of the Diocese of Brooklyn.

20. Father Guillero Flores y Flores of Guatemala on the Bayside apparitions, accessed September 20, 2012, http://www.tldm.org/news2/fr._flores.htm.

21. Charles Savitskas, "The Church and 'Apparitions,'" *Visitor* (August 8, 1982): 4.

22. Bayside Hills Civic Association to Bishop Mugavero (June 19, 1974). Archives of the Diocese of Brooklyn.

23. This was the case at Necedah and probably other apparition sties. Sandra Zimdars-Swartz, "Religious Experience and Public Cult: The Case of Mary Ann Van Hoof," *Journal of Religion and Health* 28, no. 1 (Spring 1989): 48.

24. Philip Nobile, "Our Lady of Bayside," *New York Magazine*, December 11, 1978, 60.

25. Anne Cillis, "Canadian Priest Saw Veronica in Levitation" (March 1977), 103. Archives of the Diocese of Brooklyn.

26. Michael P. Carroll, *The Cult of the Virgin Mary: Psychological Origins* (Princeton, NJ: Princeton University Press, 1986), 68; Lueken, *Virgin Mary's Bayside Prophecies*, 6:254.

27. Lueken, *Virgin Mary's Bayside Prophecies*, 6:253.

28. See the vigils described in Garvey, *Waiting for Mary.*

29. A similar problem developed in Conyers, Georgia, where an apparition attracted priests from the Atlanta diocese. A memorandum from Bishop Lyke explained that while priests could freely visit the apparition site at Conyers, they could not lead others on pilgrimages. Bishop Lyke explained, "It is important that we not create the perception or impression that I or the Archdiocese endorse or authenticate these alleged apparitions." Memorandum of Archbishop Lyke to archdiocesan priests (January 17, 1992), quoted in Brian Britt, "Snapshots of Tradition: Apparitions of the Virgin Mary in Georgia," *Nova Religio* 2, no. 1 (October 1998): 111.

30. Marlene Maloney, "Necedah Revisited: Anatomy of a Phony Apparition," *Fidelity* (February 1989); 28.

31. Charles Savitskas, "The Church and 'Apparitions,' " *Our Sunday Visitor*, August 8, 1982, 4.

32. Tavard, *The Thousand Faces of the Virgin Mary*, 180–81.

33. Other diocesan officials have explained that the reform of 1966 applies only to books that the Catholic Church had once banned. Chancellor James P. King to Ann Ferguson (January 2, 1975). Archives of the Diocese of Brooklyn.

34. James J. LeBar, *Cults, Sects, and the New Age* (Huntington, IN: Our Sunday Visitor Pub.), 209–10.

35. "Bishop Rejects Apparition Claims," *The New York Times*, February 15, 1987, 67; "El Movimiento 'Bayside,' " *The Tidings*, December 26, 1986, 6. The grammar of the Spanish in this article is flawed and it may have been translated by Mugavero himself; "Rapped Once, Seer Again," *New York Post*, December 9, 1986.

36. "Bishop Rejects Apparition Claims," 67.

37. This use of the terms church and sect was popularized in the Western scholarship by H. Richard Neibuhr. However, they were previously used in slightly different senses by Max Weber and Ernst Troeltsch. See H. Richard Niebuhr, *The Social Sources of Denominationalism* (New York: Meridian Book, 1975).

38. Finke and Stark, *The Churching of America*, 42.

39. The rejection of worldly culture in favor of an otherworldly orientation is an ongoing process with no limits to how many aspects of culture can be sacrificed. At a banquet to honor the forty-second anniversary of the apparitions at Bayside, Antonia Rehrl described the vision she experienced at Flushing Meadows of an enormous communion host that filled the sky. She said that after this experience she had become a less worldly person. My impression was that Mrs. Rehrl had never been a very worldly person to begin with and had few vices to rid

herself of. She was a talented dancer and had won several waltzing competitions with her husband. After experiencing her vision, she gave up waltzing in order to devote even more time to prayer. Field notes (June 16, 2012).

40. According to Jeremy Lueken (Phone interview May 21, 2013), some members of New York's Italian mafia families were interested in the Bayside Prophecies. The mother of John Gotti, boss of the Gambino family, was rumored to be an avid fan of Lueken.

41. Samuel G. Freedman, "Abortion Bombings Suspect: A Portrait of Piety and Rage," *The New York Times*, May 7, 1987, http://www.nytimes.com/1987/05/07/ nyregion/abortion-bombings-suspect-a-portrait-of-piety-and-rage.html.

42. Lueken, *Virgin Mary's Bayside Prophecies*, 4:473.

43. Freedman, "Abortion Bombings Suspect: A Portrait of Piety and Rage."

44. Marie Stan Adellee, "Like a Prayer," *New Republic*, July 6, 1992, 11; Ed Vulliamy, Henry McDonald, and Stuart Jeffries, "Abortion Death Hunt Muzzles 'Atomic Dog,' " *The Guardian*, March 31, 2001, http://www.guardian.co.uk/world/2001/ apr/01/edvulliamy.henrymcdonald.

45. Lueken, *Virgin Mary's Bayside Prophecies*, 1:106.

46. Joseph Bottom, "When the Swallows Come back to Capistrano: Catholic Culture in America," *First Things: A Monthly Journal of Religion and Public Life* 166 (October 2007): 30.

47. Freedman, "Abortion Bombings Suspect: A Portrait of Piety and Rage."

48. Bruce Frankel, "Pair's Prayers Piercing/Pa Women Defy Court's Order," *USA Today*, April 14, 1995, 3A.

49. Dennis B. Roddy and Mackenzie Carpenter, "Praying or Braying?," *Pittsburgh Post-Gazette*, April 12, 1995, A1–7B.

50. "Judge Drops Contempt Charges Against 'Rosary Ladies," *Associated Press*, June 2, 1995.

51. "Rosary Ladies' Won't Pray Quietly," *United Press International*, April 18, 1995, retrieved on January 6, 2011, from Lexis Nexus Academic database.

52. Dennis B. Roddy, "New Place to Pray; Greenburg Women Who Roared the Rosary Worship in Ohio Church," *Pittsburgh Post-Gazette*, June 28, 1995, B1.

53. Cuneo, *Smoke of Satan*, 164–66.

54. E. Michael Jones, "The Cult, the Statue, and the Fall of the Canadian Layman," *Fidelity* (May 1989): 33.

55. Paul Hamilton, "The Reality behind the Roses," *Sancta Maria* (December 8, 1986): 5–8.

56. Hamilton, "The Reality behind the Roses," 5–8.

57. Jones, "The Cult, the Statue, and the Fall of the Canadian Layman," 35.

58. Hamilton, "The Reality behind the Roses," 5. I spoke with a shrine worker who remembered working alongside Tony Bronson. He shook his head as he recalled receiving a series of irate phone calls from Charles Bronson. Field notes (June 3, 2012).

59. Charles Montgomery, "Charles Bronson's Secret Heartache: His Son Drops Out of Graduate School to Join Religious Cult," *The National Enquirer*, August 23, 1985, 3.

60. Montgomery, "Charles Bronson's Secret Heartache." A Baysider told me that none of Lueken's four surviving children believe in her visions. Field notes (June 16, 2012).

61. Hamilton, "The Reality behind the Roses," 6.

62. Anthony Shupe, "The Role of Apostates in the North American Anti-Cult Movement," in *The Politics of Religious Apostasy: The Role of Apostates in the Transformation of Religious Movements*, ed. David G. Bromley (Westport, CT: Praeger, 1998), 212.

63. Paolo Apolito, *The Internet and the Madonna: Religious Visionary Experience on the Web* (Chicago: University of Chicago Press, 2005), 76.

64. Lueken, *Virgin Mary's Bayside Prophecies*, 6:149.

65. An important deviation was a shrine worker I spoke with who regarded miraculous signs as true but ultimately a distraction from the message of heaven. He explained that heaven was bestowing so many miracles at Flushing Meadows because modern people are "touchy-feely" and require such signs to inspire their faith. Field notes (June 3, 2012).

66. These Last Days Ministries, accessed September 20, 2012, http://www.tldm.org/misc/Pgss6_9.htm. Luminous doves have become a common trope in modern Marian apparitions. For instance, Coptic Christians reported seeing luminous doves during a series of apparitions in al-Warraq, Egypt, in 2009. See Angie Heo, "The Virgin Made Visible: Intercessory Images of Church Territory in Egypt," *Comparative Studies in Society and History* 54, no. 2 (2012): 367.

67. Michael Mangan and Antonia Rehrl, June 2004, available on Saint Michael's World Apostolate "Is Bayside Condemned?" (Audio CD); Field notes (June 17, 2012).

68. Apolito, Paolo. *Apparitions of the Madonna at Oliveto Citra: Local Visions and Cosmic Drama*, trans. William Christian Jr. (Philadelphia: Pennsylvania State University Press, 1998), 101.

69. Paula M. Kane, "'She Offered Herself Up': The Victim Soul and Victim Spirituality in Catholicism," *Church History* 71, no. 1 (March 2002): 80–119.

70. Zimdars-Swartz, *Encountering Mary*, 17; Deborah Halter, "Field Note: Charisma in Conyers: A Journal from Visionary to Apparition Site to Church," *Nova Religio* 14, no. 3 (February 2011): 108–10.

71. Frances Duke to Bishop Francis J. Mugavero (August, 28 1979).

72. Susan Borham and Rosa Maiolo, "Prophet & Loss: How an Australian Cult Leader Duped the Faithful," *Sydney Morning Herald*, December 24, 1993, 1.

73. Elizabeth Isichei, "Visions and Visionaries: The Search for Alternative Forms of Authority among Catholic Conservatives," *Archives de Sciences Socials des Religions* 36, no. 75 (July–September 1991): 119–21.

74. Jodie Duffy, "Master Manipulator," *Illawarra Mercury*, December 8, 2007, 9; Isichei, "Visions and Visionaries," 121.

75. Lueken, *Virgin Mary's Bayside Prophecies*, 6:120.

76. Associated Press, "Cult Leader Jailed for more Sexual Abuse," *The Age*, August 24, 2007, accessed July 2, 2011, http://www.theage.com.au/news/National/Cult-leader-jailed-for-more-sexual-abuse/2007/08/24/1187462512116.html.

77. Lueken, *Virgin Mary's Bayside Prophecies*, 6:268.

CHAPTER 6

1. Saint Michael's World Apostolate, "Veronica of the Cross: Her Final Agony, Scourging and Heroism," accessed September 20, 2012, http://www.smwa.org/Veronica_of_the_Cross/Document_Veronicas_final_agony.htm.

2. Lueken, *Virgin Mary's Bayside Prophecies*, 6:4–5.

3. Michael Cuneo, *The Smoke of Satan: Conservative and Traditionalist Dissent in Contemporary American Catholicism* (New York: Oxford University Press, 1997), 154, 175. Early in the study of new religious movements, it was assumed that movements die with their leaders because they are simply extensions of the leader's charisma. This assumption has been dispelled. J. Gordon Melton ("Introduction" in *When Prophets Die: The Postcharismatic Fate of New Religious Movements*, ed. Timothy Miller (New York: SUNY, 1991), 9) explains: "When a new religion dies, it usually has nothing to do with the demise of the founder; it is from lack of response of the public to the founder's ideas or the incompetence of the founder in organizing the followers into a strong group." Lueken is an interesting case study in this regard because she never intended to create a separate Church. Many of those attending vigils were not interested in Lueken's "ideas." People came for a variety of reasons including curiosity, a sense of propinquity with the divine, and an opportunity to ritually express their objection to liturgical reform. Without Lueken, these desires could be satisfied in other ways or even through other Marian seers. The Baysiders who remained after Lueken's death were likely those who had become significantly invested in the Baysider culture of prophecy and the worldview provided through Lueken's messages.

4. Max Weber and Shmuel N. Eisenstadt, *Max Weber on Charisma and Institution Building: Selected Papers* (Chicago: University of Chicago Press, 1968), 57.

5. Ronald Brown, Interview (September 24, 2012).

6. Lueken, *Virgin Mary's Bayside Prophecies*, 5:174–75.

7. Cuneo, *Smoke of Satan*, 176.

8. Alice Feinstein, "Many Believe N.Y. 'Miracle,'" *Spokane Daily Chronicle*, December 1, 1979, 8; Frank Albas, "Resolving the Leadership Crisis at Bayside," accessed September 20, 2012, http://www.rosesfromheaven.com/bayside_crisis.htm.

9. Saint Michael's World Apostolate, "Alleluia! Great Warning Delayed" (April 1998), accessed September 20, 2012, http://www.smwa.org/Documents/Great_Warning_Delayed/Document_Great_Warning_Delayed.htm.

10. Ann Ferguson (January 8, 1997), accessed September 20, 2012, http://www.roses.org/news/annferguson.htm.

11. Frank Albas "January 1998 Newsletter," accessed September 20, 2012, http://www.rosesfromheaven.com/january.html.

12. Daniel Wojcik, "Bayside (Our Lady of the Roses)," in *Encyclopedia of Millennialism and Millennial Movements*, ed. Richard A. Landes (New York: Routledge, 2000), 92.

13. Frank Albas, "January 1998 Newsletter."

14. Field notes (June 3, 2012); Jeremy Lueken, phone interview (May 21, 2013).

15. Frank Albas, "NEWS FLASH: Lueken Wins Court Case!," accessed September 20, 2012, http://www.rosesfromheaven.com/court.html.

16. Daniel Wojcik, *The End of the World as We Know It: Faith, Fatalism, and Apocalypse in America* (New York: New York University Press, 1996), 92. This conditional understanding of prophecy relates to a general characterization about the Catholic worldview made by Andrew Greeley. Greeley argues that the fundamental difference between Protestants and Catholics is that Protestants see God as dialectical and separated from the world while Catholics see God as analogical and present in the world. Within the Catholic worldview, Greeley argues, society is not necessarily "God-forsaken." Andrew M. Greeley, *The Catholic Myth: The Behavior and Beliefs of American Catholics* (New York: Scribner, 1990), 44–45.

17. Charles Savitskas, "The Church and 'Apparitions,'" *Visitor* (August 8, 1982): 4.

18. Saint Michael's World Apostolate, "Alleluia! Great Warning Delayed."

19. Lueken, *Virgin Mary's Bayside Prophecies*, 6:148; Field notes (June 14, 2012). In the seminal study *When Prophecy Fails*, Leon Festinger argued that failed prophecies create cognitive dissonance leading to increased proselytization. Several scholars have since produced more nuanced models of how religious movements handle failed prophecies. Joseph Zygmunt argued that groups employ a repertoire of responses, one of which is to simply assign blame to factions within the group, thus using the failed prophecy as an opportunity to redirect resources. This is essentially what Arthur Lueken sought to do. J. Gordon Melton has noted that millennial movements rarely invest their entire worldview in a single prophecy. As Lorne L. Dawson explains, "Festinger et al. were misguided in seeing prophecies in simply true or false terms." See Leon Festinger, Henry W. Reicken, and Stanley Schachter, *When Prophecy Fails: A Social and Psychological Study of a Modern Group that Predicted the Destruction of the World* (New York: Harper Torchbooks, 1965); Joseph F. Zygmunt, "When Prophecies Fail: A Theoretical Perspective on the Comparative Evidence," *American Behavioral Scientist* 16, no. 2 (Nov/Dec 1972): 245–68; J. Gordon Melton,

"Spiritualization and Reaffirmation: What Really Happens When Prophecy Fails," *American Studies* 26, no. 2 (Fall 1985): 19; Lorne L. Dawson, "When Prophecy Fails and Faith Persists: A Theoretical Overview," *Nova Religio* 3, no. 1 (1999): 73.

20. Saint Michael's World Apostolate, "Jesus and Mary Chose Michael Mangan," *Golden Warrior* 1 (December 1998), accessed September 20, 2012, http://www.smwa.org/Golden_Warrior/GW_1Golden_Warrior_1_Jesus_and_Mary_chose_Michael.htm.

21. Field notes (June 14, 2012).

22. Albas, "NEWS FLASH: Lueken Wins Court Case!"

23. Ann Ferguson, "My Memories of Veronica Lueken by Mrs. Ann Ferguson," accessed June 30, 2012, http://www.tldm.org/news4/MemoriesOfVeronica.htm.

24. Frank Albas, "July 1998 Newsletter," accessed September 20, 2012, http://www.rosesfromheaven.com/july98.html.

25. "You Are There; Waiting for the Virgin," *The New York Times*, July 26, 1998, 9.

26. Michael Mangan, "Saint Michael's World Apostolate Blest and Thriving," *Golden Warrior* 1 no. 1 (December 1998): 2, http://www.smwa.org/Golden_Warrior/Pdf/GW-1.pdf.

27. William E. Dykes, "SMWA Proud Owners of Impressive 5000 sq. ft Complex," *Golden Warrior* 1, no. 2 (June 1999): 4, accessed September 20, 2012, http://www.smwa.org/Golden_Warrior/Pdf/GW-2.pdf.

28. Corey Kilgannon, "Visions of Doom Endure in Queens; Prophecy, and a Rift, at a Shrine," *The New York Times*, October 9, 2003, 1.

29. Field notes (June 10, 2012).

30. Lueken, *Virgin Mary's Bayside Prophecies*, 6:382–83.

31. Albas, "January 1998 Newsletter."

32. Phone interview (May 21, 2013).

33. Saint Michael's World Apostolate, "Arthur Lueken Funeral," accessed September 20, 2012, http://www.smwa.org/Documents/Mr_Lueken_Funeral/Arthur_Lueken_Funeral.htm.

34. Michael Mangan to Vivian Hanratty (March 8, 2005), accessed September 20, 2012, http://www.smwa.org/documents/Letter_to_Vivian_at_OLR_Corporation/Letter_to_Vivian_at_OLR_Corporation.html.

35. Field notes (June 14, 2012).

36. See Paul Sullins, "The Stained Glass Ceiling: Career Attainment for Women Clergy," *Sociology of Religion* 61, no. 3 (2000): 243–66; Catherine Wessinger, *Women's Leadership in Marginal Religions: Explorations Outside the Mainstream* (Chicago: University of Illinois Press, 1993).

37. Field notes (June 16, 2012).

38. Kilgannon, "Visions of Doom Endure in Queens," 1.

39. Lueken, *Virgin Mary's Bayside Prophecies*, 2:476; James L. Franklin, "Movie 'Hail Mary' Stirs Controversy in Boston," *Boston Globe*, November 17, 1985, accessed

through Boston Globe, ProQuest Web; Carol Beggy, "400 Protest Showing of 'Hail Mary,'" *Boston Globe*, December 1, 1985, accessed through Boston Globe, ProQuest Web.

40. Kenneth Jones, "Those For and Against, Some Angrily, Protest *Corpus Christi*," *Playbill*, October 14, 1998, accessed August 8, 2012, http://www. playbill.com/news/article/41422-Those-For-and-Against-Some-Angrily-Protest-Corpus-Christi; Saint Michael's World Apostolate, "Disciples in Action," accessed September 20, 2012, http://www.smwa.org/documents/ Mary_Like_a_Virgin_Protest/Protesting_Blasphemous_Play.htm; "Disciples in Action: *Da Vinci Code* Movie Protest," accessed September 20, 2012, http:// www.smwa.org/documents/The_Da_Vinci_Code_movie_protest/Da_Vinci_ Movie_Protest_Photos.htm.

41. Amy Welborn, "Author Provides a Revealing Look at Mary Visions," *Tampa Tribune*, October 31, 1998, 3; Field notes (June 16, 2012).

42. Jim Remsen, "Some See Signs of Apocalypse in Attacks," *The Philadelphia Inquirer*, October 4, 2001.

43. Michael Mangan, "Armageddon Rages," *Golden Warrior* 5, October 2001, accessed September 20, 2012, http://www.smwa.org/Golden_Warrior/ GW_5/Golden_Warrior_5_Armageddon_rages.htm; "9/11 Statement from the President," September 11, 2002, accessed September 20, 2012, http://www. smwa.org/Documents/Attack_on_America/Document_Statement_9_11_02_ from_President.htm.

44. Vivian Hanratty, Online tribute to Digna Alexandra Rivera Costanza (March 17, 2009), accessed September 20, 2012, http://www.9-11heroes.us/v/Digna_ Alexandra_Rivera_Costanza.php.

45. Our Lady of the Roses Shrine, *Rose Notes*, September 2002, accessed April 21, 2012, http://www.ourladyoftheroses.org/rose_notes/rose-notes_1 .htm.

46. Veronica Lueken, "Message Given to Veronica by our Lady on December 18, 1991," accessed September 20, 2012, http://www.tldm.org/Bayside/Messages/ bm911218.htm.

47. Gary Wohlsheid, Newsletter (December 22, 2001), accessed September 20, 2012, http://www.tldm.org/newsletters/FR0112.htm.

48. Lueken, *Virgin Mary's Bayside Prophecies*, 2:164.

49. Frederic J. Baumgartner, *Longing for the End: A History of Millennialism in Western Civilization* (New York: St. Martin's Press, 1999), 204.

50. Sally Cunneen, *In Search of Mary: The Woman and the Symbol* (New York: Ballantine Books, 1996), 194–95.

51. Richard Dawkins, *Unweaving the Rainbow: Science, Delusion and the Appetite for Wonder* (New York: Mariner Books, 1998), 133–35.

52. Chancellor James P. King "Memorandum" (October 9, 1973). Archives of the Diocese of Brooklyn.

234 Notes

53. Andrew Greeley, *Ecstasy: A Way of Knowing* (Englewood Cliffs, NJ: Prentice-Hall, 1974), 18–19. Wade Clark Roof makes a similar argument. He suggests that the modernity's emphasis on reason, which draws strength from Protestant theology, has led to a loss of the sacred and of mystery. This spiritual malaise has contributed to a religious "culture of questing." See *Spiritual Marketplace: Baby Boomers and the Remaking of American Religion* (Princeton, NJ: Princeton University Press, 1999).

54. James Donovan, "Bayside Unveiled: The Blessed Mother Takes a Beating from Her 'Friends,'" *Fidelity* (March 1988): 42.

55. In 1966, *Time* magazine ran its famous cover asking, "Is God Dead?" A Gallup poll taken in January 1970 indicated that 75 percent of survey respondents thought that religion was losing influence. This is the highest percentage ever recorded since Gallup began this poll in 1957 Lydia Saad, "Americans Believe Religion Is Losing Clout" (Gallup, 2009), accessed September 1, 2012, http://www.gallup.com/poll/113533/Americans-Believe-Religion-Losing-Clout.aspx. For critiques of the secularization narrative, see José Cassanova, *Public Religions in the Modern World* (Chicago: University of Chicago Press, 1994); William H. Swatos and Kevin J. Christiano, "Secularization: The Course of a Concept," in *The Secularization Debate*, ed. William H. Swatos and Daniel V. A. Olson (Lanham, MD: Rowman and Littlefield, 2000), 1–20; Rodney Stark, "Secularization, R.I.P.," *Sociology of Religion* 60, no. 3 (1999): 249–73.

56. Eugene Cullen Kennedy, "Set-decorator Catholicism: Clericalism Thrives in a New Phase of the Sex Abuse Crisis," *National Catholic Reporter*, June 30, 2011, http://ncronline.org/blogs/bulletins-human-side/set-decorator-catholicism-clericalism-thrives-new-phase-sex-abuse-crisis; Paul Vitello, "For Catholics, a Door to Absolution Is Reopened," *The New York Times*, February 9, 2009, http://www.nytimes.com/2009/02/10/nyregion/10indulgence.html?pagewanted =1&_r=.

57. Erik Eckholm, "Wisconsin on the Map to Pray with Mary," *The New York Times*, December 23, 2010, http://www.nytimes.com/2010/12/24/us/24mary.html?_r=1.

58. Joachim Bouflet and Philippe Boutry, *Un signe dans le ciel: les apparitions de la Vierge* (Paris: Grasset, 1997), 396–99.

59. Landislas Orsy, Electronic communication with the author (September 5, 2011).

60. "Marian Apparitions of the Twentieth Century," The Marian Library/International Research Institute (August 8, 2011), accessed August 23, 2011, http://campus.udayton.edu/mary/resources/aprtable.html.

61. Quoted in Bouflet and Boutry, *Un signe dans le ciel*, 396 (My translation from the French).

62. William J. Levada, "Preface to Norms Regarding the Manner of Proceeding in the Discernment of Presumed Apparitions or Revelations," accessed October 2, 2012, http://www.catholicculture.org/culture/library/view.cfm? recnum= 9951#_ftn1.

CHAPTER 7

1. Laycock, "Controversial Mary Statue Weeps Because 'We're Killing this World.'"
2. Asia News, "Vatican Sustains Ruling on Korean Visionary," *Spero News*, February 27, 2009, http://www.speroforum.com/site/article.asp?idCategory=33&idsub=122&id=18310&t=Vatican+sustains+ruling+on+Korean+visionary.
3. Edicion Impressa, "Independientes: en La Ermita se impone 'un cacicazgo tremendo'" *La Jornada Michoacan*, September 3, 2012, http://www.lajornadamichoacan.com.mx/2012/09/03/independientes-en-la-ermita-se-impone-un-cacicazgo-tremendo/.
4. BBC News, "Vatican Declares Mexican Folk Saint Blasphemous," May 9, 2013, http://www.bbc.co.uk/news/world-latin-america-22462181.
5. R. Andrew Chestnut, *Devoted to Death: Santa Muerte: The Skeleton Saint* (New York: Oxford University Press, 2012).
6. Peter Jan Margry, "Global Network of Divergent Marian Devotion," in *New Religions: A Guide: New Religious Movements, Sects and Alternative Spiritualities*, ed. Christopher Partridge (New York: Oxford University Press, 2004), 98–102.
7. David Bromley and Rachel S. Bobbitt, "Visions of the Virgin Mary: The Organizational Development of Marian Apparitional Movements," *Nova Religio* 14, no. 3 (February 2011): 7.
8. Bromley and Bobbitt, "Visions of the Virgin Mary," 30.
9. Robert Orsi, "Everyday Miracles: The Study of Lived Religion," in *Lived Religion in America: Toward a History of Practice*, ed. David D. Hall (Princeton, NJ: Princeton University Press, 1997), 8.
10. See David D. Hall, "Introduction," in *Lived Religion in America: Toward a History of Practice*, ed. David D. Hall (Princeton, NJ: Princeton University Press, 1997); as well as Nancy Ammerman, "Observing Religious Lives," in *Everyday Religion: Observing Modern Religious Lives*, ed. Nancy Ammerman (New York: Oxford University Press, 2007), 3–20.
11. Robert Orsi, *Between Heaven and Earth: The Religious Worlds People Make and the Scholars Who Study Them* (Princeton, NJ: Princeton University Press, 2005), 167.
12. Thomas A. Tweed, *Crossing and Dwelling: A Theory of Religion* (Cambridge, MA: Harvard University Press, 2006), 54. His complete definition is as follows "Religions are confluences of organic-cultural flows that intensify joy and confront suffering by drawing on human and suprahuman forces to make homes and cross boundaries."
13. Orsi, "Everyday Miracles," 9.
14. Anthony F. C. Wallace, "Revitalization Movements," *American Anthropologist* 58, no. 2 (1956): 264–81.
15. Clifford Geertz, *Islam Observed* (Chicago: Chicago University Press, 1968), 23.
16. Meredith B. McGuire, *Lived Religion: Faith and Practice in Everyday Life* (New York: Oxford University Press, 2008), 43.

Bibliography

This book relied heavily on letters, memorandum, and other primary sources made available by the archives of the Diocese of Brooklyn. The archive has collected five large files boxes of material concerning Veronica Lueken. Due to the archive's policy, I was only able to access material that was at least thirty years old. There remain numerous letters concerning Veronica Lueken and her movement from the 1980s and 1990s which researchers have not yet been able to see.

Fidelity magazine, which frequently covered the Baysiders, was available through the library of Boston College. Newspapers on the Baysiders were accessed through Google news and Lexis Nexus databases as well as the archives of *The New York Times* and *The Weekly World News*. *Newsweek* was accessed through the Briscoe Center for American History at the University of Texas at Austin. In one case, I contacted the archivist for *The Tidings*, the newsletter of the Diocese of Los Angeles. The website <http://www.tldm.org> contains all of the Bayside prophecies as well as back issues of the newsletter "Directives from Heaven." <http://www.swma.org> offers information on the current state of the Baysider movement as well as back issues of their newsletter, *Golden Warrior*.

Abbott, Walter M., ed. *The Documents of Vatican II*. Translated by Joseph Gallagher. New York: Guild Press, 1996.

Albanese, Catherine L. *America, Religions, and Religion*. Belmont, CA: Wadsworth, 1999.

Albanese, Catherine L. *A Republic of Mind and Spirit: A Cultural History of American Metaphysical Religion*. New Haven, CT: Yale University Press, 2007.

Ammerman, Nancy T., ed. *Everyday Religion: Observing Modern Religious Lives.* New York: Oxford University Press, 2007.

Anderson, Benedict. *Imagined Communities: Reflections on the Origin and Spread of Nationalism.* Rev. and extended ed. London: Verso, 1991.

Apolito, Paolo. *Apparitions of the Madonna at Oliveto Citra: Local Visions and Cosmic Drama.* Translated by William Christian Jr. Philadelphia: Pennsylvania State University Press, 1998.

Apolito, Paolo. *The Internet and the Madonna: Religious Visionary Experience on the Web.* Chicago: University of Chicago Press, 2005.

Bader, Christopher David, Frederick Carson Mencken, and Joe Baker. *Paranormal America: Ghost Encounters, UFO Sightings, Bigfoot Hunts, and Other Curiosities in Religion and Culture.* New York: New York University Press, 2010.

Barkun, Michael. *Disaster and the Millennium.* New Haven, CT: Yale University Press, 1974.

Barkun, Michael. "Politics and Apocalypticism." In *The Encyclopedia of Apocalypticism,* edited by Stephen J. Stein, 3:442–60. New York: Continuum, 1998.

Barkun, Michael. "Conspiracy Theories as Stigmatized Knowledge: The Basis for a New Age Racism?" In *Nation and Race: The Developing Euro-American Racist Subculture,* edited by Jeffrey Kaplan and Tore Bjorgo, 58–72. Boston: Northeastern University Press, 1998.

Barkun, Michael. *A Culture of Conspiracy: Apocalyptic Visions in Contemporary America.* Berkeley: University of California Press, 2003.

Barkun, Michael. "Myths of the Underworld in Contemporary American Millennialism." In *Experiences of Place,* edited by Mary N. MacDonald, 147–62. Cambridge, MA: Harvard University Press, 2003.

Baudrillard, Jean. *America.* Translated by Chris Turner. New York: Verso, 1989.

Bax, Mart. *Medjugorje: Religion, Politics, and Violence in Rural Bosnia.* Amsterdam: VU Utigeverij, 1995.

Berryman, Edward. "Taking Pictures of Jesus: Producing the Material Presence of a Divine Other." *Human Studies* 28, no. 4 (2005): 431–52.

Bobbitt, Rachel S. "Applying Movement Success Models to Marian Apparition Movements." Masters thesis, Virginia Commonwealth University, 2008.

Bottom, Joseph. "When the Swallows Come back to Capistrano: Catholic Culture in America." *First Things: A Monthly Journal of Religion and Public Life* 166 (October 2007): 27–40.

Bouflet, Joachim, and Philippe Boutry. *Un Signe Dans le Ciel:les Apparitions de la Vierge.* Paris: Grasset, 1997.

Braude, Ann. *Radical Spirits: Spiritualism and Women's Rights in Nineteenth-Century America.* Bloomington: Indiana University Press, 2002.

Britt, Brian. "Snapshots of Tradition: Apparitions of the Virgin Mary in Georgia." *Nova Religio* 2, no. 1 (October 1998): 108–25.

Bromley, David, and Rachel S. Bobbitt. "Visions of the Virgin Mary: The Organizational Development of Marian Apparitional Movements." *Nova Religio* 14, no. 3 (February 2011): 5–41.

Bullard, Thomas E. "UFOs: Lost in the Myths." In *UFOs and Abductions: Challenging the Borders of Knowledge*, edited by David M Jacobs, 141–90. Lawrence: University of Kansas, 2000.

Bynum, Caroline Walker. *Jesus as Mother: Studies in Spirituality of the High Middle Ages.* Berkley: University of California Press, 1982.

Campbell, Colin. "The Cult, the Cultic Milieu, and Secularization." In *The Cultic Milieu: Oppositional Subcultures in an Age of Globalization*, edited by Jeffrey Kaplan and Heléne Lööw, 12–25. Walnut Creek: AltaMira Press, 2002.

Cardone, Dino. "Programming the Apocalypse: Recombinant Narrative in Cyberspace." PhD diss., University of Southern California, 2007.

Carroll, Michael P. *The Cult of the Virgin Mary: Psychological Origins.* Princeton, NJ: Princeton University Press, 1986.

Carter, Stephen L. *The Culture of Disbelief: How American Law and Politics Trivialize Religious Devotion.* New York: BasicBooks, 1993.

Cassanova, José. *Public Religions in the Modern World.* Chicago: University of Chicago Press, 1994.

Catechism of the Catholic Church. New York: Continuum International Publishing Group, 2002.

Chestnut, R. Andrew. *Devoted to Death: Santa Muerte: The Skeleton Saint.* New York: Oxford University Press, 2012.

Chidester, David, and Edward T. Linenthal, eds. *American Sacred Space.* Bloomington: Indiana University Press, 1995.

Christian, William, Jr. *Local Religion in Sixteenth-Century Spain.* Princeton, NJ: Princeton University Press, 1981.

Christian, William, Jr. "Religious Apparitions and the Cold War in Southern Europe." In *Religion, Power and Protest in Local Communities: The Northern Shore of the Mediterranean*, edited by Eric Wolf, 239–66. New York: Walter de Gruyter, 1984.

Cousineau, Christy. "The Age of Mary." In *Encyclopedia of Millennialism and Millennial Movements*, edited by Richard A. Landes, 11–18. New York: Taylor & Francis, 2000.

Crouch, Ben, and Kelly Damphousse. "Law Enforcement and the Satanic Crime Connection: A Survey of 'Cult Cops.'" In *The Satanism Scare*, edited by James T. Richardson and Joel Best, 191–204. New York: Walter de Gruytner, 1991.

Cuneo, Michael. *The Smoke of Satan: Conservative and Traditionalist Dissent in Contemporary American Catholicism.* New York: Oxford University Press, 1997.

Cunneen, Sally. *In Search of Mary: The Woman and the Symbol.* New York: Ballantine Books, 1996.

Davis, Phillip W., and Jacqueline Boles. "Pilgrim Apparition Work: Symbolization and Crowd Interaction When the Virgin Mary Appeared in Georgia." *Journal of Contemporary Ethnography* 32, no. 4 (August 2003): 371–402.

Dawkins, Richard. *Unweaving the Rainbow: Science, Delusion and the Appetite for Wonder.* New York: Mariner Books, 1998.

Dawson, Lorne L. "When Prophecy Fails and Faith Persists: A Theoretical Overview." *Nova Religio* 3, no. 1 (1999): 60–82.

Dolan, Jay P. *In Search of an American Catholicism: A History of Religion and Culture in Tension.* Oxford: Oxford University Press, 2002.

Eliade, Mircea. *The Sacred and the Profane.* Translated by Willard R. Trask. New York: Harcourt Brace, 1961.

Ellis, Bill. *Raising the Devil: Satanism, New Religions, and the Media.* Lexington: University Press of Kentucky, 2000.

Festinger, Leon, Henry W. Reicken, and Stanley Schachter. *When Prophecy Fails: A Social and Psychological Study of a Modern Group that Predicted the Destruction of the World.* New York: Harper Torchbooks, 1965.

Finke, Roger, and Rodney Stark. *The Churching of America, 1776–2005: Winners and Losers in Our Religious Economy.* New Brunswick, NJ: Rutgers University Press, 2005.

Fisher, James T. *The Catholic Counterculture in America, 1933–1962.* Chapel Hill: University of North Carolina Press, 1989.

Flinn, Frank K., and J. Gordon Melton. *Encyclopedia of Catholicism.* New York: Checkmark Books, 2008.

Flowers, Ronald B. *Religion in Strange Times: The 1960s and 1970s.* Macon, GA: Mercer University Press, 1984.

Forster, Marc R. *The Counter-Reformation in the Villages: Religion and Reform in the Bishopric of Speyer, 1560-1720.* Ithaca, NY: Cornell University Press, 1992.

Foucault, Michel. *Society Must Be Defended: Lectures at the College de France, 1975-76.* New York: Picador, 2007.

Frankfurter, David. *Evil Incarnate: Rumors of Demonic Conspiracy and Ritual Abuse in History.* Princeton, NJ: Princeton University Press, 2006.

Freud, Sigmund. *Civilization and Its Discontents.* New York: Norton, 2005.

Friedland, Roger and Richard Hecht. "The Bodies of Nations: A Comparative Study of Religious Violence in Jerusalem and Ayodhya." *History of Religions* 38, no. 2 (November 1998): 101–49.

Garvey, Mark. *Waiting for Mary: America in Search of a Miracle.* Cincinnati, OH: Emis Books, 2003.

Geetz, Clifford. *Islam Observed: Religious Development in Morocco and Indonesia.* Chicago: University of Chicago Press, 2004.

Graham, Billy. *Angels: God's Secret Agents.* Garden City, NY: Doubleday, 1975.

Greeley, Andrew. M. *Ecstasy: A Way of Knowing.* Englewood Cliffs, NJ: Prentice-Hall, 1974.

Greeley, Andrew M. *The Catholic Myth: The Behavior and Beliefs of American Catholics.* New York: Scribner, 1990.

Groeschel, Benedict J. *A Still, Small Voice: A Practical Guide on Reported Revelations.* San Francisco, CA: Ignatius Press, 1993.

Gunning, Tom. "Phantom Images and Modern Manifestations: Spirit Photography, Magic Theater, Trick Films, and Photography's Uncanny." In *Fugitive Images: From Photography to Video,* edited by Patrice Petro, 42–71. Bloomington: Indiana University Press, 1995.

Gurvis, Sandra. *Way Stations to Heaven: 50 Major Visionary Shrines in the United States.* New York: Macmillan, 1996.

Hall, David D., ed. *Lived Religion in America: Toward a History of Practice.* Princeton, NJ: Princeton University Press, 1997.

Halter, Deborah. "Field Note: Charisma in Conyers: A Journal from Visionary to Apparition Site to Church." *Nova Religio* 14, no. 3 (February 2011): 108–14.

Hamington, Maurice. *Hail Mary?: The Struggle for Ultimate Womanhood in Catholicism.* New York: Routledge, 1995.

Heal, Bridget. *The Cult of the Virgin Mary in Early Modern Germany: Protestant and Catholic Piety, 1500-1648.* Cambridge, UK: Cambridge University Press, 2007.

Hennesey, James J. *American Catholics: A History of the Roman Catholic Community in the United States.* New York: Oxford University Press, 1981.

Heo, Angie. "The Virgin Made Visible: Intercessory Images of Church Territory in Egypt." *Comparative Studies in Society and History* 54, no. 2 (2012): 361–91.

Heo, Angie. "The Bodily Threat of Miracles: Security, Sacramentality, and the Egyptian politics of public order." *American Ethnologist* 40, no. 1 (2013): 149–64.

Hervieu-Léger, Danièle. *Religion as a Chain of Memory.* New Brunswick, NJ: Rutgers University Press, 2000.

Horsfall, Sara. "The Experience of Marian Apparitions and the Mary Cult." *The Social Science Journal* 37, no. 3 (2000): 375–84.

Howard, Robert Glenn. *Digital Jesus: The Making of a New Christian Fundamentalist Community on the Internet.* New York: New York University Press, 2011.

Ireland, John. *The Church and Modern Society: Lectures and Addresses.* New York: D.H. McBride & Co., 1896.

Isichei, Elizabeth. "Visions and Visionaries: The Search for Alternative Forms of Authority among Catholic Conservatives." *Archives de Sciences Socials des Religions* 36, no. 75 (July–September 1991): 113–25.

Jenkins, Philip. *The Next Christendom: The Coming of Global Christianity.* New York: Oxford University Press, 2002.

Kane, Paula M. "'She Offered Herself Up': The Victim Soul and Victim Spirituality in Catholicism." *Church History* 71, no. 1 (March 2002): 80–119.

Kripal, Jeffrey J. *Authors of the Impossible: The Paranormal and the Sacred.* Chicago: University of Chicago Press, 2010.

Kselman, Thomas A., and Steven Avella. "Marian Piety and the Cold War in the United States." *Catholic Historical Review* 72 (July 1986): 403–24.

Kurluk, Ewa. *Veronica and Her Cloth: History, Symbolism, and Structure of a "True" Image.* Cambridge, MA: Basil Blackwell, 1991.

Laurentin, Rene. *The Apparitions of the Blessed Virgin Mary Today.* Translated by Luke Griffin. Dublin: Veritas Publications, 1991.

LeBar, James J. *Cults, Sects, and the New Age.* Huntington, IN: Our Sunday Visitor Pub. Division, Our Sunday Visitor, 1989.

Lewis, I. M. *Ecstatic Religion: An Anthropological Study of Spirit Possession and Shamanism.* Harmondsworth, UK: Penguin, 1978.

Lindsey, David M. *The Woman and the Dragon: Apparitions of Mary.* Gretna, LA: Pelican Pub, 2000.

Lueken, Veronica. *The Incredible Bayside Prophecies on the United States and Canada.* Lowell, MI: These Last Days Ministries, 1991.

Lueken, Veronica. *Virgin Mary's Bayside Prophecies: A Gift of Love.* 6 vols. Lowell, MI: These Last Days Ministries, 1998.

Margry, Peter Jan. "Global Network of Divergent Marian Devotion." In *New Religions: A Guide: New Religious Movements, Sects and Alternative Spiritualities,* edited by Christopher Partridge, 98–102. New York: Oxford University Press, 2004.

Martin, Daniel. *Vatican II: A Historic Turning Point.* Bloomington, IN: AuthorHouse, 2011.

Martin, Malachi. *Hostage to the Devil.* New York: Reader's Digest Press, 1976.

Martin, Malachi. *The Final Conclave.* New York: Stein and Day, 1978.

Martins, Antonio Maria. *Novos Documentos de Fátima.* São Paulo: Edições Loyola, 1984.

Marty, Jean. *Warnings from Beyond: Warnings from the Other World to the Contemporary Church (Confessions of Hell).* Translated by Nancy Knowles-Smith. Fort Lauderdale, FL: Catholic Books and Tapes, n.d.

Matovina, Timothy M. *Latino Catholicism: Transformation in America's Largest Church.* Princeton, NJ: Princeton University Press, 2012.

Massa, Mark, ed. *American Catholic History: A Documentary Reader.* New York: New York University Press, 2008.

Matter, E. Ann. "The Virgin Mary: A Goddess?" In *The Book of the Goddess,* edited by Carl Olson, 80–96. New York: Crossroad, 1983.

Matter, E. Ann. "Apparitions of the Virgin Mary in the Late Twentieth Century: Apocalyptic, Representation, Politics." *Religion* 31, no. 2 (2001): 125–53.

McDannell, Colleen. *The Spirit of Vatican II: A History of Catholic Reform in America.* New York: Basic Books, 2011.

McGuire, Meredith B. *Lived Religion: Faith and Practice in Everyday Life.* New York: Oxford University Press, 2008.

McKay, Alison. *Bayside.* Portsmouth, NH: Arcadia Publishing, 2008.

Melton, J. Gordon. "Spiritualization and Reaffirmation: What Really Happens When Prophecy Fails." *American Studies* 26, no. 2 (Fall 1985): 17–29.

Melton, J. Gordon. *Encyclopedic Handbook of Cults in America*. New York: Garland Pub, 1992.

Melton, J. Gordon. "Our Lady of Roses Shrine." In *The Encyclopedia of American Religions*, 5th ed, 229. Detroit, MI: Gale Research Inc., 1996.

Miller, Timothy, ed. *When Prophets Die: The Postcharismatic Fate of New Religious Movements*. New York: SUNY, 1991.

Morgan, David. *Visual Piety: A History and Theory of Popular Religious Images*. Berkeley: University of California Press, 1998.

Niebuhr, H. Richard. *The Social Sources of Denominationalism*. New York: Meridian Book, 1975.

Oakes, Len. *Prophetic Charisma: The Psychology of Revolutionary Religious Personalities*. Syracuse, NY: Syracuse University Press, 1997.

Orsi, Robert. *The Madonna of 115th Street*. New Haven, CT: Yale University Press, 1985.

Orsi, Robert. *Thank You, St. Jude: Women's Devotion to the Patron Saint of Hopeless Causes*. New Haven, CT: Yale University Press, 1999.

Orsi, Robert. *Between Heaven and Earth: The Religious Worlds People Make and the Scholars Who Study Them*. Princeton, NJ: Princeton University Press, 2005.

Orsi, Robert. "The 'So-Called' History of the Study of Religion." *Method and Theory in the Study of Religion* 20, no. 2 (2008): 134–38.

O'Toole, James M. *The Faithful: A History of Catholics in America*. Cambridge, MA: Belknap Press of Harvard University Press, 2008.

Pagliaroli, Jessy C. "Kodak Catholicism: Miraculous Photography and Its Significance at a Post-Conciliar Marian Apparition Site in Canada." *Historical Studies* 70 (2004): 71–93.

Partridge, Christopher. *The Re-Enchantment of the West: Alternative Spiritualities, Sacralization, Popular Culture, and Occulture*. 2 vols. London: T & T Clark International, 2004.

Peers, E. Alison. *The Life of Teresa of Jesus: The Autobiography of Teresa of Avila*. New York: Doubleday, 1991.

Primiano, Leonard Norman. "Vernacular Religion and the Search for Method in Religious Folklife." *Western Folklore* 54 (January 1995): 37–56.

Richardson, James T., Joel Best, and David G. Bromley. *The Satanism Scare*. Hawthorne, NY: Aldine de Gruyter, 1991.

Roof, Wade Clark. *Spiritual Marketplace: Baby Boomers and the Remaking of American Religion*. Princeton, NJ: Princeton University Press, 1999.

Rosenberg, Chaim M. *America at the Fair: Chicago's 1893 World's Columbian Exhibition*. Chicago: Arcadia Publishing, 2008.

Rubin, Miri. *Gentile Tales: The Narrative Assault on Late Medieval Jews*. New Haven, CT: Yale University Press, 1999.

Shupe, Anthony. "The Role of Apostates in the North American Anti-Cult Movement." In *The Politics of Religious Apostasy: The Role of Apostates in the Transformation of Religious Movements*, edited by David G. Bromley, 209–18. Westport, CT: Praeger, 1998.

Sharkey, Don. *The Woman shall conquer; the story of the Blessed Virgin in the Modern World*. Milwaukee, WI: Bruce Pub. Co., 1952.

Smith, Jonathan Z. *Imagining Religion: From Babylon to Jonestown*. Chicago: University of Chicago Press, 1982.

Smith, Jonathan Z. *Map Is Not Territory: Studies in the History of Religion*. Chicago: University of Chicago Press, 1993.

Stark, Rodney. "A Theory of Revelation." *Journal for the Scientific Study of Religion* 38, no. 2 (1999): 287–308.

Stark, Rodney. "Secularization, R.I.P." *Sociology of Religion* 60, no. 3 (1999): 249–73.

Swatos, William H., and Kevin J. Christiano. "Secularization: The Course of a Concept." In *The Secularization Debate*, edited by William H. Swatos and Daniel V. A. Olson, 1–20. Lanham, MD: Rowman and Littlefield, 2000.

Tavard, George H. *The Thousand Faces of the Virgin Mary*. Collegeville, MN: Liturgical Press, 1996.

Turner, Victor W, and Edith L. B. Turner. *Image and Pilgrimage in Christian Culture: Anthropological Perspectives*. New York: Columbia University Press, 1978.

Tweed, Thomas A. *Crossing and Dwelling: A Theory of Religion*. Cambridge, MA: Harvard University Press, 2006.

Wallace, Anthony F. C. "Revitalization Movements." *American Anthropologist* 58, no. 2 (April 1956): 264–81.

Weaver, Mary Jo. *New Catholic Women: A Contemporary Challenge to Traditional Religious Authority*. Bloomington: Indiana University Press, 1986.

Weaver, Mary Jo, and R. Scott Appleby, eds. *Being Right: Conservative Catholics in America*. Bloomington: Indiana University Press, 1995.

Weber, Max, and Talcott Parsons. *The Theory of Social and Economic Organization*. New York: Free Press, 1964.

Weber, Max, and Shmuel N. Eisenstadt. *Max Weber on Charisma and Institution Building: Selected Papers*. Chicago: University of Chicago Press, 1968.

Weber, Max, and Talcott Parsons. *The Protestant Ethic and the Spirit of Capitalism*. Mineola, NY: Dover Publications, 2003

Weiner, Isaac. *Religion Out Loud: Religious Sound, Public Space, and American Pluralism*. New York: New York University Press, 2013.

Wessinger, Catherine. *Women's Leadership in Marginal Religions: Explorations Outside the Mainstream*. Chicago: University of Illinois Press, 1993.

Wojcik, Daniel. *The End of the World as We Know It: Faith, Fatalism, and Apocalypse in America*. New York: New York University Press. 1996.

Wojcik, Daniel. "Polaroids from Heaven: Photography, Folk Religion, and the Miraculous Image Tradition at a Marian Apparition Site." *Journal of American Folklore* 109, no. 432 (Spring 1996): 129–48.

Wojcik, Daniel. "Bayside (Our Lady of the Roses)." In *Encyclopedia of Millennialism and Millennial Movements*, edited by Richard A. Landes, 85–93. New York: Routledge, 2000.

Wojcik, Daniel. "Spirits, Apparitions, and Traditions of Supernatural Photography." *Visual Resources: An International Journal of Documentation* 25, nos. 1–2 (March–June 2009): 109–36.

Wuthnow, Robert. *After Heaven: Spirituality in America Since the 1950s.* Berkeley: University of California Press, 1998.

Yamane, David. "Narrative and Religious Experience." *Sociology of Religion* 61, no. 2 (2000): 171–89.

Yager, Jane. *The Rosary and the Lawnmower: The Making of Public Religion in the Contemporary American City.* Honors paper, Macalester College, 2001.

Yoder, Don. "Toward a Definition of Folk Religion." *Western Folklore* 33 (January 1974): 2–15.

Zablocki, Benjamin D, and Thomas Robbins. *Misunderstanding Cults: Searching for Objectivity in a Controversial Field.* Toronto: University of Toronto Press, 2001.

Zimdars-Swartz, Sandra. "Religious Experience and Public Cult: The Case of Mary Ann Van Hoof." *Journal of Religion and Health* 28, no. 1 (Spring 1989): 36–57.

Zimdars-Swartz, Sandra. *Encountering Mary: From La Salette to Medjugorje.* Princeton, NJ: Princeton University Press, 1991.

Zygmunt, Joseph F. "When Prophecies Fail: A Theoretical Perspective on the Comparative Evidence." *American Behavioral Scientist* 16, no. 2 (Nov/Dec 1972): 245–68.

Index